WORLD CLASS!

WORLD CLASS!

Strategies for winning with your customer

TONY MANNING

1991
JUTA & CO, LTD

First published in 1991

Copyright © Juta & Co, Ltd
PO Box 14373, Kenwyn 7790

ISBN 0 7021 2663 2

Printed and bound by
Creda Press, Solan Road, Cape Town.

Last year, each of our 10 million customers came in contact with approximately five SAS employees, and this contact lasted an average of 15 seconds each. Thus SAS is "created" 50 million times a year, 15 seconds at a time. These 50 million "moments of truth" are the moments that ultimately determine whether SAS will succeed or fail as a company.

JAN CARLZON, CEO of Scandinavian Airlines System (SAS)[1]

In marketing . . . the object is to get and keep a customer, and also to get existing buyers to prefer to do business with you than with your competitors. In marketing, therefore, the imagination must constantly focus on that objective.

THEODORE LEVITT[2]

What the customer thinks he or she is buying, what he or she considers value, is decisive — it determines what a business is, what it produces, and whether it will prosper.

PETER F. DRUCKER[3]

1   Jan Carlzon, *Moments Of Truth*, Ballinger, 1987
2   Theodore Levitt, *The Marketing Imagination*, The Free Press, 1983
3   Peter F. Drucker, *Management: Tasks, Responsibilities, Practices*, Harper College Press, 1977

We have learned more about the right way to run a business in the 1980s than in the preceding half century. In a nutshell, we've learned this: that world-class performance is *dedicated to serving the customer.*

RICHARD J. SCHONBERGER[4]

... not one state in the world today can regard itself isolated from others in the economic respect.

MIKHAIL GORBACHEV[5]

4   Richard J. Schonberger, *Building A Chain Of Customers*, The Free Press, 1990
5   Richard J. Kirkland, "Entering A New Age Of Boundless Competition," *Fortune*, March 14, 1988

CONTENTS

INTRODUCTION

During the 1970s and 1980s, managers everywhere talked about building a "sustainable competitive advantage." Today, that's virtually impossible. In the 1990s and beyond, companies will have to learn to survive and grow despite *unsustainable* advantages.

Obsessive attention to customers has become a key strategic weapon. Showing companies how to use it has become a major industry for academics, consultants, and trainers. But most firms have yet to advance from being merely customer-aware to being customer-*driven*. They must learn that business is about marketing and that customer service is everybody's business. And they need to understand that customer service as most people understand it is an *unsustainable* competitive advantage. It's just too easy to copy, too easy to beat.

Around the world today, there's a new breed of customer, making new demands on the firms they buy from. To win them over, leading edge companies have become increasingly competitive. With astonishing speed they develop and launch breakthrough products and services. They constantly upgrade and add features, starting the instant their wares reach the market. They improve quality, slash costs, drive down prices, and extend distribution through hybrid channels. They restructure and downsize . . . they automate and they enter strategic alliances . . . they spend increasing amounts on R&D,

1

training, and promotion . . . and they pour resources into building "global brands."

Along the way, a new term — "world class" — has crept into the language of business:

❑ ". . . we acquired a world-class paper company. . . ." (Ad for Georgia-Pacific.)

❑ "Introducing a whole new class of American sedan: world class." (Ad for Buick.)

❑ ". . . General Motors" commitment to exploring new ideas and revolutionary ways of building world class American cars and beating the competition. . . ." (Ad for GM's North American vehicle range.)

❑ "World Class." (Slogan used by Imperial Chemical Industries.)

❑ "For advertisers seeking to create a world image, sell to the world's markets or position a worldclass product, it is one medium that is the perfect vehicle." (Ad for *Newsweek*.)

❑ ". . . when a hotel is world-class, its cuisine should be, too." (Ad for Four Seasons hotels.)

"World class" is taking over from "excellence," which had its run in the 1980s. Excellence is a fuzzy notion, open to any number of interpretations. World class is far more specific. It's a real objective for the 1990s. And it's a moving target.

It all begins with the customer

Business fads come and go, and right now customers are clawing their way to the top of many executive's agendas. Competitiveness is the hot new issue. There's a great deal of real interest in "customer care." More and more of the calls I get are from companies who want to sharpen up in this area. Yet most managers have a very superficial view of what it's about and how to make it a reality.

To most of them, customers are almost entirely the concern of people on the front line. That, after all, is where the "moment of truth" occurs . . . where "the rubber meets the road" . . . where sales and service people meet customers, and customers make their critical judgements.

Because of this, many managers think that a brief training course for front line people will do the trick. So they send Mary the receptionist to a morning seminar that promises to put a "smile in her voice." Or they send John the salesman for "handshake training." The CEO makes a few speeches, the employees watch a Tom Peters film, and posters exhort them to love their customers.

However, as I'll show, creating and keeping customers in the new competitive environment is a complex process. World class customer service comes only when you do *everything* better — when you anticipate customers' needs, when you reach way down into the organization and become "best of breed" in everything you do, and when your entire business system empowers front line people to meet or exceed customers' expectations.

Becoming world class demands total commitment to customers, and a company-wide drive to "dazzle them." It demands totally new standards of performance, new attitudes to people both inside and outside the organization, and a new willingness to change.

Above all, it requires that *continuous change* becomes the norm . . . that *continuous improvement* becomes a way of life for everyone . . . and that every person, in every function, becomes a *leader* at his or her own level.

Success in tomorrow's world demands that you change both *what* you do and *how* you do it. So this book is a call for radical surgery, not for a dab of antiseptic and a piece of sticking plaster. This is a book about holistic change management.

Needed: more than good intentions

Customers exist both inside and outside of an organization's walls. The external customer is the one to focus on, the one who ultimately accounts for a company's results. But each person in the organization also has *internal* customers who depend on him or her. These internal customers make results happen. And as the saying goes, "You have to show that *you* care, if you expect them to show that *they* care."

Walt Disney once said, "You can dream, create, design, and build the most wonderful place in the world . . . but it requires people to make the dream a reality." And as Ted Levitt wrote in his classic 1960 *Harvard Business Review* article "Marketing Myopia," building an effective, customer-oriented company "involves more than good intentions or promotional tricks; it involves profound matters of human organization and leadership."[1]

The starting point to success is to look outside your organization at the customer who finally buys, uses, or consumes your product or service. Then, to do everything necessary to meet or exceed that person's expectations.

Long-term competitive advantage is possible only when you treat customers as partners in profit — when you develop a win-win relationship that benefits you both.

What are you really selling?

The mid-1950s marked a major shift for business. Computers began appearing in large firms, and, for the first time in advanced countries, more people were employed in service industries than in manufacturing. It was the start of the Infor-

1   Theodore Levitt, "Marketing Myopia," *Harvard Business Review* 1960

mation Age. "Second Wave" industrial society began giving way to the "Third Wave" knowledge society.[2] Since then, we've talked of the "service economy."

Service providers sell a "product." American Express's "product" range includes cheque accounts, savings accounts, credit cards, home loans, and merchant banking. Roto Rooter sells clean drains. Avis sells the temporary use of a car, wherever you are. Sheraton Hotels sell home-from-home accommodation and food. British Airways sells air transport. Sketchley sells laundered work clothes and linen. Arthur Anderson sells auditing and management advice. Federal Express sells overnight delivery. Your doctor sells health care.

In general, service "products" are different from manufactured products such as cameras or a TV sets in several ways:

1. They're intangible — you can't see them, hold them or stockpile them (if you miss a sale today, you won't sell two tomorrow!)
2. They don't exist until they're consumed.
3. The user is often a partner in their production.
4. The person providing the service is part of its perceived value.
5. They can't be fixed or replaced.

But service is not the preserve of car hire companies, advertising agencies, auditors, management consultants, hotels, retailers or banks. It's also a vital factor in the sale of tangible products. As manufacturers strive to add value for customers, and to differentiate themselves from their competitors, the line between products and services becomes increasingly blurred. It's hard to tell where a product ends and the service that sells it begins. If their "knowledge content" once separated them, it does so less and less often today.

2   See Peter F. Drucker, *The Age Of Discontinuity*, William Heinemann Ltd 1969, and Alvin Toffler, *The Third Wave*, William Collins and Sons 1980

Despite the obvious differences, "hard" products and "soft" services are marketed using similar tools and techniques. Customers use many of the same criteria to judge them. The basics are the same, and the differences are narrowing.

World class manufacturers are closing the gap between production and consumption by manufacturing only to order. And the customer is often a partner in almost every step of the production, delivery, and support process.

Personal attention ("customer care" or "customer service") is obviously vital in a restaurant, a health club or a bank. It's also an increasingly important factor in the sale of any manufactured product. It forms part of the product in a customer's mind. People need information to help them make buying decisions. They need advice and instructions. They need help with installation or use. They need after-sales support and technical assistance. They need to be made to feel important, and they want approval, image, "sex appeal," and reassurance.

So whatever business you're in, you need to carefully examine both the product you sell — whether it's a motor car, a camera, a bank account, lawn care, or a movie — and the service you wrap it in. For both shape the customer's perception of value.

Examples:

❏ The housewife who buys an Empisal sewing machine buys more than a piece of hardware. She buys *the ability to make clothes.* So she needs patterns, and she needs training. These are both part of the "product." The "hard" element — the machine — might be less important than the "soft" stuff that enables her to use it.

❏ When ICL's computer plants order components from outside suppliers, they don't just buy chips and cables. They also buy *advanced design and engineering, and on-time de-*

liveries in precise quantities. These service elements can make all the difference when it comes to choosing between suppliers.

❏ Ken Kirsten's nursery in Johannesburg, South Africa, sells pretty much the same shrubs and trees you could buy anywhere. But his TV programmes have positioned him as an expert horticulturist. Gardeners know that when they buy from him they'll get good advice about what will grow where, when to plant, and how to care for plants. They buy *beautiful gardens* — not just plants in a pot.

❏ Gemstar Development Corp. sells a remote control device called Plus+ which makes it easy for TV watchers to record their favourite shows. But people who buy the $59,95 VCR programmer are really buying *information.* So Gemstar has persuaded major newspapers and TV guides to print "PlusCodes" in their programme schedules. The product is made whole by this service; the service, in turn, depends on the product.

Very few products have a chance in the marketplace without an element of service. Wrapping your product in superior service is one of the most powerful ways to differentiate it from the competition. As features and benefits converge, it's often the only way.

"There is a growing realization," says John Humphrey, chairman of Boston's Forum Corporation, a leading firm of consultants, "that most companies today are primarily service businesses, even if they manufacture products."[3]

Says Harvard marketing guru Ted Levitt: "When we know enough about a business it becomes clear that its 'product' is much more than what's generically at the core of what's expected by the customer and offered by the seller."[4]

3 "Focusing On The Customer," a special advertising section in *Fortune,* June 5, 1989
4 Theodore Levitt, *The Marketing Imagination,* The Free Press 1983

And Californian marketing consultant Regis McKenna recently wrote, "The product is no longer just the thing itself; it includes service, word-of-mouth references, company financial reports, the technology, and even the personal image of the CEO. As a result, product marketing and service marketing, formerly two distinct fields, have become a single hybrid."[5]

But the man who put it best of all was Elmer Wheeler, the legendary sales trainer. Whatever you're selling, he counselled, "Sell the sizzle, not the steak!"

Success begins "out there"

Hungry entrepreneurs will do virtually anything to create and keep customers. They're not wedded to ways of doing things, or to satisfying "the system." They don't have rules to bend. They don't have to worry about layers of people protecting their turf. When a customer calls, they act. And they can be as creative about it as they like.

But success almost always puts a stop to all that freewheeling inventiveness. As soon as organizations start to mature, their people start spending a lot of time gazing at their own navels. They get busy with things that are important to themselves. They develop complicated systems and bureaucratic procedures which tie them up, slow them down, and don't create value for anyone. The organization chart becomes a map of who can do what to whom. Communication bogs down and paper proliferates. Policy manuals appear. Fun disappears.

When managers in established firms aim for improvement, they generally work from the inside out. They redesign the organization to suit themselves. They give people titles that suggest power or prestige, but mean nothing. They adapt or

5   Regis McKenna, "Marketing In An Age Of Diversity," *Harvard Business Review*, September-October 1989

refine existing structure or systems — and they're careful not to raise too many hackles in the process. Corporate politics directs people's energy into pursuits that add costs rather than value.

To become world class, however, requires an outside-in, zero-based approach. People must learn to work "backwards" from the external customer, through every function in the firm. Before they do anything, or incur any expense, they must ask, "Will this add value for my customer?"

Each individual in the team must recognize that he or she is both a supplier and a customer, in that they provide certain value and they need certain support. Together, they form a "value chain" (Michael Porter[6]) or a "chain of customers" (Richard Schonberger[7]).

There are many ways to get this message across. One recent survey showed that companies take some of the following steps to boost customer satisfaction:

❑ A mission statement which includes a customer service goal — 92 per cent.

❑ Customer service training — 85 per cent.

❑ Customer-focused training for new employees — 84 per cent.

❑ Companywide customer service communication — 79 per cent.

❑ Reviews of customer service systems/technology — 76 per cent.

❑ Audits of customer service policies/practices — 75 per cent.

❑ Senior management meetings on customer satisfaction — 75 per cent.

6   Michael E. Porter *Competitive Advantage*, The Free Press, 1985
7   Richard J. Schonberger, *Building A Chain Of Customers*, The Free Press, 1990

❑ Set and measure customer satisfaction standards — 75 per cent.[8]

Unfortunately, as good as all this sounds, it's nowhere near good enough. As I've said, becoming world class is a whole lot harder than just becoming customer-aware. It's possible only when an organization becomes customer-*driven*. That requires that the entire organization be redesigned, and that everything it does be reviewed, and if necessary, reinvented.

Aiming for superior customer service is not just a fad or a project to tackle as an adjunct to "real work." It's the objective that *directs* real work. The needs of customers should define what the organization looks like, what it does, and how it does things. No one in the firm should waste time on anything that doesn't add value for customers.

It's all about increasing profits

This is a book about making profits. It's addressed to managers who want to transform their organizations so they can survive and thrive in an increasingly hostile world. It's a "how-to" manual that provides a practical, step-by-step approach to world class performance.

Its central theme is the why and the how of building win-win relationships with your customers, starting with the resources you've got right now. But while it's far broader in scope than most books of this genre, it skims over issues which are adequately dealt with in other publications.

The first edition of *World Class!* was wonderfully received and became the basis of many companies' change programmes. Many readers gave me constructive feedback, asked for more information about particular issues, or suggested improvements. In addition, I've run many seminars and workshops on customer service since the book was published, and

8   Ibid

those experiences, too, have provided invaluable ideas and information.

So, taking my own advice, this second edition really is "new and improved!" I've included a lot of additional information and ideas, expanded many areas, chopped others, and added many new checklists plus a lot of extra illustrations.

Many people have asked why I called this book *World Class!* Some say, "I don't sell internationally; I sell right here, in my back yard. Why should I aim to be 'world class?'"

There are essentially three reasons:

1. *World class is the new business standard, wherever you are, and wherever you trade.* Today's customers shop around the corner — and around the world. Consumer tastes are converging, and buying behaviour is becoming more similar across countries and cultures (though not quite as much as some prophets predicted).

   In response to these changes, companies have been forced to improve the value they offer, and to drive down their costs and their prices. This has required huge investments in R&D, design, technology, production, and marketing. Result: in many industries you simply can't stay in the game if you're not world class.

2. *No matter what business you're in, chances are that you'll face competition from a world class player sooner or later.* Whether you compete in foreign markets or close to home, there's no place to hide and hardly any way to avoid an ugly confrontation. World class competitors are everywhere and they're continually seeking out new opportunities. Protectionist barriers rise in one place as fast as they fall elsewhere. Deregulation is changing the rules of the game in industry after industry.

   It's tempting to think that your knowledge of your home market guarantees your security; in fact, it's no guarantee at all. *Fortune* recently sounded a clear warning: "See how foreign manufacturers, including many from the so-called Third World, hastened the industrial sunset for USX, LTV, and America's other stay-at-home steelmakers."[9] Companies in every industry, take note. Now, as never before in business, the best defence is attack!

3. *If your standards are not world class, you're not using your resources as well as you might do.* Someone out there is producing better quality, more productively. They're winning more customers — and those customers are coming back for more. Their return on investment is higher than yours. They're probably more profitable. By becoming world class, those rewards can be yours.

What does it mean to be "world class?"

Quite simply, it means being at least as good as the best player anywhere, in everything you do. That's a heck of an objective, but it's the only one to aim for. Second best just doesn't shape in this tough new world!

Outstanding performance occurs when you:

1. Understand and clearly define your customers' needs.
2. Design your total business system to meet those needs.
3. Monitor changes in what customers want and what competitors offer.
4. Continually improve everything you do.

The title of this book is not just a catchy set of words. Rather, it's a *philosophy of business.* And it's a philosophy that every business must adopt or die. For the only way to survive and thrive in the increasingly competitive global marketplace is to be world class.

Of course, getting there is a big job. It won't happen overnight. It's not a task you can delegate to the human resources

9   Richard J. Kirkland, "Entering A New Age Of Boundless Competition," *Fortune,* March 14, 1988

department or to the sales manager. It requires the total involvement and commitment of every person in your firm, from the top down.

So don't expect this book to be a miracle cure — it's not, nor can any book or programme possibly be. All I offer is a road map. The rest is up to you.

You can't get half pregnant!

Before you embark on the journey to world class performance, remember that you can't get half pregnant. It's all or nothing!

Efforts to improve customer service fail time and again because they're seen as a *programme* rather than a *process*.

Managers view them as a special effort that can be made from time to time, in isolated areas, and in addition to everyday work. Seldom, if ever, do they understand that customer service has to be a companywide obsession . . . a driving force . . . part of the mind-set . . . and a way of life for everyone.

You can plaster as many slogans on the walls as you like, or put all your people through a training course, and your customers might just notice a difference. But chances are it'll be for a short while only.

If I refer many times in this book to Japanese work practices, it's because they've worked spectacularly. Also, because Japanese firms show so well how *managing a complex array of very basic issues adds up to world class performance.*

Real change needs intense effort and companywide commitment over a long period. The process is never complete.

As you begin, think about the wise words of my friend Mike Parker of Imperial Chemical Industries Plc.: "Customer care is like sex. A hell of a lot of people are talking about it but only a few actually do it!"

Tony Manning
July 1991

PART I

WHAT IT MEANS
TO BE A "KILLER COMPETITOR"
IN THE 1990s AND BEYOND

CHAPTER ONE

CONFRONTING THE FUTURE

What the hell is going on out there?

As we entered the 1990s, *Fortune* hailed this as "The Era of Possibilities."[1] Just one year later *Newsweek* called it "The Age of Anxiety."[2] New forces swirl around us, altering politics, society, and business. The competitive environment is heating up and changing at a frenetic pace and in unexpected ways.

Countries and companies around the world are in the throes of radical transformation. Reform and renewal are key concerns. Many organizations, especially in Japan, the U.S., and Europe, have been working at them for a decade or more. Managers who haven't begun the task must move especially fast and with extra determination if they're to survive and thrive in the new arena.

That said, you need to recognize that the future is a matter of choice, not chance. You are where you are today because of decisions you took — or *didn't* take — sometime in the past. And the shape of tomorrow depends entirely on how you act right now.

In other words, as turbulent and surprising as the world may be, you do have a great deal of control over your own destiny. Whether you succeed or fail is in your hands.

1   "The Era Of Possibilities," *Fortune*, January 15, 1990
2   Cover story, *Newsweek*, January 7, 1991

Opposite trends

On a macro scale, two trends move in opposite directions.
The first, says Robert Reich, professor of political economics
and management at Harvard University, is a trend toward
"managed trade" with nations agreeing how much to buy or
sell from each other."[3]

This is a potentially dangerous development. The devastating effects of America's Smoot-Hawley tariffs in the 1930s
offer ample reason to avoid it at all costs. Barriers inevitably
serve small interest groups at the expense of consumers. All
evidence suggests that markets do better than lobbyists and
politicians in deciding what should be made, bought or sold.

But, says *The Economist*, "The size and persistence of
America's trade deficits have inspired in its politicians the
urge to 'do something' about trade. The world's other big
trading powers, Western Europe and Japan, are unable or
unwilling to take up the role of defender of free trade that
America seems ready to give up."[4]

The second trend Reich sees is a move towards "the globalization of production, through which corporations make,
buy, and sell their wares all over the planet."[5]

Not long ago, these headlines appeared on a single page of
the *Financial Times*:

❏ "Boeing spots demand for eastern European travel."
❏ "Malaysia steel mill contract goes to Italy."
❏ "Austrian-led group to finance Polish hotel and office
complex."
❏ "Latin America anxious to boost Japanese investment."
❏ "Japan machine tool maker sets up UK technical centre."

3   Robert B. Reich, "Whither Protectionism?" *Harvard International Review*,
    Tenth Anniversary Issue 1989
4   "The Ravishing Of Trade," *The Economist*, March 25, 1989
5   Robert B. Reich, ibid.

❏ "Belleli awarded Dutch topside platform order."
❏ "Fujikura-Pirelli cable deal."
❏ "French win Bolivian gas contract."[6]

Reich isn't the first person to comment on this development; others including Marshall McLuhan, Peter Drucker, and Theodore Levitt were there a long time ago. Until fairly recently, however, relatively few companies have taken note of it. Most are still parochial: back yard players who persist in thinking small. But now they must wake up.

A third trend — and one which makes it vital that firms think big — is the evolution of giant trading blocs. Markets were once defined by national borders. Now, common interests — commercial, social, political, security, and others — make those borders "porous" and encourage trade across them. Groups of countries are ganging up to give themselves a competitive advantage, and to keep "outsiders" at bay.

The "triad" of the United States, the European Economic Community, and Japan have in recent years been key targets of opportunity. However, these markets are being re-defined by new trade pacts between the U.S. and Canada and the U.S. and Mexico . . . by the dramatic enlargement of Europe to include not just the 12 EC members, but also Eastern Europe, the Scandinavian countries, and even the Soviet Union . . . and by rising living standards and consumer demand in the Pacific Rim countries.

"Protectionism" is a dirty word, and "industrial policy" is a controversial issue. But even as loud voices call for freer trade, and for market forces to determine who wins and who loses, defensive barriers are being built. National and regional interests will play a growing role in determining which countries and companies come out on top.

6 *Financial Times*, April 4, 1991

The competitive arena is changing, and will change
further and faster in the future. The rules of competition are also changing. Survival will be an uphill battle
for many companies. Creating a sustainable competitive advantage will be impossible.

Sweating the assets

Back in the early 1980s, companies everywhere took defensive
action in the face of a worldwide recession. They fought for
survival by furiously cutting costs. They fired people, sold off
excess plant and equipment, cancelled leases, and closed
down sluggish operations.

But now they're back on the offensive.

Having cut the fat, and learned how painful that is, they're
now "sweating their assets." Managers everywhere are working on productivity and going for growth.

They're thinking more strategically and more boldly.
They're learning new habits, sharpening up, and becoming a
lot more aggressive. They're more innovative and they're
spending more on R&D. They're investing more in technology
and paying more attention to people — and they're working
harder to bring man and machine together.

It's going to be a "white-knuckle decade for global business," says Jack Welch, chairman of General Electric Co.[7] "The
pace of change in the Nineties will make the Eighties look like
a picnic — a walk in the park. Competition will be relentless.
The bar of excellence in everything we do will be raised every
day."[8]

"This may be a time of immense uncertainty," says Walker
Lewis, head of Strategic Planning Associates, a Washington

---

7   "Managing Now For The 1990s," *Fortune*, September 26, 1988
8   John F. Welch, "Today's Leaders Look To Tomorrow," *Fortune*, March
    26, 1990

D.C. consulting firm, "but it is a *certainty* that Western companies are in for ten years of competitive hell."[9]

Some managers will respond by throwing up their hands. Others will go for the gold. "We can't sit around and commiserate with one another," says Lee Iacocca. "We've got to get good, we've got to compete, we've got to be worldclass. We can't just shout about it, we've got to be it."[10]

Changes to watch

The new conditions have evolved with unprecedented speed. Managers largely ignored a 1982 *Newsweek* cover story which asked, "Can the U.S. compete?" They paid scant attention to the same headline on a *Business Week* cover story in 1987. And chances are many skimmed a 1990 *Time* cover story which asked, "Can America Still Compete?" But now they're on red alert — and for good reason.

The massive changes occurring all around us trigger a stream of new and unpredictable consequences. The astonishing advance of technology from the mid-1950s has made knowledge universally available. Now we're caught up in a maelstrom of conflict and cooperation, of shifting power balances and of pressures that did not exist only a short time ago.

Here are just a few of the changes to watch:

❑ The failure of communism and socialism and the global spread of democracy.

❑ Global economic inter-dependence (what McKinsey consultant Kenichi Ohmae calls the "inter-linked economy, or ILE).[11]

9 Ronald Henkoff, "How to plan for 1995," *Fortune*, December 31, 1990
10 Lee Iacocca, interviewed in "Today's Leaders Look To Tomorrow," *Fortune*, March 26, 1990
11 Kenichi Ohmae, *The Borderless World*, Harper Business, 1990

❑ A worldwide slowdown in economic growth after eight years of uninterrupted improvement (the longest stretch in the post-World War II period).

❑ Huge overcapacity in many industries.

❑ Shrinking corporate profits.

❑ Shorter product life cycles

❑ A proliferation of innovative new products.

❑ More demanding, more fickle customers.

❑ An increasingly diverse workforce, with complications of language, culture, political views, values, and behaviours.

❑ A shrinking, ageing labour pool in most industrialized countries.

❑ A new focus on corporate ethics.

❑ The rise of the "green" movement.

❑ Deregulation and privatization.

❑ 1992 in Europe.

Then, there's the shifting balance of trade power. In 1960, America did almost twice as much trade with Europe as with Asia. By 1986, U.S. trade with the Pacific rim countries was 50 per cent ahead of its trade with Europe.

Just two decades ago, U.S.-based multinationals were far bigger than their competitors at home and abroad. Eighteen of the top 20 companies in the world were American. Only about 5 per cent of American firms faced foreign competitors.

In the 1950s, America was the clear leader in high-tech, and made more than 80 per cent of the world's cars and TV sets. But from 1960 to 1978, U.S. firms' share of world markets fell 30 to 50 per cent in such vital industries as pharmaceuticals, chemicals, electronics, and aviation. Today, America accounts for less than 30 per cent of auto and TV production. Fully 75 per cent of American products face foreign competition.

The astonishing rise of Japan

After World War II, Japan was in ashes. Its people were dispirited and demoralized. Massive aid programmes were necessary to rescue them from disaster. Yet today, Japan is an industrial colossus, a socio-economic miracle, a proud nation that has become a role model for many others.

In 1960, Japan's gross national product was smaller than that of England, France, or West Germany. Now, it's 30 per cent greater than that of England and France combined, and more than twice that of West Germany. In 1988, Japan passed America as the world's biggest aid donor.

A 1983 study by Japan's Ministry of Trade and Industry (MITI) put America ahead of Japan in 40 key technologies. By 1988, however, MITI put the U.S. ahead in just one — database software.[12] What's really alarming is that America has lost ground in technologies critical to a number of industries. What's particularly galling is that since World War II, Japan has paid less than $10 billion for scientific know-how estimated to have cost western R&D labs more than *$50 billion* to develop!

In only 30 years — from 1957 to 1987 — the U.S. and Japanese semiconductor industries traded places.[13] During the 1980s, American auto companies closed seven plants in America, while their Japanese competitors opened seven.

Japan now holds 26 per cent of the U.S. car market. Toyota sells more cars in America than every GM division except Chevrolet. Both Toyota and Honda have passed Chrysler in the number of vehicles produced in America. (Honda sells more cars in America than in Japan.) Nissan is currently spending $490 million to double its production capacity in the

12 Peter Petre "Lifting American Competitiveness," *Fortune*, April 23, 1990
13 For a fascinating account of how it happened, see Clyde V. Prestowitz, Jr., *Trading Places*, Basic Books, 1988

U.S., and by the end of the 1990s it will produce nearly half its vehicles outside of Japan.

Fortune's 1990 list of the "Global 500" includes 167 American firms and 111 Japanese. American firms rank first in 14 of the 25 industries that are included — more than Japan, West Germany, and Canada combined. But, warns the magazine, "Impressive as those numbers are, U.S. dominance is slowly giving way. In 1980, 23 U.S. companies made the top 50, compared with only five Japanese. Now, there are 17 American and ten Japanese. And two of the largest corporations, Samsung (No. 20) and Daiwoo (No. 47), are South Korean."[14]

Eight of the top ten banks in the world ranked by assets are now Japanese. The 30 Japanese banks on *Fortune*'s 1990 list control $5,6 trillion in assets — more than the banks of the U.S., West Germany, France, Britain, and Italy together.[15] Nomura Securities is 20 times as big as Merrill Lynch, and makes as much profit as the entire U.S., securities industry. Sumitomo Bank has a market valuation bigger than the top 23 American bank holding companies together. The market capitalization of the Tokyo Stock Exchange is about 50 per cent bigger than that of the New York Stock Exchange. And Japan's overseas investments are about twice those of OPEC at its peak.[16]

According to *Business Week*, six of the world's top ten companies by market value are Japanese. Three are American, and one — Royal Dutch Shell — is Netherlands/British. In the top 100, Japan beats the United States 37 to 35.[17]

Forbes gives Japan the top six spots for the biggest public companies outside the U.S., and 16 of the top 25. Its list of the biggest privately-owned firms has Japan in the top three

14 "Japan Is Still No. 1," *Fortune*, July 30, 1990
15 Ibid.
16 Mortimer B. Zuckerman, "Time To Bank On The Future," *U.S. News & World Report*, July 10, 1989
17 "The Business Week Global 1000," *Business Week*, July 16, 1990

places, and with ten mentions in all. (The list also includes three Korean companies and six from Germany.)[18]

A 1991 study by the International Institute for Management Development and the World Economic Forum ranked Japan the world's most competitive nation for the sixth straight year. It came top in six of the eight key measures, with its greatest strengths in management, the economy, science, and technology.[19]

A report from MIT's Commission on Industrial Productivity warns that "American industry . . . shows worrisome signs of weakness." In industry after industry, U.S. firms are losing ground to foreign competitors. The MIT Commission concluded that this isn't just because of a few isolated or random events. Rather, it's symptomatic of "more systematic and pervasive ills."[20]

Most Americans now believe Japan to be a more serious threat to them than is the U.S.S.R. "Suddenly," says *Fortune*, "the Japanese have become the people it's O.K. to hate."[21]

European attitudes, too, are hardening. A recent article in the *International Herald Tribune* began: "A new wave of anti-Japanese sentiment is spreading across Europe as public admiration for Japan's remarkable postwar recovery is rapidly running to fear that its economic juggernaut will smash key industries, conquer the unifying European market and transform the Continent into an industrial colony."[22]

This feeling was summed up French Prime Minister Edith Cresson, just before she took office in May 1991. "They sit up

18 "The 500 Largest Foreign Companies," *Forbes*, July 24, 1989
19 William Dullforce, "Japan stays well clear of the field," *Financial Times*, June 20, 1991
20 Michael L. Dertouzos, Richard K. Letser, Robert M. Solow, and the MIT Commission on Productivity, *Made In America*, The MIT Press, 1989
21 Lee Smith, "Fear And Loathing Of Japan," *Fortune*, February 26, 1990
22 William Drozdiak, "In a fearful Europe, Japan's new clout prompts a backlash," *International Herald Tribune*, June 17, 1991

all night thinking of ways to screw the Americans and the Europeans," she said. "They are our common enemy."[23]

What makes Japan such a fearsome competitor? Admirers and critics list a host of factors, from a homogeneous population, a remorseless education system and an intense work ethic, to unfair trade practices, "Japanese management," "enterprise" unions, and the long-term orientation of investors. All of them no doubt play a role. But above all, Japan has been successful because of its unswerving attention to the basics.

❑ Japan spends 2,8 per cent of GNP on civilian R&D, vs. 1,8 per cent by the U.S. and 2,6 per cent by West Germany. That's over 100 per cent more per employee than American companies. (In 1990, while U.S. and European computer manufacturers were losing money and shedding people because of looming recession, Japan's Big Five computer makers increased their R&D spend by 10 per cent to $15 billion. Their goal: to take the global lead in the next generation of computers!)

❑ Japanese firms pay far more attention to customers than do most of their western competitors; they know that market share creates profits, and that customers are a firm's most precious invisible asset. (As former U.S. President Jimmy Carter recently said, "The Japanese are much more familiar with the preferences and needs of customers in our country than we are of the Japanese."[24])

❑ Quality and productivity are *policy* — not optional programmes or projects which can be started and stopped at will. The Japanese have paid attention to Deming, Juran, Feigenbaum, Drucker, and other experts for 40 years; Americans are only now waking up to the wisdom of their own prophets.

23 Ibid.
24 Inaugural speech in the Ohira Memorial Lecture Series to the Japan Society, quoted in "Know your customers," *Forbes*, April 29, 1991

❏ Japanese companies know that people are their most important resource, and they treat them as such. They invest heavily in the education and training of their full-time employees, with an emphasis on lifelong learning.

❏ Japanese companies don't try to be all things to all people, nor do they try to do everything themselves. They create dense networks of design specialists, suppliers, component manufacturers, distributors, and so on. These encourage narrow specialization, but also make for close cooperation.

❏ They understand the importance of building key skills, and leveraging them across various fields.

❏ They rely on teams to get things done. Their reward systems make it important for people do achieve great things together rather than through individual excellence.

Taken together these factors add up to formidable firepower. But they're bolstered by another strength which is often overlooked. This is the *gambatte* ethic — "do your best, try harder, persist" — which is instilled in Japanese children, and impacts later on their work practices.[25]

Japanese firms are incredibly patient. They make more mistakes than anyone notices, but they push past failure towards distant and, some would say, over-ambitious goals. Unlike so many western companies, which flit from opportunity to opportunity, companies like Honda, Canon, Kyocera, Matsushita, Shiseido, and Kao will stick to a particular course for ten, 15, or 20 years, despite heavy financial losses. They seem to have no "deadline for success."[26]

According to Sony chairman Akio Morita, "The United States looks ten minutes ahead while Japan looks ten years

25 Simon Holberton, "Why sheer persistence is the key to Japanese success," *Financial Times*, June 21, 1991
26 Ibid.

ahead."[27] There's more than a little truth in his scornful obser-
vation. Japan's competitive strengths were not built overnight.
The island nation, blessed with virtually no natural resources,
has invested for decades in the skills and technologies which
make today's innovations possible, and which now give it
growing advantage in the race to the future.

The scramble for Europe

In 1900, Europe accounted for about 36 per cent of world trade.
The great colonial powers virtually controlled the economies
of North America, Asia, and Africa. More recently, European
nations have traded mostly with each other. Their global
influence has waned.

Until late 1989, "Europe 1992" conjured up a picture of one
market of some 320 million people, with a combined gross
national product of $4,5 trillion — the biggest, richest con-
sumer market in the world. Companies everywhere scrambled for a share of the pie.

Then Mikhael Gorbachev's early moves towards *perestroika*
and *glasnost*, the crumbling of the Berlin Wall, and the changed
order in Eastern Europe created a whole new set of possibilities. Virtually overnight, Europe became a market of *850
million people in 25 countries!*

If competition was hot before, it's blistering now. Even
though things have gone somewhat sour in the Soviet Union
and a number of East European countries, Europe has become
the most interesting of the triad of major markets which includes North America (the U.S., Canada, and Mexico) and East
Asia (Japan, Hong Kong, Taiwan, Singapore, Thailand, the
Philippines, Malaysia, Australia, New Zealand, etc.).

To make sure they get a fair slice, European firms are
spending sharply more on R&D, slashing staff, restructuring,

27 Shintaro Ishihara, *The Japan That Can Say No*, Simon & Schuster Ltd, 1991

and honing their strategies. According to a recent report in *Fortune*, 62 per cent of them are "actively considering merging or acquiring another European company."[28] Sir John Harvey Jones, former chairman of ICI, and now chairman of *The Economist*, predicts that by the year 2000 fully half of Europe's factories will close and half its companies will disappear through sales or mergers.[29]

Foreign invaders, watching this new competitive spirit and worried about new trade barriers, are using tough tactics. In the first quarter of 1989, foreign companies bought 240 European firms for $5,8 billion. American companies alone spent twice as much as in 1988. In addition, these aggressors are tying up strategic alliances, buying European brands, establishing new factories inside Europe, hiring European managers, investing heavily in both promotion and in community projects, and working to expand distribution.

So far, Japan has been relatively slow in attacking the European market. For every $100 that British consumers spend on Japanese products, only $10 has been made in the U.K. In contrast, for every $100 spent on American products, $85 has been made in American-owned factories in the U.K. American multinationals employ more than 500 000 people in Britain, while Japanese firms employ just 25 000.

Of the 929 alliances tied up between Soviet firms and outsiders from January 1987 through September 1989, Japan accounted for just 18. A mid-1991 study by Japan's Association of Corporate Executives revealed that only 26 Japanese firms had actually invested in eastern Europe.[30]

But don't expect this situation to last. Japan Inc. is working hard to be well entrenched in western Europe before any

28 "Merger Mania is Sweeping Europe," *Fortune*, December 19, 1988
29 Clemens P. Work, "The Great Global Buying Binge," *U.S. News & World Report*, July 3, 1989
30 Robert Thompson, "Japanese study how to invest in E Europe," *Financial Times*, June 18, 1991

protectionist walls can be raised. An article in *Eurobusiness* warns, "It is a fair bet that the Japanese are better informed about 1992 than the British. . . . Japanese companies do not come to the U.K. (60 have arrived since 1987) for philanthropic reasons. . . . They come to Europe as part of their global strategies. . . . The Japanese are aware that 1992 is a process of gradual evolution, not of sudden revolution. Their interest in Europe is not going to come to a sudden halt on December 31, 1992."[31]

Lars Sjogrun, managing director of the U.K. arm of Mercuri International, a leading European sales training consultancy, reports that much of his new business growth comes from Japanese firms anxious to learn how to compete against the *gaijin* in Europe.

There are signs that a concerted drive into the eastern bloc will begin soon. The Japanese government recently launched a programme to train managers to invest there. The Ministry of Labour is to sponsor 20 executives on a year-long study trip, saying, "Before they can invest, companies have to learn how to deal with local people."[32]

In *A Japan That Can Say No*, a book that raised a furore in America, Shintaro Ishihara hints at the thinking that might underpin Japan's interest in eastern Europe. "Here is a probable scenario for Eastern Europe: Our funds and technology will resuscitate the region. Then the former satellites will gradually transfer know-how to the Soviet Union, bringing it within our technological sphere of influence. From Tokyo to Moscow via Warsaw and Prague will be a short journey."[33]

Does Japan have national ambitions and a national strategy for world domination? Does it really matter? The fact is, Japanese firms now dominate many industries simply because

31 Christopher McCooey and Tim Hindle, "A Mixed Blessing For The
    UK," *Eurobusiness*, January 1990
32 *Financial Times*, ibid.
33 Shintaro Ishihara, *The Japan That Can Say No*, Simon & Schuster Ltd, 1991

their strategies are better than those of the companies they once trailed.

As tough as things are today, this is just warm-up time. The battle for global market share will intensify much faster, and become much more bitter, in the years ahead.

Where is the real enemy?

For the past decade, Japan has turned heads with its assault on global markets, and newer competitors from the Pacific rim have kept our attention focused on the East. But Mexico, Mauritius, and India have joined the ranks of the newly industrialized countries (NICs), and added a new dimension to global competitiveness. Hungary is seen as a future challenger. And Israel has absorbed so many highly-trained East Germans that it must surely become a threat in many industries in a few years' time. Now, it seems, as fast as one country makes its mark, another steals its thunder.

As recently as 1965, there wasn't a single developing country among the world's top 30 exporters of manufactured goods. Since then, their share of world exports has soared from 7,3 per cent to more than 17 per cent. Now, the World Bank ranks Hong Kong, Singapore, South Korea, and Brazil among the top 20.[34]

However, with all eyes on Japan and the newly industrializing countries (NIC's), what's been missed is the astonishing performance of many young companies in *Europe* and *America*, and the powerful resurgence of many older firms in the West.

From 1979 to 1988, U.S. manufacturing productivity grew by 3,3 per cent a year, compared to Germany's 2,6 per cent, France's 3,1 per cent, Britain's 4,7 per cent, and Japan's 5,8 per

34 Richard I. Kirkland Jr., "Entering A New Age Of Boundless Competition," *Fortune*, March 14, 1988

cent. Yet even though Japan's productivity is improving faster than America's, some experts predict that it'll take from 30 to 200 years for Japan to catch up. American firms start from a high base, and are aggressively improving all the time.

It's not generally recognized that the U.S. is still 30 per cent more productive than Japan in terms of gross domestic product per employee. (And 14 per cent ahead of France, 19 per cent ahead of West Germany, and 60 per cent ahead of South Korea.)

And if you're worried by the pace at which Japan Inc. is "buying up" America, relax. Right now, Japan owns maybe 1 per cent of U.S. manufacturing capacity. By the year 2 000, it may own 2 to 3 per cent. There's so much heat on Japanese firms that they're now thinking twice about buying American land or companies.

In contrast, consider America's stake in Europe: its book value was up to almost $150 billion in 1987 — more than its total worldwide direct foreign investment in 1977, and eight times higher than its 1967 investment.[35]

During the 1980s, there have been positive political, economic and social changes in England, France, Spain, and Italy — and a host of other countries. And for real competitiveness just watch the former West Germany, the world's biggest merchandise exporter (12,1 per cent of the world's total in 1990).

For the past decade, managers in these countries have been rethinking and overhauling their rusty charges. They've poured millions — even billions — into major surgery. Now, they face the 1990s in great shape. Even "sunset industries" such as steel and autos are back in the game, and facing the future with confidence.

"Europe 1992" has clearly been a massive spur to change. A survey by the American Management Association revealed

35 Robert Ball, "The Big U.S. Non-News," *Time*, April 24, 1989

that 69 per cent of U.S. firms with sales of more than $500 million were gearing up specially to compete in Europe, as were almost half of smaller firms.[36]

When a *Fortune* poll asked American CEOs how they felt about their chances in the global business war, 67 per cent said they were more competitive than five years ago, and 59 per cent said they planned to increase their foreign investment.[37]

But "1992" is not the only reason for all this new activity. Managers everywhere have recognized that their world is different and more dangerous than ever. At the same time, they've seen the new opportunities brought about by the discontinuities.

The competitive arena is thus being fundamentally restructured. The rules of the business game are changing forever — but even more important, *the game itself is changing*.

Forward-thinking companies are responding in totally new ways to the new imperatives. Alert executives are questioning the "what," the "why," and the "how" of everything they do. They're putting ever more time, money, energy, and imagination into their competitive strategies.

Paradoxically, the more changes there are, and the faster they occur, the wider the range of competitive possibilities becomes. But taking advantage of them is a hell of a job.

---

36 "Preparing For 1992," American Management Association, July 1989, reported in *Inc.*, October 1989
37 Susan E. Kuhn, "Eager To Take On The World's Best," *Fortune*, April 23, 1990

CHAPTER TWO
INDUSTRIES IN TRANSITION

Like products and companies, industries have their own life cycles. From time to time, great upheavals turn them on their heads. They evolve over many years, then suddenly everything changes.

These discontinuities are triggered by many factors: innovation, economics, politics, trading laws, and so on. But above all, they're triggered by the changing demands of customers.

Customers for everything behave differently today than yesterday. In developed countries they're older, better educated, richer, more discriminating. Families are disintegrating, women are out at work, values are under threat, time has become a precious commodity, and people put leisure and entertainment ahead of their careers.

Buyers of consumer goods are increasingly self-conscious, health-conscious, brand-conscious, and price-conscious. They're "information junkies" who know their options and their rights. Their definitions of "value" change with the speed of light. Today's fad is tomorrow's failure.

Industrial buyers, too, expect new standards from their suppliers. They are extremely well informed, and not easily fooled by tricks and flashy sales pitches. Because many of their purchases are big-ticket items, they make buying decisions slowly and carefully. Often, lots of people are involved. They demand hard facts, comparisons with competitive offerings, testimonials from other customers, and high levels of support.

These changes have forced companies to find new ways to compete.

Bodyshopping for knowledge and skills

Once, low price was a sure way to win customers. Companies scrambled to be the low-cost supplier their industry. But now *everyone's* aiming at that goal so it's no longer a defensible position. Third World countries have wage structures that those in the First World can't match. Where labour costs remain a problem, automation replaces people and drives down costs at an unprecedented speed. And when low wages and automation meet, the combination provides a daunting challenge to any competitor.

Manufacturers are no longer hampered by national boundaries. They simply move production to wherever it's cheapest right now. Or they sub-contract, and buy from the suppliers whose prices are most attractive.

"As cross-border trade and investment flows reach new heights," reports *Business Week*, "big global companies are effectively making decisions with little regard to national boundaries. Though few companies are totally untethered from their home countries, the trend toward a form of 'stateless' corporation is unmistakeable."[1]

In a dramatic description of what this means, Robert Reich describes how money flows when an American buys a Pontiac Le Mans from General Motors:

"Of the $10 000 paid to GM, about $3 000 goes to South Korea for routine labor and assembly operations, $1 850 to Japan for advanced components (engines, transaxles, and electronics), $700 to the former West Germany for design engineering, $400 to Taiwan, Singapore and Japan for small components, $250 to Britain for advertis-

1   "The Stateless Corporation," *Business Week*, May 14, 1990

ing and marketing services, and about $50 to Ireland and Barbados for data processing. The rest — less that $4 000 — goes to strategists in Detroit, lawyers and bankers in New York, lobbyists in Washington, insurance and health care workers all over the country, and to General Motors' shareholders all over the world."[2]

Chasing low-cost advantage

In the decade after World War II, Japan was able to enter and seize many markets through a low-cost strategy. Japanese wage rates were extremely low. But as that country has become more successful, and as per capita GDP has soared, Japanese firms have had to seek new manufacturing locations.

The same has happened to Taiwan. The average manufacturing worker there now earns about $600 a month. But in Jakarta, the official minimum factory wage is just $42 a month, including an allowance for food and transport. And in Shanghai, $1 a day is an excellent wage — and only one worker in ten earns that much.

The result is that Japan is now the biggest investor in Thailand, Malaysia, and mainland China, with Taiwan a close second. Taiwan is the biggest investor in the Philippines and the sixth biggest in Indonesia.

Today the locus of low cost might be Manila; tomorrow it's Bangkok . . . Sao Paulo . . . Bombay . . . or wherever. Satellite dishes, fax machines, and 747s make everywhere "next door."

The capacity of international data circuits is rising by 40 per cent a year, and the cost of using them will fall by as much as 40 per cent by 1996. The cost of computing power will fall by about 100 times by the year 2 000. A study of the computer market in the mid-1950s predicted that 57 units might be sold world-wide. By 1970, about 50 000 were in use; now 50 000 are

2 Robert Reich, "The myth of 'made in the U.S.A.,'" *The Wall Street Journal Europe,* July 9, 1991

sold each day, and there are about 100 million computers and terminals at work altogether. The Chunnel tunnel will carry passengers, cars, trucks, and busses between Britain and France in just 20 minutes. New fibre-optical circuits will carry huge volumes of messages along a "global digital highway" that will circle the world (in 1985 alone, more than 1 million kilometres of cable were sold). Already, executives "meet" via satellite, conversing with colleagues virtually anywhere without leaving their own offices. There are more than three million fax machines in the U.S., including 2 000-plus that a Miami company has placed in hotel lobbies around the country. The number in Europe will rise from 2 million to 6 million in the next three years. More than 4 million cellular phones are already in use in 50 countries, and France's Alcatel estimates there will be ten million subscribers in Europe alone by 1998.

The new communications links facilitate a new phenomenon known as "body shopping" or "cross-border data flows." London-based service firms process paperwork in Taiwan. American Airlines processes its ticket coupons in Barbados. New York Life Insurance Co. processes claims in Castleisland, a town in southwest Ireland. Filipino programmers in Manila helped Arthur Anderson & Co., a Chicago-based consulting firm, upgrade a computer operating system for a client in Atlanta. Indian firms, whose programmers are estimated to be 150 per cent more productive than Americans, write programmes for Hewlett-Packard, Citicorp, and Digital Equipment Co.[3]

The globalization of *knowledge* will have even more impact than the globalization of manufacturing. Together, these forces will alter forever the way people think, the way they shop, and the way business is done.

3   Richard Ernsberger Jr., "Business Goes Body Shopping," *Newsweek*, July 10, 1989

The age of "lean production"

Once it was vital to drive up volumes in order to cut costs. Strategists love "cost curves" and "experience curves." So market share was a vital goal. Wherever possible, manufacturers aimed at the longest possible production runs with few switchovers. Mass production underpinned the concept of globalization.

Henry Ford dominated the motor business by making his Model-T easily affordable. He drove down costs by offering it to customers in "any colour you like, as long as it's black." The Ford plant was a vast, totally integrated organization which took raw materials in at one end, and spewed cars out the other.

Today, however, economies of scale are often irrelevant. Far more important in many industries are customization, speed, and flexibility. "Lean production" is the new dogma.[4] British management guru Charles Handy talks of the "new equation of half the people, paid twice as much, working three times as effectively. . . ."[5]

In the early 1960s, efficient production volume for colour TVs started at about 50 000 sets. By 1980, a factory had to turn out 2 million to be profitable. But small is beautiful once again. Simplified design, CAD/CAM and CAE, automated production lines, and a new generation of knowledge workers can make money from much smaller runs. Standardized products are losing their appeal to both customers and manufacturers. "One-off" production, zero-inventories, and radically reduced forecasting periods are the new goals.

4   For an excellent in-depth study of this concept, see *The Machine That Changed The World*, James P. Womack, Daniel T. Jones, and Daniel Roos, Rawson Associates, Macmillan Publishing Company, 1990
5   Charles Handy, *The Age of Unreason*, Business Books Limited, 1989

According to U.S. management consultant Michael Kami, something like 75 per cent of all machined parts in the world are currently made in batches of 50 or less.[6] Mazda is working towards model runs of just 100 motor cars. With only 20 employees, the National Bicycle Industrial Company in Japan builds bicycles to order in 14 days — and offers 11 231 862 variations on 18 models, in 199 different colours![7]

Factory workers everywhere are learning to use the latest technologies. They're working in teams to cut change-over times, produce a wider range of products — and do it all a lot faster and cheaper than before. Result: distribution channels carry less stock and marketers can keep up with fast-changing customer demands.

Take, for example, how things work in The Limited, America's biggest retail fashion chain. Merchandisers check out the latest fashions at shows in Paris and Milan. Using ink jet printers, they're able to include up to 16 million colours in their designs. Then, optical scanners turn their sketches into high-resolution computer images, which are flashed by a private satellite system from their U.S. home office to factories in the Far East. Altogether, it takes a mere 1 000 hours — about 41 days — to put a new range on the shelves.[8]

Or consider Benneton, the family-owned Italian company which has made a world wide hit with its fashion sportswear. CAD systems slash design time, and transmit patterns directly into computer numerically-controlled cutting machines. When stores call for stock, fabric is cut and dyed and garments are made up. They're on sale in just 15 days.

Closer to home, shopping for food at Woolworths is always a pleasing surprise because brand new items arrive on shelf

6   Michael J. Kami, *Trigger Points*, McGraw-Hill, 1988
7   Susan Moffat, "Japan's new personalized production," *Fortune*, October 22, 1990
8   "For Apparel, New Look Is Global," *International Herald Tribune*, May 15, 1990

virtually every day. Stock levels are kept low to ensure freshness, so if you don't get there early, you'll miss out.

Speed, customization, quality, productivity, and innovation are all indispensable weapons in the war for market share. However, none of them is effective on its own in this strange new world. Virtually everyone aims to cut "cycle time" . . . "zero defects" is a common objective . . . productivity is everyone's responsibility, from executive suite to shop floor . . . and constant improvement is a commodity.

Rise of the "prosumer"

Traditional business thinking draws a definite line between companies and their customers. One produces, the other consumes. The roles are clear. And most business systems are designed around the differences.

Increasingly, however, says David McKinney, head of IBM Europe, "those who were once simply our customers, may now be our partners in the morning, our suppliers in the afternoon, competitors in the evening and customers again at midnight."[9] A decade ago, Alvin Toffler observed that a "progressive blurring of the line that separates producer from consumer" was changing the relationship between companies and their customers.[10] Where once customers were "out there," and got whatever a firm chose to deliver, now they were being actively hooked into the value-creating process as early as possible. The result, said Toffler, was the rise of the "prosumer." Now, watch his prediction come true in a growing array of industries:

❏ The Mike's Kitchen family restaurant chain has marvellous salad bars where diners mix their own salads. You take

9   David E. McKinney, "Europe, open for business," in *1992 NOW*, IBM
     Europe's quarterly review
10 Alvin Toffler, *The Third Wave*, Collins, 1980

what you like — as much as you want. And a range of
sauces lets you add the final personalized taste.

❏ If all goes well for General Motors, buyers of its revolutionary Saturn motor car will literally co-design their vehicles
on a dealership computer console. When they push the
"go" button, their order will zip through to the factory; at
the same time, components will be called up from suppliers. The car will then be built in *a run of one*. Quite a feat
of engineering, when you consider that a motor car is a
complex high-tech product, and that the average GM car
today carries as much computing power as the lunar landing module took to the moon in 1969!

❏ In more than 100 record stores in New York and California,
customers mix their own 40-minute music tapes from a
catalogue of over 4 000 jazz, rock, rhythm and blues, and
classical numbers. Music buffs choose the tunes they want,
then tape them in just five minutes through a digital recording system called Personics. The cost: 50 cents to $1,50 a
song.

❏ Electronic home banking has taken off slowly, but experts
say that within a decade 20 per cent of bank accounts will
be with banks that offer this service. Auto teller machines
(ATMs) enable customers to choose from a menu of transactions, and to conduct their financial affairs after hours,
or without going into a bank. Banque Bruxelles Lambert,
Belgium's second largest retail bank, goes one further, with
machines called "banquettes." Fitted with comfy seats,
they not only let customers check their balances, call up
foreign exchange rates or run through their securities port-
folios, but also work out hire-purchase financing plans,
and complete their tax returns. Citibank in the U.S. has a
system called ET (Enhanced Telephone), which lets customers see transactions on a small screen on a specially-de-
veloped telephone. Gotabanken, a large Swedish bank, has

plans for a system called World Banking, which will give customers access to their accounts from their office computer terminals.[11]

❑ Bespoke tailors, dress designers, architects, decorators, and hairdressers all collaborate closely with their clients to create a uniquely personal look. Insurance agents help clients structure financial cover by choosing from a variety of possible packages. Management consultants act as facilitators, guiding clients through the development and implementation of "co-authored" strategies.

Technology is one factor that makes it possible for companies to get closer to their customers at every step in the value chain, from concept through to consumption or use. Technology not only speeds the flow of information, but it also enables customers to do things — draw, match colours, visualize what a product might look like — which they could not do on their own.

Says *Fortune*: "Your broker doesn't merely have a desk, a chair, and a telephone anymore — she's wired to a huge back office in the suburbs where floors of communication and data-processing equipment link her to the global financial marketplace. Hotel chains are becoming hotbeds of technology, far beyond electric blankets: Microcomputers are automating everything from menu planning to maintenance scheduling. Guests can plug into a host of new services, including in-room VCRs, computerized wake-up calls, and even TV checkout."[12]

That said, no company can afford to wait for "the right" technology before it acts. Encouraging "prosumption" relies heavily on the human touch. Japanese auto manufacturers, for

---

11 Peter Knight, Banks Cash In On Automated Future," *Financial Times*, Thursday January 3, 1991
12 Maureen F. Allyn, "Services are supplying the steam for business investment," *Fortune*, June 5, 1989

example, use continuous, rich feedback from dealer salesmen to improve their products. This task might be helped by technology, but doesn't depend totally on it. What it does depend on is training sales people to ask the right questions and interpret the answers accurately, on motivating them to make the effort, on listening to what they say — and on doing something about it.

The notion of the "prosumer" suggests all sorts of possibilities for virtually every company. When customers are involved in creating what they buy, they "own" the outcome. Their choices reflect extremely accurately what they really want. And, most important of all, the "prosumption" process is the ultimate form of lean production.

When big really is better

Becoming a world class competitor in many industries requires vast amounts of money, invested for a long time. It also requires large-scale production facilities, global distribution, and internationally-recognized brand names. So the only survivors will be a few real giants at the top end, and some niche players at the bottom end. Medium-sized firms without either economies of scale or the advantage of specialization and focus will simply not stay the pace.

This is especially true in high-tech fields. There, in fact, the sums required are often so enormous that even the biggest firms can't afford to act independently.

❏ In the 1970s, it cost about $16 million and took four to five years to develop a new drug. Now, it costs around $250 million and can take 12 years. About 15 per cent of industry sales goes on R&D. The process of getting drugs passed by regulatory agencies is tortuous and time-consuming. Fewer companies can play the game, and fewer medicines come to market — 93 worldwide in 1961, and just 48 in

1980.[13] What's more, defending share is not easy; when patents expire, generics usually grab 50 per cent of the market within six months.

❏ Corning Glass invested 17 years and $100 million in fibre optics before landing a major order. The firm's incredible persistence paid off, because it now has a $600 million-a-year business that's the leader in an industry growing by 20 per cent a year.[14]

❏ To have a chance of survival in consumer electronics demands an investment of at least 7 per cent of net sales on research and development. Matsushita and Sony, the industry leaders, consistently spend close to 8 per cent. In addition, firms have to be able to produce their own semiconductor chips. All of which takes deep pockets — and immense courage — in a fast-maturing industry.

❏ Since 1984, more than 100 major research consortia have been formed in America alone. Many of the firms that belong to them are competitors who normally fight each other to the death. Seven major American firms got together in 1989 to form U.S. Memories Inc., with a projected three-year R&D budget of $1 billion. But they're up against Europe's Eureka project (19 countries, $413 billion for 213 projects) and Japan's Giant Electronics (15 companies, $400 million over seven years).

❏ The European Space Agency was formed in 1975, and now has 13 full members and two associates — and a budget of 1,68 billion ECUs. Its aim: to make Europe a leader in space exploration by the year 2000.

Launching a new product in most categories today is increasingly expensive and risky. Even "low-tech" products depend on high-tech processes, or have advanced technology em-

13 "Mismanaging Drug Research," *The Economist*, November 21, 1987
14 Keith H. Hammonds, "Corning"s class act," *Business Week*, May 13, 1991

bedded somewhere in their value chain. Barriers to entry are
high and costly to overcome. Building brands chews up cash.
And many products have as little as six months in the marketplace.

It's impossible to compete in a growing number of industries — 136 of them by one estimate, including autos, banking,
consumer electronics, entertainment, pharmaceuticals, publishing, travel services, and washing machines — except on a
global scale. The only firms that have a chance are those with
worldwide access to R&D, finance, labour, technology, and
customers.[15]

To overcome the hurdles, companies have resorted increasingly to mergers and acquisitions (which are relatively
permanent), and to strategic alliances (which might survive
for many years, but usually are temporary "marriages of
convenience"). When they're not killing each other, they're
getting into bed or getting married. Altogether, the competitive battlefield looks quite different today than it did even a
year ago.

Almost every auto manufacturer is somehow in cahoots
with every other one. The industry is now a dense web of
interlocking relationships. Competition is vicious, but it's increasingly hard to tell where one firm ends and its enemy
begins.

GM and Toyota compete and collaborate in the U.S. and in
Australia. Nissan sells Volkswagens in Japan, and VW sells
Nissan four-wheel drives in Europe. Honda is now America's
fourth largest car maker, and sells more cars in Japan than GM
and Ford together. (Its two-door Accord coupe is exported to
Japan with an American eagle on the badge.)

Early in 1990, while Honda was talking to Chrysler about
selling some Chrysler models in Japan, GM and Chrysler
entered a joint venture to manufacture manual transmissions

15 Jeremy Main, "How To Go Global - And Why," *Fortune*, August 28, 1989

and four-wheel-drive transfer cases. Since then, in a historic attempt to defend their turf against the Japanese, the Big Three American automakers have joined hands in a race to develop a new environmentally-friendly battery before the Japanese. Their chief executives recently met with President Bush to discuss trade policy, and afterwards appeared together on TV in a unique show of solidarity.

When an article in the *International Herald Tribune* reported in August 1990 that Chrysler was talking to Fiat, Renault, and Volvo about possible links, chairman Lee Iacocca responded, "Everybody is talking to everybody. I think over time everybody will need some kind of affiliation or partnership."[16]

And it really is happening, in industry after industry.

In the electronics field, Philips (Holland), NBC-TV (America), and Thomson (France) have created a joint venture to research advanced HDTV systems. Two other American companies, Zenith and AT&T, are also collaborating.

Philips and Matsushita have a Japanese joint venture to develop the Domestic Digital Bus (DB2) standard for consumer electronics. It will let consumers buy products from various suppliers, and easily link them together. Both Thompson and Sony have agreed to support and promote the standard.

Whirlpool will make appliances under the Philips brand name in five European countries. General Electric of the U.S. is to invest $580 million in joint ventures with Britain's General Electric Co. In November 1988, Siemens and GEC made a hostile bid for Plessey. A month later Siemens spent $1 billion on ROLM Systems, an IBM subsidiary. Siemens also has ties to Matsushita.

16 "Chrysler Discusses Link-Up," *International Herald Tribune*, August 15, 1990

By the mid-1990s, the telecommunications hardware industry is likely to be dominated by a few transnational megafirms: AT&T, Siemens, Fujitsu, and Alcatel.[17] Giants such as ITT, GTE, and IBM have all left the business.

Or take the computer industry — now in a terrible slump.

IBM's profits plummeted 92% for the second quarter of 1991 compared to the same period in 1990. "Big Blue," once the arrogant king of data processing, now has more than 500 alliances with suppliers. It'll buy operating systems from Next, Steve Jobs' new firm, and recently signed accords with Apple Computer (his old firm, in which Canon has a $100 million stake), Lotus, Siemens, and Wang. IBM and Motorola will market a wireless communications service for computers. And Motorola is talking to Apple Computer about building radio-frequency modems into PCs.

Siemens and Nixdorf merged in an effort to become the first big European competitor in the world computer market. And Siemens and Iskra, the leading Yugoslavian electronics firm have formed a joint venture company called Iskra Tel.

Fujitsu spent $1,5 billion to buy 80 per cent of Britain's flagship computer company, International Computers Limited. Persistent organic growth and astute acquisitions like this have made it the world's No. 2 computer firm, ahead of such luminaries as Digital Equipment Corp., Hewlett-Packard, and Unysis. Today, Fujitsu makes the world's most powerful conventional supercomputers, the lightest laptops, the smallest cellular phones, and the biggest memory chips.[18]

The same things are happening in the airline industry.

Since America deregulated aviation in 1978, more than 200 airlines have been taken over or gone out of business. In 1990, British Airways and Holland's KLM each bought a 20 per cent

17 "Mobilizing For A War," *Time*, May 1, 1989
18 Brenton R. Schlender, "How Fujitsu will tackle the giants," *Fortune*, July 1, 1991

stake in Sabena, the national airline of Belgium. When the deal collapsed at the end of that year, press reports said that BA wanted to talk further about an alliance with Sabena, but would have to fight off American Airlines, Scandinavian Airlines System, and Trans European Airways.

Scandinavian Airlines System (SAS) has partnerships with eight other airlines: Finnair, Swissair, LAN Chile, British Midland, Singapore Airlines, Thai International, Continental Airlines, and Delta. CEO Carlzon sees even more shakeouts in the industry, leaving only a few very big survivors. He intends to be "One in Five in '95."[19]

Swissair has links with Singapore Airlines and Delta, and new ties are proposed with Quantas. A marketing agreement between Swissair, Finnair, Austrian Airlines, and SAS links 250 planes and 80 000 employees; in 1989 these four airlines carried 30 million passengers.

What we're seeing, in short, is a relentless shift away from the idea that it's O.K. to be good in a local market, to the acknowledgement that world class is the only standard that counts — *even if you intend to compete only in your local market*. And, flowing from this new reality, the acceptance that while small can be beautiful, big often is best in a world without borders; and that your enemy can be your best friend.

But being a global player is not just a matter of marketing muscle. It does not hinge entirely on access to big international markets. It's not just an issue for export-oriented firms.

Global competitiveness will become more and more important even in small, local market niches. In fact, to successfully penetrate and then "own" various niches will conceivably be tougher than taking on the mass market. To do it, you'll have to be able to tap into

19 Kenneth Labich, "An Airline That Soars On Service," *Fortune*, December 31, 1990

leading edge information, skills, and whatever other inputs your business uses.

... But there's a twist to this view

In his most recent work, *The Competitive Advantage of Nations*, Harvard professor Michael Porter reports that to be a world class player you have to have a number of things going for you in your own back yard. And some back yards are better than others for particular industries.

After a seminal four-year study of 100 companies in ten countries, Porter concluded that the home environment must provide four critical attributes: (1) intense competition, (2) favourable "factor conditions" such as geographic location, skills or infrastructure, (3) dedicated suppliers and supporting industries, and (4) demanding customers.

"Competitive advantage is created and sustained through a highly localized process," says Porter. "Differences in national economic structures, values, cultures, institutions, and histories contribute profoundly to competitive success."

The underlying factor driven by each of the four determinants is *pressure for continuous innovation*. "Ultimately," says Porter, "nations succeed in particular industries because their home environment is the most dynamic and the most challenging, and stimulates and prods firms to upgrade and widen their advantages over time."[20]

Every country will not be an equally good base for every kind of industry. Different nations give different industries a head start. So any firm aiming to be an international competitor must (a) weigh up its chances of success in its chosen business, and (b) do whatever is necessary to create a favourable support system.

20 Michael E. Porter, *The Competitive Advantage of Nations*, The Free Press, 1990

Companies do not function in isolation. To be successful, they have to manage their environment. Simply wanting to be good, and investing in your own resources, is not enough.

Until now, managers have largely taken the external environment for granted. They have, in a sense, developed a "victim mentality." But from now on, ambitious executives will have to spend more and more time looking beyond the boundaries of their organizations, and managing what happens "out there." Their external stakeholders will demand increasing attention.

New kinds of people needed

In this, the age of the "smart machine," of the "hollow company" or the "stateless corporation," a new breed of manager is required.

On the one hand, there is a need for "knowledge workers" — people who can think and plan and create. In 1973, 30 per cent of Honda's people were involved in "brain work" and 70 per cent in "routine work." Today, 56 per cent are brainworkers. During the 1990s the proportion will rise to 80 per cent.[21]

The same trend is evident in many other organizations. If it isn't happening in your firm already, you should ask why. It could be that you simply haven't noticed the change towards knowledge work. Or perhaps you've missed an opportunity by not forcing the change.

Skills such as creative thinking and problem-solving are already vital; they'll be at a premium during the 1990s and beyond. In addition, executives will have to learn to deal at once with high-tech, low-tech . . . and no-tech.[22] And they'll have to be familiar with terms such as CAD/CAE (computer-assisted design/computer-assisted engineering); JIT (just in

21 Setsuo Mito, *The Honda Book of Management*, Kogan Page, 1990
22 See Shoshana Zuboff's book, *In the Age Of The Smart Machine*, Basic Books, 1988

time); TQC (total quality control); ZD (zero defects); FMS (flexible manufacturing systems); AS/RS (automatic storage/retrieval systems); and TPM (total preventive maintenance).

A second major requirement is for people who are able to transcend national differences, and can function effectively outside their home environment.

Key people will be hired for their ability to speak two or more major languages. Companies will spend a lot of their training funds on language courses. Consultants will be used to teach executives about cultures and customs.

The advent of the transnational company, spanning continents and cultures, lends new urgency to the development of true global business people. Air travel puts everywhere just hours away. No businessman worth his salt can be caught without a frequent flyer card. The Concorde is regularly filled with executives hurtling to meetings across the Atlantic, and back home the same day. Fax machines and cellular telephones have already transformed communications.

Sony has two non-Japanese on its main board. Directors of ICL include two Japanese, a Greek, and a Dane. A Briton runs Nissan's U.K. operation. Board meetings at ABB Asea Brown Boveri, a $25 billion industrial firm headquartered in Zurich, are conducted in English. The company was formed through the merger of Swedish-based Asea and Swiss-based Brown Boveri. "Swenglish" is its global language.

One recent survey ranked the ideal characteristics of tomorrow's international managers like this:

1. Strategic awareness.
2. Adaptability to new situations.
3. Sensitivity to other cultures.
4. Ability to work in international teams.

5. Language skills.
6. Understanding of international marketing.[23]

A recent *Fortune* article suggests that tomorrow's MBA should "speak a foreign language and be intimate with a foreign culture . . . have a strong grasp of ethics . . . be sensitive to others' feelings . . . know how to negotiate . . . have polished business manners . . . speak and write well, and understand the uses of technology." He or she should also "be familiar with the political, economic, and regulatory situations in the U.S. and Europe, and have vision, an entrepreneurial spirit, leadership qualities, and a capacity to innovate."[24]

A growing number of top business schools now include global business in their programmes. Management journals are loaded with articles on the subject. More and more companies are making deliberate efforts to develop global managers.

Percy Barnevik, president and CEO of ABB says that "global managers are born, not made." However, he concedes, "There is no substitute for line experience in three or four countries to create a global perspective. You also encourage people to work in mixed-nationality teams. You *force* them to create personal alliances across borders, which means that sometimes you interfere in hiring decisions."[25]

In their book *Managing Across Borders*, Christopher Bartlett and Sumantra Ghoshal report that a key goal of human resources management programmes in global firms is "to develop an organization in which the individual manager's perceptions, capabilities, and relationships would become the basic

23 "When The Ideal And Reality Do Not Match," *The Financial Times*, August 13, 1990
24 Jeremy Main, "B-schools get a global vision," *Fortune*, July 17, 1991
25 William Taylor, "The logic of global business: an interview with ABB's Percy Barnevik," *Harvard Business Review*, March–April 1991

building block for an integrated, yet flexible worldwide organization."[26]

A number of Japanese firms have adopted a systematic
approach to staffing up with internationalists.

There are four steps:

1. Promising candidates are hired overseas.
2. They're trained and given their first assignments at the
    head office in Japan.
3. They're assigned to the international division within in the
    head office.
4. They return on assignment to their home country or an-
    other country.[27]

This process puts great emphasis on socializing new recruits,
and making them "part of the family." It cannot compensate
entirely for differences in language and culture, but it does
help to give executives the "shorthand" they need to network
effectively with their colleagues.

In summary:

Today's executives must become far more worldly, more
broadly educated, and more adaptable than in the past. They
must be both tough and tender. At the same time they must
become more adept at managing people: more participative,
more sensitive, more trusting and more flexible. And they
must advance from being mere managers to being leaders —
and from being *transactional* leaders to being *transformational*
leaders.

26 Christopher A. Bartlett and Sumantra Ghoshal, *Managing Across Borders*,
    Harvard Business School Press, 1989
27 Allan Bird and May Mukuda, "Expatriates in their own home: a new
    twist in the human resource management strategies of Japanese
    MNC's," *Human Resources Management*, Winter 1989, Volume 28,
    Number 4

It's your move now

By now, it should be clear you can't become a world class competitor by making a few cosmetic changes. Nor can you do it by working only on front line behaviour.

The fact is, if you want to be a player in tomorrow's tough world, you have to play the game the way the best are playing it. They're lean, mean fighting machines. They have no sacred cows. They revere innovation and change. They thrive on surprise. They aim high, they reach further than their resources realistically allow, and they never stop improving.

What's more, they operate in environments which encourage, rather than hamper, outstanding performance. This may or may not be a factor in your firm's favour, and it might not be something you can influence as well as you need to. If that's the case, you simply have to work even harder to stay up there with the best.

CHAPTER THREE

CHARACTERISTICS OF WORLD CLASS COMPANIES

What does a world class company look like? What is its character? How does it behave? What are the priorities of its managers? What holds it together? If you're going to change your own organization, what should you change *to*?

During the past decade, many studies have tried to answer these questions. *In Search of Excellence*[1] is the most famous of them, but there have been lots of others.

In their efforts to uncover the "secrets" of success, and to explain them to busy managers, it was natural that students of business would try to simplify things. So they used analogies and metaphors. And since organizations are social organisms, "corporate culture" was a natural hit.

It became a faddish issue in the early 1980s, and has taken up a lot of time and attention ever since. Fiddling with it has cost companies a fortune — with dubious results. It would be safe to say that most efforts to change corporate culture have not achieved their original aims.

❏ "The notion that executives can come in and change culture is just a misuse of the concept and the term," says MIT professor Edgar Schein.[2]

---

1 Thomas J. Peters and Robert H. Waterman, *In Search of Excellence*, Harper and Row, 1982
2 Fred Luthans, "Conversation With Edgar H. Schein," *Organizational Dynamics*, May 1989

❑ In a recent article in *Organizational Dynamics* Thomas H.
Fitzgerald wrote, *"Of course,* there has been a gratifying
improvement in the products and processes of American
industry, but little evidence nationally indicates that cultural transformation, rather than astute management, was
responsible."[3]

❑ Allan Kennedy, author of the best-selling book, *Corporate
Cultures,* recently lamented, "If I'd had any idea I was going
to contribute to spawning this huge industry of people
who think you can manage culture and therefore affect the
world, I'd probably have tried to suppress the book!"[4]

❑ Tom Peters, one of the first and loudest exponents of
culture, now says that companies waste a fortune "taking
people through God-only-knows what kind of exercise
about how to change their inner thinking and inner being
and make them externally oriented, or whatever other kind
of bullshit those programs tend to peddle."[5]

❑ "The fact is that there are no techniques for building ideo-
logies, no five easy steps to a better culture," says McGill
University professor Henry Mintzberg. "These are built
slowly and patiently by committed leaders who have
found interesting missions for their organizations and care
deeply about the people who perform them."[6]

Yesterday's survival strategies

Corporate culture is the end result of many things. It's the sum
total of an organization's basic beliefs — an expression of
"what counts around here, why those things are important,
and how we act." It is, in essence, a "tape recording" of the

3   Thomas H. Fitzgerald, "Can Change in Organizational Culture Really
    Be Managed?" *Organizational Dynamics,* Autumn 1988
4   "Coming Of Age," *Inc.,* April 1989
5   In an interview with Jack Gordon, editor of *Training* magazine, June 1989
6   Henry Mintzberg, *Mintzberg on Management,* The Free Press, 1989

organization's past and how it has coped with various challenges.

But while culture provides an intriguing picture of yesterday, and while it obviously influences current behaviour, it does not necessarily equip an organization to deal with the future in the best way. On the contrary, *culture can be as easily become a deadly drag on a company as a dynamic driving force.*

On one level, culture is observable: people in one company handle situations quite differently than those in another; certain behaviour is O.K. in one firm, but not in another. But at a deeper level, culture is invisible: behaviour is shaped by values which in turn have been shaped by people's assumptions.[7]

Unfortunately, we don't yet have a proven theory of how values change or can be changed. Nor is there an easy way to surface people's assumptions. And no one knows which cultural variables really matter, anyway.

Yet when managers set about improving customer service, they very quickly lock in on the culture issue. They know that to deliver superior service, they must change "what counts around here, why those things are important, and how we act."

But to say you're aiming at "a new culture" is a very squishy objective. What exactly are you talking about? Precisely what should you change — and why? How will you do it? And how will you know when you've got there?

What is the best culture for an engineering firm? For an advertising agency? For a chemical company? For an organization that sells consumer goods? The simple answer is: no one knows.

And should GM, Ford, and Toyota all strive towards the same culture, just because they all sell cars? That would be ridiculous, wouldn't it.

7   Edgar H. Schein, *Organizational Culture and Leadership*, Jossey-Bass, 1985

Yet everywhere you look, managers toy with culture and talk about "excellence" as an ideal. What does it all mean? What is excellent performance? Who's the judge?

It's all very well discussing these things, but so often it's a waste of time and money. In this competitive environment, managers can't afford the indulgence. Most firms will start making real progress when they stop talking about the things they can't easily manage and can't do much about in the short term, and instead get to work where they can make a rapid and meaningful impact.

Watch the Japanese

With the popularity of culture in the past decade, climate has been largely overlooked as a factor in making strategy come true. But it's a powerful moderating influence because it affects the way people feel about their jobs, and thus their motivation to work. For proof, one has only to watch the incredible changes that occur when Japanese managers take over a typical western workforce.

Time and again we've seen it happen. A company is in terrible trouble. Morale is low, productivity is sliding, and creditors are knocking at the door. In many cases, trade unions have caused problems for years. Then in come Japanese rescuers, and the very workers who were blamed for causing the problems suddenly "change their attitudes."

How does it happen? What's the secret?

What makes the difference is not a secret at all. It's certainly not some mythical "Japanese management" technique, and it doesn't happen because the new owners push a single "hot button." The improvement occurs largely through a return to common sense. Those Japanese managers know that if they want to fix anything, they'd better fix the fundamentals. So they dive in and simultaneously attend to many very basic things that transform the workplace.

One factor that appears to get a lot of attention is the climate in the their organizations. The new managers quickly get busy building new kinds of relationships, training and re-training people at all levels, and discussing ambitious new goals. They involve employees in talking about opportunities and solving problems. They share information. They remove layers of hierarchy to improve communication.

Some years ago, after Bridgestone (the Japanese tyre company) bought Firestone (a U.S. company), employees were asked about the difference between the Japanese and the Americans. Said one: "It's quite easy. When I worked for the Americans, they expected me to park my brains at the gate. Now that I work for the Japanese, they expect the whole person to come to work each day." Or consider the remarkable performance of New United Motor Manufacturing Inc. (NUMMI), a joint venture between General Motors and Toyota. The two motor giants joined hands so that GM could learn about Japanese management and production methods, and Toyota could learn about managing an American work-force. The plant they run together in Fremont California was once one of GM's worst. In fact, it was shut down in 1982 because of a long list of problems: lousy quality, poor productivity, labour-management conflict, absenteeism. Today, however, NUMMI "has managed to convert a crew of largely middle-aged, rabble-rousing former GM workers into a crack force that is beating the bumpers off the Big Three plants in efficiency and product quality."[8] One indication of the new commitment of workers: the company's suggestion scheme drew 1 716 ideas in 1986, 5 225 in 1987, and 10 671 in 1988![9]

8 "Gung ho to repeat assembly-line errors," *The Wall Street Journal*, March 27, 1986
9 Dean M. Schroeder and Alan G. Robinson, "America's most successful export to Japan: continuous improvement programs," *Sloan Management Review*, Spring 1991, Volume 32, no. 3

Changes of this magnitude don't happen overnight. It takes time to win back employees' loyalty and commitment, time to install new systems, time to change work practices. The organization has to unlearn old habits and learn new ones. It has to be coaxed gently — towards ever-tougher goals.

Not "the happiness factor"

Organizational climate is a controversial and misunderstood area. Some would say that the only difference between culture and climate is a semantic one. But I'd argue that *while culture describes every aspect of an organization's mind-set, climate is just one aspect of culture.*

Changing the climate and encouraging new kinds of behaviour ultimately changes the culture.

Too often, climate is confused with morale. Yet analysis of literally hundreds of studies shows little or no correlation between morale and productivity. Managers monitor the "happiness factor" but it doesn't necessarily tell them what they need to know. One recent survey, comparing employee attitudes and management practices in 106 factories in the U.S. and Japan, concluded:

> "... it appears that commitment to the company is essentially the same in our American and Japanese employee samples. . . . American employees seem much more satisfied with their jobs than do the Japanese. . . . Every prior survey contrasting Japanese and Western work attitudes has likewise found work satisfaction to be lowest among the Japanese."[10])

10 James R. Lincoln, "Employee Work Attitudes and Management Practice in the U.S. and Japan: Evidence From a Large Comparative Survey," *California Management Review*, Fall 1989, Vol. 32, No.1

Climate may be defined as "the sum of the perceptions of the individuals working in an organization."[11] These perceptions are shaped by a number of factors, including:

❏ The amount of freedom and involvement people feel they're allowed.
❏ The sense of challenge they get from their jobs.
❏ Rewards and recognition.
❏ The warmth and support of colleagues.
❏ The presence or absence of conflict.
❏ The way managers treat people.

Climate is both a *cause* and a *result* of the way people feel about an organization. It's affected by the leader's style, by systems, procedures, and policies. Also by such factors as pressure of work, the mix of people in the workplace, and "housekeeping" or "hygiene" arrangements.

But equally important is people's understanding of:

❏ Where the organization is going.
❏ How it'll get there.
❏ What they must do to make it happen.
❏ How they'll be rewarded.

Climate and strategy are thus tightly interlinked — in fact, inter-*dependent*. Each has a direct impact on the other. And the good news is, both can be deliberately managed.

Few managers understand all this. So while they might design the most elegant strategy, they overlook the fact that the damned thing won't work without the support of a lot of people.

They don't think about all the factors which turn people on — or turn them off. Nor do they bother to "count their people

---

11 George H. Litwin and Robert A. Stringer Jr., *Motivation And Organizational Climate*, Division Of Research, Graduate School Of Business Administration, Harvard University, 1968

in" at an early stage, so they lose their commitment later when it's needed.

Most people in most companies don't know what's going on. They don't know what's required of them. They get too little information, and virtually no feedback. They're not involved in decisions that directly affect their performance. When it comes to strategy, they're in the dark.

This causes them to see their roles in very limited terms, to do as little as possible, to withhold ideas, and to pull in different directions. Ignorance about their employer's strategy makes it easy for them to under-perform.

Make them important

Developing a healthy, productive climate begins with making clear the firm's purpose and its strategy. In addition, it depends upon a rich flow of information in all directions, and on an open, involving management style. People must be helped to see the real meaning in their jobs. They must want to come forward with new ideas, take responsibility for their own performance, and think for themselves. This happens when they're treated like adults, and when they're forced to reach beyond their own, often self-imposed, limits.

In their best-selling book *The One Minute Manager*, Ken Blanchard and Spencer Johnson advise, "Help people reach their full potential. Catch them doing something right."[12] Wise words! But don't stop there.

> It's easy to catch someone doing something right, and to make them feel important. But if you expect world class performance, you have to take them beyond just *feeling* important, to actually *being* important. And that's a hell of a leap.

12 Kenneth Blanchard and Spencer Johnson, *The One Minute Manager*, William Morrow and Company, 1982

You can make someone feel important by patting them on the back, by saying, "Well done" or by giving them some kind of reward. In other words, *recognition* is the key. But to make them important you have to give them something quite different, something that could carry a risk, something you may be loath to let go of. In a word: *power.*

There's no doubt that you can motivate people — for a while at least — by "catching them doing something right." But if it's long-term performance you're after, and if your standard is world class, you'd better share the most critical information, decisions, and actions.

This is easy to say and tough to do. Most managers won't even try. So making a real effort could give you a powerful advantage over your competitors.

The value of climate surveys

Structured climate surveys provide reasonably objective data on how people feel about such factors as working conditions, communications, pay, training, the management style, and so on. This information can be used as a benchmark for change.

Over time, such records track what's happening in an organization. Management gets useful feedback, and opportunities for further improvement are highlighted.

But helpful though they may be, climate surveys are not a panacea. Nor do you have to wait for one before you can start shaping up. If you simply wandered around and talked to your people for a while, you'd find out pretty much everything that a structured survey might tell you.

One CEO I know has a regular breakfast to which he invites 20 people from various parts of his organization. "It's very relaxed," he says, "and they talk pretty freely." Others make sure they join their staff for drinks on a Friday evening, or they make a point of travelling with different people.

Perhaps the greatest value of a structured survey (outside researchers, formal questionnaires, etc.) is that it takes the information-gathering process beyond "fingertip feel." It appears to be more objective, and thus often gives executives a real jolt. If the news is bad, they sit up and take note.

But a word of warning: if you do a survey, be sure to follow up with feedback on the results. Let people know what their opinions added up to, and what action will follow. The survey itself says, "We're interested in what you think." That gets their expectations up. Don't let them down!

The results to focus on

Deliberate organizational change seldom occurs just because someone thinks it's a good idea. It's almost always triggered by a crisis: profits or productivity are down, quality is falling, accidents are rising, industrial relations are unhealthy, and so on. In only a few cases is change promoted *in anticipation* of new circumstances.

Thus most change efforts are *reactive*. Managers invariably start with what they can see — i.e., "the numbers" — and the more pressure they're under, the more focused their concern becomes. Of course, they are quite right to act this way. Ultimately, profit is what counts. But to achieve their financial goals, two things are essential:

1. Employees must all understand the importance of profit, how it's made, and how they impact on it.
2. A climate must be created and maintained in which they not only buy into the idea, but accept it as a driving purpose in their own lives.

The climate is the underlying cause of a business's competitive standing. Managers don't understand this, or they choose to overlook it. Then, because they focus on the wrong results, they choose the wrong change strategy.

More of them would be more successful if they saw that the "soft" side of management is vital in the quest for better "hard" numbers.

Not a "touchy-feely" process

Contrary to what many people seem to think, improving a company's climate isn't a "touchy-feely" process. It has little to do with people *liking* each other or *agreeing* with each other on everything.

In many countries today, managers must deal with multi-cultural work forces. Politics, socio-economic differences, education, race, language, and religion often are used as excuses for not starting a change effort. Managers wisely shy away from any process or programme which hinges on people changing their basic beliefs.

Given half a chance, virtually any group of people will be able to find countless points of disagreement. It's far more constructive to talk about their common purpose.

The aim should be not to iron out those differences, but rather to help people learn that they can cooperate towards a goal *in spite of* their differences.

The key therefore is to focus on *work*, on *profit*, on *quality* and *productivity* and *customer service*. To talk about business and what makes it tick. To keep your feet on the ground, and to make sure that your whole team spends as much of its time as possible on those things which will make a difference to profits.

As I'll emphasise time and again in these pages, communication and involvement make all the difference in a firm's performance. But that does not mean that managers must all become "nice guys" and stop making decisions, or accept sub-standard work. In fact, quite the opposite.

To be world class, managers must be tough. They must set high standards, and keep raising them. They must

**insist that today's resources be tapped for every last
drop of profit, and that every activity builds tomorrow's resources.**

The best organizations are learning to mobilize their people by
treating them with dignity and respect — and by pushing
them like hell towards "impossible" objectives.

Shifting priorities

In business, the gap between lip service and day-to-day action
is a big one. Talking about superior customer service is easy.
"Smile" training can be delivered any day of the week.

But just as most business strategies fail through poor implementation, so are most efforts to improve customer service
likely to fail.

Nine times out of ten, "the programme" is launched with
a bang. The boss makes a speech, the troops are shown a video,
posters suddenly bloom all over the place, and a new ad
campaign starts telling the world how much "we care."

But very quickly problems arise. Customers continue to act
unreasonable, ask for the impossible, and expect the unde-
liverable. Employees get bored with the whole thing. And
managers change their priorities. Today, they talk customers.
Tomorrow, they're under pressure to deliver increased
profits. A week hence, they fret about the firm's social responsibility stance, its relations with government, or trouble with
the unions.

As CEOs come and go, attention shifts from issue to issue.
When there's a marketing man at the helm, people talk about
customers. When an accountant takes over, everyone burrows
into the numbers. I've worked with two chief executives who
were transferred just as their change programmes took hold.
The minute the news leaked out, you could sense staff heaving
a sigh of relief. The initiatives they'd begun died almost immediately.

A general manager of a third firm fell in love with the "eight basic principles" in *In Search Of Excellence*, and spent several years trying to implant them in his firm. While he was there it was hard to see their impact. (And, of course, it was impossible to tell whether any change in performance was due to the eight "excellence" factors or to his ability.) Within weeks of his transfer, his successor was doing something different.

People expect this to happen. So when a manager announces that customer service is the new priority, they all nod in agreement. Privately, however, they say, "Here we go again." Then they put their heads down below the parapets, and wait for him — and "it" — to go away.

They know, from past experience, that "this programme" will go the same way as all the others: last year's cost-cutting drive . . . the quality programme that was launched with such fanfare two years ago . . . the productivity effort that bit the dust in 1980. "We've tried that before, and it didn't work," becomes the cry.

Why should I believe you?

Trust is a key element in organizational performance. It's vital in creating a customer service ethic. Yet managers destroy it time and again. Too often they talk a great story, then fail to live it out.

When people trust each other, communication is open and honest. Ideas flow naturally. Feedback is accurate. Cooperation and teamwork typify "the way things are done around here." And even conflict is healthy.

On the other hand, when trust has not developed, or when it breaks down, dysfunctional behaviour is almost certain. That's when individuals start following their own agendas, and corporate politics becomes a problem.

Unfortunately, trust can't be demanded. It must be *earned*. And the only way to earn it is by trusting others, and by acting out your stated intentions. By doing what you say you'll do.

Share the load

Tomorrow's manager must survive in sea of paradox. He'll be faced with more decisions (and more complex ones), which need faster answers. Decisiveness will be crucial. At the same time, however, managers have to weigh the risks. With competition hot and resources scarce, each decision will have bigger consequences.

Intuitive, responsive behaviour will become more important; but so will strategy. Even while managers deal with the here and now, they'll have to think ahead and plan for tomorrow's opportunities. And even while some decisions will be best taken centrally, many others will have to be decentralized. (Not least because ideas only translate into action when they're shoved out to the front.)

> In the new world class company, more people will have to become involved in the bigger issues. Not that they'll make the final decisions, or even prescribe direction; but rather, that they'll *influence* decisions and direction.

What this means, of course, is that participative management is not an "optional extra." It's key to the sea change we need in the way we think about and execute strategy.

Factors that lead to world class performance

Like many other authors and consultants, I too have hunted for the secrets of business success. For more than a decade I've scoured the literature and watched people at work.

In the process, I've isolated ten key factors which appear essential to world class performance. These are issues to think about if you're serious about being a first-league player.

They describe the priorities and activities that command attention in the best companies, so they suggest some of the things you should look at if you want to improve your results. Think about them. Think about how much attention they get in your firm right now. Consider the impact they might have if they got more. And talk to your colleagues about what they could mean if you started working with them.

1. Vision

In this time of increasing turbulence, uncertainty, and unpredictability, a clear, long-term view is vital. Corporate strategists must ask, "Where are we going?" and they must clearly spell out their direction so their followers can support them. They must dream big dreams and set ambitious goals — and they must stretch just a little further than their capabilities allow.

Many executives shy away from spelling out a vision of the future. Their resources are limited so they feel they must be modest and conservative. They don't like to be specific, preferring to keep their options open. They argue that the future is so unpredictable one cannot sensibly make forecasts. As one executive said to me recently, "I can't see *next week*, let alone next month. So don't ask me to share my vision with you; I don't have one. The here and now is what counts for me!"

But consider the example of Konosuke Matsushita, former chairman of Matsushita Industries, one of the giants of Japanese industry. He first spelled out his strategy in 1923. At the time, he couldn't have anticipated the devastating impact of the Depression years, or of World War II. But he said to his people, in effect, *"There's* the mountain we're going to climb. Follow me."

And he never deviated from that grand purpose. When some American business leaders visited him in 1985, when he was in his nineties, they asked him about his vision. "We've heard about the long view you take in Japan," they said. "How far into the future do you look?"

The old man thought for a while, then said, "Oh . . . maybe 250 years."

They were flabbergasted. "What do you need for that?"

Matsushita pondered the question, and answered, "Patience."

Perhaps that's what we all need. Defining a vision has nothing to do with crystal-ball gazing, and everything to do with making the future a matter of choice and not chance. It's a totally pragmatic exercise, and the first step in creating a meaningful strategy.

Vision is a business tool. It's the key to empowerment. No company can afford the luxury of vagueness. As Laurence J. Peter says, "If you don't know where you're going, you'll wind up somewhere else." (And if your staff don't know where you're going, they'll help you get lost!)

Without a vision, it's impossible to delegate responsibility or to make sensible decisions about future resources. Without a vision, it's impossible to "let people go," or for them to take responsibility for their own performance. Without a vision, the people in your firm are compelled to focus on *activities* rather than on *results*.

On the other hand, when you do spell out your vision, when you do stretch people's ambitions and ignite their spirit, great things are possible. Most people respond well to big ideas and to bold goals. Most people are capable of far more than is expected of them — or than they expect of themselves. Most people have it in them to be high achievers — when their leaders create a climate of high achievement.

2. Boldness

Because the future is so hazy, virtually every decision is a risk decision. We don't know what lies ahead or how our decisions will pan out. The result, in most companies, is analysis paralysis. Decisions are delayed; action is postponed; managers talk proudly of being "risk-averse" or of their insistence on "no surprises" from subordinates.

New technology hasn't loosened things up, either. Now, facts are easy to retrieve. There's a PC on every executive's desk. And there's no end to the theories and models which managers eagerly grasp in the search for certainty.

The fact is, however, that all the sophisticated tools in the world haven't done much to improve decision-making. It's still a risky business. More than 90 per cent of all new products fail. Only about 20 per cent of new companies last five years. Yesterday's champions are today's also-rans.

So why the delay? Is one more meeting really going to make the critical difference? Is one more research report or analyst's view really going to guarantee success? Of course not. So if you're going to get it wrong, *won't you be better off failing faster, so you learn faster?*

All the evidence says yes. The best time to take advantage of a window of opportunity is the first time it opens. Getting to market late almost always carries severe penalties in terms of customer awareness, market share, costs, and profits.

World class companies understand this. Tomorrow's big wins will come to those managers who push ahead knowing that they'll make some mistakes. The biggest risk is taking no risk at all.

Unfortunately, there's a decided lack of positive thinking in business today. Virtually every company needs more people with real leadership quality, people with the guts and the go to stand up and be counted. But widespread layoffs and massive cost-cutting efforts have had a serious impact on people's willingness to take risks and on their loyalty to their employers. Many are now in defensive mode, intent only on keeping their jobs. Even those in successful firms are wary.

Management will have to work hard to restore morale. It'll take time to re-create a climate in which constructive risk-taking is lauded and rewarded. Every employee must be encouraged to take the positive view . . . to "go for it" in his or her part of the business.

This means, of course, that leaders must become more tolerant of mistakes. People must understand that it's safe to get things wrong. And personnel policies must be redesigned to support the new standards that are set.

3. Anticipation

A decade ago, when I was pitching for a health food company's advertising account, I proposed that they sponsor a major triathlon. Around the same time, I suggested to a friend in the athletics apparel business that he start making "designer" sportswear. Both ideas were ignored. Both firms lost a once-in-a-lifetime opportunity. They failed to take advantage of serious changes that had appeared on the horizon.

The future can't be precisely predicted, but if you look hard enough there are many clear signals of what does lie ahead. The most important strength of any company in the future will be its ability to learn faster than its competitors.

Managers must watch changes in the business arena — the socio-political environment, economics, population shifts, technological developments, competitor activity, and so on. But most importantly, they must stay one step ahead of their *customers*. They must not just *re*-act to customers' needs and wants, but they must *pre*-act to shape them.

To make this happen, companies are being radically redesigned. They're becoming "porous," so that information and ideas flow quickly into them and to the right people. They're also "transparent," because of their flat, lean, flexible structure and their management information systems. You can see through them from top to bottom, and out into the marketplace. There's a great deal of sharing — of information and of power.

By getting closer to their customers, companies dramatically improve their understanding of what's needed next. And through constant experiments, they get a real-time sense of what works and what doesn't.

But in addition to direct feedback from customers, there's a great deal of other information that must be examined. For example, demographic trends tell us a lot about the size and location of tomorrow's markets. Coupled with changes in spending power, they also suggest how values — and thus *psychographics* — are likely to shift.

Starting today, examine the facts that are available, scan a wide horizon, and open your mind to the great spectrum of possibilities before you. Get the rest of your team involved, too. The more eyes and ears you have, the better your chances of staying ahead of the competition.

That said, don't fall into the trap of expecting customers to give you all the answers. They don't always know what products or services they'll pay for. The Sony Walkman, for example, came from the imagination of Sony chairman Akio Morita, not from a customer survey. Which customers, ten or 15 years ago, would have asked for products like Perrier water, Kellogg's Heartwise cereal, the Reebok Pump athletic shoe, or Matsushita's Aisaigo Day washing machine, which uses "fuzzy logic" to programme itself? And who would have asked for services like outplacement counselling or temporary executives, or for processes like thin slab steel casting?

Customers are a rich source of new ideas. But most of them are not designers, they don't know what technology might be available, and they can't visualize the full range of possibilities for your business.

Anticipating their needs requires that you literally think for them, that you stay one jump ahead of them (and of the competition), and that you sometimes make a fool of yourself in trying to out-guess them.

4. Responsiveness

When the Berlin Wall fell in 1989, Heinz Wiezorek, president of Coca-Cola's German operation, was in America. He saw the news on TV, recognized an opportunity, and phoned home to say, "Get Coke out there!" The result was that thousands of East Germans who crossed the border got a free sample of the world's favourite soft drink.

Wiezorek knew the value of speed. He understood that when the East German market opened up, "There won't be two colas in restaurants and small outlets. They'll choose the one that's first in the market."[13]

The toughest competitors today are doing everything faster, with fewer resources. The accelerating pace of change doesn't allow the luxury of lengthy debate or idle contemplation. To stay ahead, companies must move fast. The need for speed is paramount.

Sony launches an average of 1,5 new products a day. Seiko launches a new watch every day. Citibank has introduced as many as three new financial services in a single week. About 25 per cent of 3M's sales come from products less than five years old. New products give Johnson & Johnson 25 per cent of its U.S. sales.[14]

John Young, CEO of Hewlett Packard, has set a goal of cutting in half the time it takes to get a new product from concept to customer. Motorola used to take three weeks to manufacture an electronic pager; now it takes just *two hours*.

13 Patricia Sellers, "Coke's brash new European strategy," *Fortune*, August 13, 1990
14 Kenneth Labich, "The Innovators," *Fortune*, June 6, 1988

When Apple Computer launched a budget model Macintosh recently, the whole process, from design to delivery, took just nine months — a saving of more than 50 per cent. Toshiba has cut the time it takes to develop a home computer from two years to less than six months. It has also increased the pace of new product introductions, launching three laptop computers in 1986, five in 1987, eight in 1990.

American steel mills now take fewer man-hours to produce a ton of steel than the Japanese. IBM has cut the development time of a new mainframe computer from three years to 18 months. Xerox trimmed about 30 per cent off the time it takes to get a new copier to market. ICI once took up to six years to roll a new drug out into several markets, but now does it in just one or two, and will soon cut the lag entirely.

Japanese auto manufacturers develop new models in under four years, compared to at least five for their western competitors. By the mid to late 1990s, they'll do it in two to three years. Most of them build only to order, and take just 16,9 man-hours to turn out a luxury car (25 per cent of the time European manufacturers need.) They deliver within ten days to three weeks, but Toyota aims to slash that to just a couple of days. The goal of zero inventories is being pursued as aggressively as that of zero defects. These Japanese firms continually excite customers with totally new vehicles, not just cosmetic changes to yesterday's basic bodies.

Companies that don't speed up won't survive. The same scenario is being acted out in industry after industry. There just is no place for constipated companies in the new go-go global market. Product life cycles are getting shorter. Customers are more impatient. Novelty is the name of the game. Just-in-time manufacturing (JIT) is replacing "just-in-case" stockpiling.

Quicker cycle times are vital to respond to pushy customers. They have a direct economic benefit as well. When you cut the slack out of the system you also cut a lot of costs. A leaner, slicker, fitter system is a whole lot healthier. Quite simply, value is added for a larger portion of the time spent in the process.[15] The results show up on the bottom line.

So, on the one hand, be prepared to act before all the facts are in. When a customer calls with a request, a complaint or a suggestion, do something about it right away. When an employee offers an idea, cut through the paperwork and put it into action fast.

On the other hand, start redesigning your business system right now. Start experimenting. Take some chances. Try some of the things you'll read about in this book. Don't wait till you've got the resources you need — you may never get them if you don't start building them today!

Of course, this will go against the grain in many organizations. Their systems, policies, and procedures all are designed for certainty. But be warned: windows of opportunity open for only the briefest moment. The best time and the cheapest time to get through them is the first time. The surest way to be shut out of the game is to drag your feet.

5. Focus

Every strategist since Clausewitz has underlined the importance of focusing strength against weakness. Military theory suggests that to be successful in a head-on clash, an attacker should have at least a three-to-one advantage in terms of resources. But as many guerilla wars have shown, sheer firepower can often be çountered by speed and agility when limited resources are carefully aimed at a few weak spots.

In the new global economy, all managers face an abundance of opportunities with a shortage of resources. There are just too many possibilities. Given the chance, any management team could come up with a list of two

15 "The Merit Of Making Things Fast," Roger W. Schmenner, *Sloan Management Review*, Fall 1988

dozen priorities. But the 80/20 rule always applies, so tough choices must be made.

In the contest for customers, world class firms gain valuable advantage by looking for the chinks in their enemies' armour, and targeting them with precision. The challenge is to accurately pick the areas that on the one hand are especially vulnerable or unguarded, and on the other, promise the biggest payoff if they're successfully breached.

This may mean, for example, that you use direct response techniques to tackle a competitor with a big sales force. Or that you attack their German market (which has potential, but is being ignored right now) rather than their home market in Portugal. Or that you attack one of their "cash cows" (a product, a market, a technology) so they can't fund their next move.

Alternatively, it might mean that you send a "Trojan horse" into one of their markets — to seize one small slice, then another, then another.

But the need for focus does not just apply to markets and strategies. It applies equally to people.

An organization's people are all important. They all have infinite potential. In an ideal world, they'd all deliver "turbocharged" performance. But in real life, there are always a few key individuals who really make the difference. Find them, put them in the right jobs, motivate them, and empower them to perform — and watch them turn the others on.

World class leaders concentrate their efforts where they'll do the most good. They look for leverage in everything they do. They choose the few things that'll make the biggest difference, and go at them with a vengeance.

6. Commitment

The Japanese kamikaze pilot who flew 100 missions was involved, but not committed. In the same way, managers who keep themselves busy with too many priorities confuse involvement with commitment.

One reason that projects, products, people, and companies fail is that there's not a critical mass of money, time, energy or other resources behind them. This is quite natural because most of us don't like risks. We prefer to move cautiously, a step at a time, building a solid base as we go. And we try to juggle many balls at once, so even if we drop one or two, several others stay in the air.

But face facts: you can't be all things to all people. You have to make choices. You have to give yourself wholeheartedly to one direction or another. Success in any field requires real commitment.

The Japanese are often criticized for the time they spend debating new opportunities or a change in direction. Conversation goes around and around, up and down. No one appears to want to make a decision. The need for consensus slows things to a snail's pace. But they're successful because when they do finally choose a course of action, they put everything into it and they move with lightning speed. They're single-minded, and they play to win.

When you know where you're going, be sure you commit sufficient resources to getting there. When you decide on a strategy, put enough behind it to give it a chance. And stay with it when the going gets tough — as it most assuredly will. Giving up too soon never made a winner of anyone.

Flexibility

Modern business is full of paradoxes, and here's one of them: while focus and commitment are vital, firms must be prepared to change direction fast if a strategy isn't working.

And here's a second paradox: while tight controls and a clear structure are absolutely necessary, world class companies are increasingly becoming more organic than mechanistic. People are cross-trained so they understand their colleagues' jobs and can easily fill in for them. Roles are often interchangeable. Teams of people with specific skills and from many areas of the business — including suppliers and subcontractors — form to tackle specific tasks, then disband. Communication occurs informally, and not just via memos and scheduled meetings.

Success is the enemy of flexibility. When we've learned how to make something work, we don't easily change our minds or our methods. We become trapped in the past.

No strategy can be cast in stone. Flexibility is vital in an ever-changing world. We must all be prepared to discard cherished ideas, to kill products that have brought profits for years, and to toss aside plans that have cost hours of toil.

A great example of strategic flexibility was Coca-Cola's about-face when consumers rejected "new" Coke. A lot of money, effort, emotion, and ego was involved in the decision to launch the new formula. But when consumers responded negatively, top management moved with surprising speed. Coke Classic — the taste that America knew and loved — was brought back virtually overnight to bolster the company's "megabrand," and to gain precious share points in the cola wars.

> **Flexibility is needed right throughout the value chain. Because customers are bombarded by new and better offerings every day, companies must learn to customize products and services. As mass marketing gives way to micro-marketing, mass production must give way to "lean" production. A "run of one" must be the new objective.**

This takes a total overhaul of virtually everything. In particular, manufacturing operations must be examined from top to bottom. Factors to review range from plant location and layout to supplier relations, design and engineering, automation, information management, and the management style.

8. Creativity

A constant stream of fresh ideas is essential in the face of shorter life cycles for virtually everything. Every person in your company must be encouraged to "find a better way." In their quest for quality, many firms have tried to reduce tasks to their essentials, to give people specific instructions and to set clear standards for them. In other words, they've tried to cut out individual initiative and imagination, and to impose a foolproof procedure.

Unfortunately, this can be terribly counter-productive. No one knows a job as well as the person doing it. No one is in a better position to reinvent it. And there's nothing motivating in doing a mechanical task over and over to someone else's specifications.

The auto industry provides endless examples of good and bad management. One study showed that U.S. firms involved just 12 per cent of people at all levels in problem solving and decision making. In contrast, Japanese firms involved some 70 per cent.

Another study compared the U.S. operations of the top three American motor manufacturers (General Motors, Ford, and Chrysler) with those of the top three Japanese motor manufacturers (Toyota, Nissan, and Honda). The American firms got an average of one suggestion per 37 employees, and implemented about 20 per cent of those ideas. The Japanese got 27 suggestions *per person*, and implemented more than 90 per cent. Toyota alone implemented 3 365 suggestions a day![16]

Altogether, Japanese firms are streets ahead in exploiting the potential of their "knowledge workers." In 1986, for

16 John J. Nora, C. Raymond Rogers, and Robert J. Stramy, *Transforming The Workplace*, Princeton Research Press, 1986

example, they coaxed almost 48 million ideas for improvement from their workers; American companies got just 1 million.[17]

> Once you unleash the brainpower in your firm, amazing things are possible. But good ideas alone aren't enough; they must be translated into action. This might seem risky at times but it's also one way to reduce risk. For when you *do*, you *learn*. And it's only by trying things that we discover whether or not they're really practical.

Says GE's Jack Welch: ". . . if we let our people flourish and grow, if we use the best ideas they come up with, then we have a chance to win. The idea of liberation and empowerment for our workforce is not enlightenment — it's a competitive necessity. When you look at the global arena, *that's what our competitive advantage is.*"[18]

> Many suggestion schemes fail because people focus on big-bang changes, or quantum leaps. Of course, those are important; but equally important are the dozens — *hundreds*, even — of small, incremental changes which the Japanese call "the samurai's 1 000 tiny cuts."

Of course, innovation cannot be just be a product of suggestion schemes. It must be encouraged in many ways. The most creative companies put people into small teams with their own budgets, their own goals — and their own rules. (And often they'll give several teams the same challenge.) They have many projects on the boil at once, to swing the odds of a few

---

17 Dean M. Schroeder and Alan G. Robinson, "America's most successful export to Japan: continuous improvement programs," *Sloan Management Review*, Spring 1991, Volume 32, No.3

18 Stratford P. Sherman, "Inside The Mind Of Jack Welch," *Fortune*, March 27, 1989

successes in their favour. They beg, borrow, and buy (and sometimes steal) ideas from outsiders. They tackle different parts of a project "in parallel," both to speed it up and because discoveries in one area often trigger breakthroughs elsewhere. In short, *they think creatively about how to manage creativity. They know that innovation is too important to be left to chance. They make their own luck.*

Changing any company is a long-term process. It cannot be rushed. But "quick-fixes" must be part of the formula. Everyone must be encouraged to experiment, to risk, and to improve — TODAY! And the process must be continuous. We must invent our way into the future.

9. Knowledge

"We are working towards a world in which the big change is technology of information," says Lester Wunderman, chairman of Young & Rubicam's Wunderman Worldwide unit in New York.[19] An MIT study revealed that we now have to cope with about 600 times as much knowledge as in 1980. There's as much information in one issue of *Time* magazine as an average person would have gained in a lifetime in 17th Century England.

> **One of a company's most precious "invisible assets" in this Third Wave information age is knowledge — about customers, competitors, technology, processes. But few firms have a systematic plan for collecting or analyzing it. Most ignore it or squander it.**

If organizations learn at all, it's usually very slowly. They take a myopic view of their world, information is gathered largely by accident, it's looked at superficially, and it's either filed "for

19 "Wunderman Touts New Age Of TV," *Advertising Age*, November 6, 1990

future reference" or tossed out (Figure 3-1). The result is that change comes slowly, if at all. Opportunities are easily missed. Competitive advantage is quickly eroded.

Figure 3-1
The slow-learning process

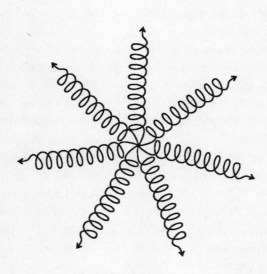

Figure 3-2
Wide scan, fast learning

Because this is such an uncertain time, fast, continuous learning is essential. World class firms scan a wide horizon for new
data. They scoop up ideas, and demand feedback on everything they do. They deliberately capture new knowledge and
use it to transform themselves (figure 3-2). Result: their people
grow, they surprise their customers with a continuous flow of
innovative ideas, and they present their competitors with a
moving target.

10. Communication

The more knowledge we accumulate, and the more things
change around us, the faster we must be able to share ideas.
Superconductive materials are still in the novelty stage. Superconductive *organizations* have yet to be designed.

In addition to speed of communication, however, new
ways must be found to improve the quality of communication
— both inside the organization, and outside with key stakeholders.

Tell your team what they need to know: your business
strategy, how your company is doing, what their roles are,
what lies ahead for them. As Jan Carlzon of Scandinavian
Airlines says, "People without information cannot take responsibility. People with information cannot help but take
responsibility."[20]

Most people in most firms get far too little information.
They can't reach their potential because they really don't know
what to do. Nobody listens to them, and nobody reacts to their
suggestions. A huge amount of valuable energy is lost.

The fact is, you can't over-communicate the critical messages. No firm that I know does even a halfway decent job of
spreading the world class gospel.

20 Jan Carlzon, op. cit.

Communication is a competitive weapon that is almost universally overlooked and under-exploited. Any company that makes a determined effort to improve it gains an advantage that is not only hard to detect, but also very hard to copy. For like all other "invisible assets," communication doesn't just happen. You can't buy it and install it. It takes time to implant, and effort to keep it alive. And best of all, the more you "use" it, the better it gets.

CHAPTER FOUR

CUSTOMER SERVICE STINKS!

No matter what you buy, parting with your cash is seldom easy. Companies seem to have some sort of built-in resistance to their most valuable asset: their customers. Products don't work. Administrative systems cause endless foul-ups and delays. Front line people are often ignorant and unhelpful. The most vital factor of all in business success — extraordinary attention to customers — is not yet common practice.

A shocking number of firms just don't understand the pivotal role of customers in their lives. They fail to treat customers the way we all like to be treated: with care and respect, trust and dignity. They don't build the total business system which is needed to make superior front line performance possible. They focus inwards, on *activities* that keep them busy, rather than outwards on customers who give them *results*.

The first priority of business

Peter Drucker said perhaps three decades ago that *the first priority of business is to create and keep a customer*. Ted Levitt has repeated the same thing over and over, and any number of other authorities have drummed home the message.

But for many people, this amazing insight is a brand new idea. Says Jack Falvey, contributing editor to *Sales & Marketing Management*: "Top executives at many companies have just discovered what most sales managers have known since their days in a territory — that the customer is an important element of their business."[1]

Only somewhat tongue-in-cheek, *Training & Development Journal* advises, "Please assemble whatever pain relievers you normally require in stressful situations, get a glass of water, sit down, and take a deep breath. What you are about to read may shock you. *Customer service drives very few American businesses.*"[2]

Actually, customer service drives very few businesses anywhere in the world. Instead, paperwork and politics, machines, and obsolete procedures get most attention.

A simple process

When you get down to it, business is an incredibly simple process. You take some resources (money and minds), and turn them into value that a customer will pay for . . . then you use that revenue to buy more resources. Round and round it goes, like a little engine — as long as you put in more "fuel" (Figure 4-1).

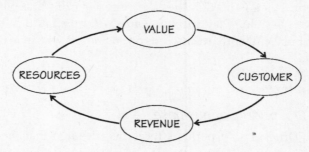

Figure 4-1
The business process

---

1   Jack Falvey, "Get The Lowdown On Your Customers," *Sales & Marketing Management,* May 1989
2   John Wilcox, "Do As I Say, Not As I Do," *Training & Development Journal,* December 1988

Trouble comes when you forget that the only source of power is the customer; and that's what happens throughout most organizations. People everywhere keep themselves busy with agendas that have nothing to do with creating value for their customers.

For some reason, most companies seem to view customer service as a "zero-sum" game in which one side (the customer) wins at the expense of the other (the company).

Because they have this resentful attitude, they don't pay nearly enough attention to anyone who volunteers to keep them in business. Marketing is just a "function," a "department," a bunch of crazies who spend money on advertising and lunch. Other activities — finance, administration, quality control — are far more important. The result is that many companies are their own worst enemies in the marketplace.

Customers are a "product"

Customers aren't an issue you can talk about from time to time. Nor are they the sole preserve of just a few specialists in Marketing or Sales. Rather, they are a *result* or a *product*. They are created when you anticipate their needs and wants, and when you make effective use of your resources to meet or exceed their expectations.

Customers pay for a product's features and performance. "Value" to them means tangible things such as function, appearance, feel, fit, finish, reliability, serviceability, guarantees, and resale value. It also means intangibles: image, empathy, courtesy, and respect.

In return, you get not just money, but equally important, such vital "invisible assets" as information, ideas, skills, vision, confidence, trust, a brand reputation, and a positive attitude within your organization (Figure 4-2). Competing is learning. The faster you learn, the more knowledge you can

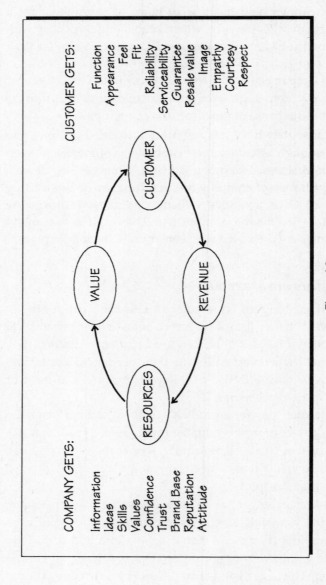

Figure 4-2
The rewards of customer service

assimilate and use, the better your chances of survival and growth.

Everyone in your firm needs to know this. Most people don't, so they spend a lot of time complaining about "ungrateful bloody customers," and working out how to do as little as possible for them.

Most people aren't trained to deliver out-of-the-ordinary service, nor do they get the kind of management support that makes it a way of life. They beaver away doing the wrong things the wrong way because their real purpose is unclear.

If you recognize this, and do something serious about it fast, you can look forward to some exciting times. If you don't, expect deep trouble. The new business arena is an unforgiving place.

Managing your "moments of truth"

Customers get a very superficial view of most firms. They're routed by a receptionist . . . a sales person wraps their purchases . . . a credit clerk phones for payment. But those brief encounters shape customers' perceptions. The behaviour of the individuals they deal with makes an indelible impression.

In the eyes of a customer, your front line representative *is* your company. Your company's total image is shaped by the way that person looks, acts, and speaks. At the "moment of truth" the customer doesn't know about your wonderful executive development programme, doesn't see your wonderful factory, and doesn't care about your strong balance sheet. He doesn't appreciate your concern for the environment, your progressive employee benefits programme or your "flat" organization. All he sees is Suzanne or Joe delivering the goods or screwing up. So before you read any further, ask:

❏ Do you have the nicest possible people managing your moments of truth? (Some people simply are better at the job than others!)

❑ Do your people look clean, smart, efficient, and friendly?
❑ Do they know enough about your products and services, and your business procedures, to be able to do the right thing, fast, when customers ask a question, present a problem, or complain?
❑ Are they prepared to stick their necks out for customers, to buck the system or bend the rules if need be?
❑ Do they have the imagination to anticipate customers' needs, and to be creative about meeting them?
❑ Can they take the strain of dealing with particularly rude or demanding customers?

Many interactions with customers last just a few minutes, or even seconds. But even the briefest of them leaves a snapshot of the total organization. Customers have nothing else by which to judge you. And once they form a view, it's hard to change their minds.

Managing those "moments of truth" is the ultimate objective in making your company more customer-friendly. Making it happen is hard work. It's not enough to run a few workshops for your people. Nor is it as simple as trying to motivate them with a pep talk by the current hotshot on the lecture circuit. And putting up posters that proclaim your commitment to customer care, or issuing pocket cards to remind everyone of what that means, can be the kiss of death.

> Customer service is far from reality in most organizations. Most moments of truth are a disaster. The only way to improve is through a massive, company-wide effort. Real change involves every employee, every system, every process. It requires leadership of the highest order. And it needs enduring commitment over the long run.

Bad service makes headlines

Often, as a workshop exercise, I ask customers to describe a particularly satisfying shopping experience and an especially bad one. They battle to recall good ones, but they come back with long lists of bad ones.

Here's how they sum up the treatment companies dish out:

> "Most companies do things for their own convenience; the customer likes it or lumps it."

> "When you ask for information or help, they either can't give it to you, or can't be bothered."

> "It's a waste of time complaining. You can't find the right person, and then they don't do anything anyway."

Time magazine felt strongly enough about the lousy level of service to feature it as a 1987 cover story. The headline screamed, "Pul-eeze! Will Somebody Help Me?" Some quotes:

> "Personal service has become a maddeningly rare commodity in the American marketplace."

> "... many U.S. companies today are failing to achieve the right balance of high-tech expedience vs. personal attention."

> "... workers spoil an otherwise fine job with an almost creatively bad gesture."

> "... the deterioration of basic, personal service is taking the fun out of new offerings."

> "... some businesses feel they have an abundant supply of customers, and thus are not dependent on long-term relationships with the shopper."[3]

3   "Pul-eeze! Will somebody help me?" *Time*, February 2, 1987

Personal experiences

Here are some of my own recent experiences as a customer:

❑ When I tried to buy a car for my wife, deliveries were being delayed by a strike at the factory. I called five dealers, and placed a firm order with each of them. Only one bothered to call back. The manufacturer has spent a fortune implanting and publicizing a customer care programme; it clearly doesn't work as well as the MD thinks!

❑ When my own car was new, everything seemed to go wrong with it. Every time it went in for attention, it came back with a new problem. I started joking that the company and I shared the car — we each had it for half the time. Midway through the hassles, I called the dealer principal to complain. He promised to personally sort things out — but that was the last I heard from him. I sent a ten-page fax to the managing director of the manufacturing company; an assistant wrote back assuring me everything was under control. The problems continued.

❑ I recently sent off a cheque to pay for service to my photo-copier. A week later I got a call from an accounts clerk who asked what the money was for. It turned out that my name was in their computer as "Mister Manning" but my cheque was in the name of "Tony Manning" so they couldn't put the two together. When I suggested that they re-name my account, the clerk asked me to put the request in writing as she wasn't allowed to make such adjustments on the basis of a phone call.

❑ Over the last 25 years, I've bought life assurance from a succession of brokers. They've virtually all disappeared as soon as they've sold me. So the last time I needed a policy, I called my bank manager for help. He introduced me to a top agent associated with the bank. After we'd discussed my needs, and filled in all the forms, this man suggested that I update my will. He promised to send me the necessary documents the next day, and to help with the changes. Four weeks later, my new policy arrived in the mail. Six weeks after that, the will form arrived with an unsigned compliment slip. My only other contact with that hot-shot broker has been a Christmas card. Right now I need more insurance . . . so I'm looking for a new broker yet again.

❑ After I'd waited ten days to have a pen repaired, it fell apart in my hands while I was paying for it. The shop assistant told me it would take another ten days to fix, but if I took it to the workshop myself I'd probably get it back faster.

❑ When I had some copy typed by a secretarial bureau, it came back on a floppy disc infected with a virus. Repairing my computer cost five times as much as the typing. I called to tell the bureau owner what had happened, so she wouldn't make the same mistake for someone else. She said, "Oh, that's awful. We had the same thing happen a few months ago." No apology. No question of making up in any way. I'm still trying to clean the gobbledygook off my hard drive.

Corporate suicide

If you asked any of the above firms how they felt about customer service, they'd tell you it was one of their major concerns, and a key reason for their success. In fact, it's costing them dearly, and they don't even know it.

The two motor companies spend colossal amounts each year raising customers' expectations through advertising, promotions, and public relations. The motor industry suffers from serious over-capacity. You'd think that dealers would bust a gut to make every possible sale — and then to keep customers happy, so they might one day come back.

The copier company is world famous, and ranks among the few firms that really can be called world class. It faces intense competition, so every sale is important. What's more, a large chunk of its revenue comes from supplies and support rather than from copier sales, so customer relationships are critical. The person most often in contact with me — and probably with most other customers — is the credit clerk. But she's stuck with a system that prevents her from dealing with customers in a halfway sensible fashion.

If the insurance broker looked after his existing clients, he'd probably never have to prospect again. My policy puts money in his pocket for as long as I keep paying the premiums. Every year my financial needs change, and I become a sitting duck for new insurance products. However, he's lost me, and will now have to waste time and energy replacing me with another client.

The stationery shop I went to with my broken pen is more interested in selling new products than fixing old ones. However, like any other retailer it depends on customers walking in through the door more than once. The person who buys an expensive ballpoint pen must be a prospect for a matching fountain pen or pencil. I could have become a lifetime customer worth a great deal of money. But the sales assistant saw me as a one-time, one-sale P-R-O-B-L-E-M!

The secretarial bureau depends on small businessmen like me to keep it busy. It can't afford to run ads or send out mail shots, so it depends on customers hunting it down and then calling in with their work. Any number of housewives and office temps offer at least equal service — and they're possibly quicker and cheaper. The bureau simply cannot afford to lose a single customer.

It's the same everywhere — but things are changing

As these few examples show, shoddy service is easy to find. It doesn't matter how much money you have to spend or what you buy, the problem is endemic. You're just as likely to be messed around when you buy a motor car as when you buy a loaf of bread.

When you shop for luxury items, or want really personal service, your choices are obviously limited. Famous brand names, special expertise, custom design, or particular specifications aren't available everywhere. Superior products, exclusive ambience, and exceptional attention usually come at a high price. A reputation for quality and service is earned over a long time, and at great cost. Most luxury goods firms depend on a relatively small target market for their income, so repeat sales and word-of-mouth recommendation are essential. Yet these companies often harm themselves at the moment of truth, because their staff are snooty and intimidating.

The corner store that sells milk and cigarettes is just as uncaring. Far too often, the owner is surly and unhelpful. He takes your money without a word, doesn't offer carrier bags (and snarls when you ask for one), and has a take-it-or-leave-it attitude when you ask if the bread really is fresh.

Fortunately, these firms' days are numbered. Customers are becoming more discriminating, more demanding, and quicker to complain. Consumer watchdogs pounce on them in the media. And competitors are forcing standards relentlessly upwards.

The high cost of screwing up

Customer dissatisfaction is a major business cost. A wide range of studies from various countries tell us:

❑ It costs about five times as much to get a new customer as it does to keep an existing one. Far better, then, to keep the customers you've got — they're your most precious "invisible asset." (Hence the rush by many British companies to place a value on their brands.)

❑ Almost five times as many customers switch because of poor service than because of poor product quality or price.

❏ Almost three out of four people think product and service quality is slipping.

❏ More than 80 per cent of customers say they'll stop dealing with an organization which doesn't meet their service expectations.

❏ About 15 per cent of customers stop buying a product because they're unhappy with it. Almost 70 per cent stop because they think the company doesn't care.

❏ Up to 45 per cent of people who are unhappy about service don't complain. They just go away. You don't even know you've lost them!

❏ 20 per cent of people who get a positive response when they complain, feel more confident about dealing with the supplier; but negative treatment makes 40 per cent feel less confident.

❏ More than 50 per cent of people who complain are dissatisfied with the response. More than 50 per cent stop buying from the offending firm.

❏ Satisfied customers tell between three and five people about their experience; unhappy ones tell 11 to 15.

❏ For every complaint you hear, between ten and 50 go unreported.

There's plenty more of this stuff. The evidence is overwhelming. Getting on the bad side of customers just doesn't pay. Yet how many firms see poor customer service as a cost. How many measure the damage it does? And how many work as slavishly to cut this cost as they do in other areas that don't have the same devastating impact?

A lifetime investment

When you look at customers on a sale-by-sale basis, it's often easy to wonder whether they're worth the effort. (Judging by the way most companies treat customers, this is exactly how they think. When you buy a can of beans, they seem to see a little sign on your forehead that says, "79 cents" — and you get the 79-cent treatment!)

But look at a customer's lifetime investment in whatever you sell, and the picture changes. Imagine a massive flashing sign on the housewife's head that reads "$100 000" (for ten years' worth of groceries), or one saying "$100 million" on an airline manager's head (for some new planes), and suddenly you see a valuable asset. The problems these people present today are simply part of the price you pay for a long-term stream of income and profits.

The average individual might spend $200 000 on motor cars in a lifetime (some spend that on just one car!) or $100 000 on clothes. And some of those "average" people will spend a heck of a lot more on a fleet of aircraft or a major computer system.

Getting these people through the door in the first place is not cheap. It might take years in some industries. So once you've got a customer it's worth hanging onto him with everything you've got.

Finally, remember that the value of a customer can't be measured purely in terms of costs and financial benefits. Customers provide feedback, insights, and ideas which trigger innovation. Also, they talk about their buying experiences; their word-of-mouth recommendation is worth a fortune.

More than a front line problem

If we all like good service and agree that it makes good business sense, and if we quickly recognize lousy service, why is superior customer service so rare?

The "moments of truth" that customers experience are largely shaped by front line people. Their actions and their attitudes get the blame for a host of corporate ills. But the "service problem" isn't one of service alone. *It comes from a whole attitude to business.* Yes, shoddy front line performance is the norm; but so are shoddy products and sloppy marketing practices. And behind those are a host of other factors which virtually guarantee their inadequacy.

Whatever happens on the front line is a direct reflection of what happens on a moment-to-moment basis elsewhere in organizations. The way people are managed, the firm's strategy, climate, systems, policies, and procedures all play a part.

The bad news for top management is that these problems start right at the top.

Even today, a remarkable number of managers haven't woken up to the "marketing revolution." They still don't understand that customers drive business performance. They haven't bought into the notion of customer care. Quality is a new-fangled job for which they employ inspectors.

The management style in most companies works against great customer service. Most managers are autocrats. They claim to be enthusiastic about participative management, but what they really mean is that it's O.K. for someone else. They don't really trust their people, they don't empower them to perform, and they don't allow risk-taking or initiative. Result: their people don't trust them, they don't take responsibility, and they don't take chances or buck the system to help customers.

Other reasons for bad service

In addition to the causes of poor service I've already mentioned, here are some other problems:

1. Many companies have yet to face real competition. Some have been protected by legislation. Some belong to cartels whose members agree (illegally) on prices and trade practices. Some have enjoyed monopoly status for years, because they established themselves in an industry when the

market was unexploited and entry costs were low. And of course, there are often cosy arrangements between competitors, which are not good for customers.

2. Most of us have grown up experiencing nothing but lousy service. So now we know "that's the way you do things" in business. We've been conditioned to expect shoddy standards, and we model our behaviour on the worst possible examples.

3. The business system doesn't "fit" the customer profile closely enough. This might be because customers were not clearly enough identified, or because the system was designed to be "all things to all men." It also happens when customers change and management fails to keep up.

4. Policies and procedures are all too often designed by bureaucrats or functional specialists. They're seldom as "customer-friendly" as they should be. So when customers call for help, employees can't respond fast or with any flexibility. And the system feeds off itself: people are appointed to check on other people ... paper creates paper ... backup systems for everything cost a fortune, waste space, and take up endless time and effort.

5. People in front line roles aren't hired carefully enough. They don't like their jobs, and it shows. Or they don't like *people* — and that shows even faster. Factors that should be considered are: personality, willingness to take responsibility, initiative, resilience under fire, and readiness to "go the extra mile" (and do it with a smile). There's no doubt about it: some people are better suited to the rigors of front line life than others. So why start with a handicap? Get the best people right off, and train them to be super-stars!

6. People throughout most firms don't get enough training. They're not told that customers are Priority No.1, and they're not taught to do their jobs properly. What's more, they seldom know enough about their colleagues' jobs, so

they don't understand how they mesh with the rest of the team.

7. People don't get enough *relevant* information about the organization, the challenges it faces, or its strategy. Japanese companies are "information-rich." Employees are showered with facts, ideas, feedback. Most western firms, by contrast, are "information-poor." The grapevine is the most powerful source of information and disinformation. When the boss makes a speech, he carefully says nothing — and everyone knows it. Potentially valuable media like company newsletters talk about Mary's new baby, Joe's golf score, and the fact that Dick just won a bursary. But that "hatch, match, and dispatch" stuff doesn't do anything for performance. It doesn't tell people what they really want to know: the company's strategy, how it's doing, how they can be more productive, how they can progress.

In most companies, customer service is a task tacked on after everything else. It's not a central theme. It's not an integrating concept. It's not an attitude, a driving force or an unshakeable value. And it's not something that *involves everyone.*

The fact that customer service was poor in the past was easy to understand. That it remains a costly weakness in so many firms is a surprise.

The "iceberg factor"

A key cause of inadequate performance in the marketplace is what I call "The Iceberg Factor." It can best be explained by a look at the world's most famous marketing war: the battle between Coke and Pepsi.

For many years, the two companies have run neck-and-neck in their quest for market share in the U.S.. Other markets around the world are important, but the home market is the prize: one share point is worth around $300 million a year.

Both companies have traditionally concentrated on the 16–24 age group. That's their core target market, as that's where the heavy cola drinkers are. But in the early 1970s Pepsi decided on a new strategy. The firm aimed at an even younger group with a view to luring them early, to make them committed Pepsi drinkers before they hit their peak years of cola consumption. A new advertising campaign was launched to position Pepsi as the "Choice of a New Generation."

Then Pepsi research revealed an interesting fact. Where people had no choice in the product they bought — i.e., in outlets such as McDonald's, with whom Coke had a supply contract — Coke naturally outsold Pepsi. But where people had a choice — in drugstores, supermarkets, and so on — Pepsi often outsold Coke. Taste tests showed that when people were offered the two products in plain cups, Pepsi was frequently chosen first.

An alert Pepsi executive got a Texas-based advertising agency to stage some tests and film them, and he ran a few local commercials showing the results of the "Pepsi Challenge."

Initially there was some resistance within Pepsi to the "Challenge" spots. The company's advertising experts warned that the "youthful, heartwarming imagery" of the "Pepsi Generation" campaign would be lost. Short-term market-share gains would be traded off against greater longer-term benefits.

The experts argued that each advertisement should help build the product's brand image, and define its personality. But market research showed that the "Challenge" didn't harm it at all.

The results of the campaign far exceeded anyone's expectations. Pepsi sales took off in the territory where the "Challenge" ads ran. Other bottlers jumped on the bandwagon. More commercials were shot. And the "Pepsi Challenge" drove Coke crazy.

At first, the Atlanta giant responded in a pretty rational way with some good, solid commercials. Later, as the "Challenge" rolled out across America, Coke became desperate. It tried all sorts of ideas, to no avail. It even made one silly commercial which featured two chimps tasting competing products.

As so often happens, Coke's marketing team focused on the wrong things. They saw the tip of a threatening iceberg, so that's where they attacked; they saw TV commercials, so they countered with commercials of their own.

What they couldn't see was the seven-eighths of the iceberg that was under water. And that was the part that weighed most heavily in the cola wars. The "Pepsi Challenge" began as a TV commercial, but quickly embraced a host of other — equally important — activities.

"We treated each Challenge as a major event, a battle to be fought in our long-term war against Coke." says John Sculley, former president and CEO of Pepsi Cola, and now chairman of Apple Computer.[4]

Weeks before a "Challenge" was mounted in a particular area, Pepsi began working with the local bottler to improve quality. When commercials were shot, the company wanted to be sure to win. Better long-term quality was also an important spin-off.

The evening before a "Challenge" was to debut, Sculley often flew in to give bottlers and their families a pep talk. Truck teams were highly motivated. Special displays were erected in key outlets. Dealers got extra incentives. Prices were cut.

What Pepsi did, in other words, was what any sensible marketer should do: it created a *holistic attack plan* in which all the parts worked together.

4   John Sculley with John A. Byrne, *Odyssey*, William Collins and Sons, 1987

By starting with attention to product quality, it made sure that Pepsi-Cola would, in fact, win the on-camera taste tests. Then it made sure that when customers went shopping, Pepsi would be easy to find and attractively priced. It motivated its people to make the "Challenge" a roaring success. And "Challenge" success stories were then used to keep the momentum going — and, incidentally, to seriously demotivate Coke people.

Stew Leonard shows how

Stew Leonard, owner of Stew Leonard's Dairy in Norwalk, Connecticut, is one of the shining stars in American business folklore. He was "discovered" by Peters and Waterman when they did the research for *In Search Of Excellence*, and has since become something of a celebrity. He appears regularly on TV and radio shows, and is often quoted in the business press.

According the Grocery Marketing Association of America, the average dairy store in the U.S. makes an annual profit of about $300 a square foot. Stew makes $3 000! And he does it against 93 competitors within a 15-mile radius of his store.

Quite clearly, the man has a secret. So I asked him, "If you're such a public figure, and if what you do is so well-known, how do your competitors let you get away with it? What do they do to counter you?"

Stew chuckled. "You know," he said, "it's a funny thing. Every day about 30 of them come stomping around my store. We know who they are because they're not shopping, just looking, and they're all wearing suits. And they walk around searching for 'the secret.' But they can't see it, because the secret's in the way we treat our people and the way we treat our customers."

As so often happens, Stew's competitors look in the wrong direction, focus on the wrong things, and are prisoners of their industry's conventional wisdom.

They "know" that you win the grocery war by cutting prices, by advertising "specials," by building displays, and by using the latest checkout technology. That's the way they've been brought up, and that's the way they think.

And that's the reason Stew Leonard beats them to death.

He wins because he does the things that really add up to profit. He wins because he focuses on things his competitors can't see. And above all, he wins because he loves his customers. Some ways he shows it:

❏ There's a big rock outside his store, with the "rules of the store" carved on it:
   "Rule No.1 — The customer is always right.
   "Rule No.2. — If the customer is wrong, re-read Rule No.1!"

❏ There's a suggestion box at his front door. Customers provide an average of *100 suggestions a day.* They're typed and circulated to all his staff before the store opens next day. Within 24 hours, every customer who has left a phone number is contacted for a chat about their ideas. Result: staff have their finger on the customers' pulse, and customers are delighted to know they're heard.

❏ Every week, a small group of customers is invited for tea and cookies at the store. Stew and his people sit around and listen to them, asking their opinions and advice on how to improve their service. This market research method is a lot less sophisticated than many marketing professionals might like, but it works. Stew not only gets right under his customers' skin and into their minds, but he also builds close personal relationships with them. Conducting these "focus groups" costs almost nothing, and there's no delay in getting a report-back. Stew can do something about suggestions or complaints right away.

❏ He *acts* on suggestions. For example, when customers complained that they often found squashed strawberries at the bottom of punnets, he asked what he could do. "Don't pack them for us," was the answer. "Just pile them up, and we'll pick and pack our own." Stew did, even at the risk of lots of squashed strawberries at the bottom of the big pile. He figured that was a small price to pay for satisfied customers. The result was happy customers — and unexpectedly high strawberry sales!

❑ He hires nice people. "They've got to have genuinely pleasant personalities and positive attitudes," he says. "They really must like people and want to help others." With this as the starting point, Stew doesn't waste time trying to create a silk purse from a sow's ear. He begins with good raw material (the hard bit), then provides the professional skills (the easy bit).

Stew Leonard is an unusual man in a highly competitive industry. His cheery manner, ready smile, and genuine care for others are obviously advantages. He's naturally an excellent leader. He's always alert for new ideas, and prepared to test and discard dozens in search of the few that work.

But when you really analyze what he does and how he does it, there's no hidden formula. Any store — or any other business, for that matter — could do the same. His brand of personal leadership might not be easy to copy, but his methods are. So why doesn't it happen?

The evolution of management thinking

The fact that customers still get a raw deal so often should be no comfort to any company. Things are moving. As the competitive arena evolves, managers are changing their minds about what leads to success. Consider:

❑ As recently as November 1983, *Business Week* saw fit to run a cover story headlined, "Marketing: The New Priority."[5]

5 "Marketing: The New Priority," *Business Week*, 21 November 1983

This, despite the fact that the "marketing revolution" occurred back in the early 1960s.

❏ In their influential 1985 book, *Kaisha,* James Abbeglen and George Stalk Jr. reported that the top three priorities of American managers were: (1) return on investment, (2) share price increases, and (3) market share. In contrast, Japanese managers ranked market share their top priority, with return on investment second, and new product launches third.[6] (*Forbes* reports that in terms of sales, six of the top ten companies in the world are Japanese; but Toyota is the only Japanese firm among the top ten *profit*-makers.[7])

❏ When a 1986 survey asked what they'd do next to compete with the Japanese, senior executives in 300 large U.S. manufacturing companies ranked their plans like this:
  • Invest in new plant and equipment — 27 per cent.
  • Spend more on R&D — 23 per cent.
  • Improve customer service — 23 per cent.
  • Become more aggressive marketers — 14 per cent.
  • Cut wages — 6 per cent.
  • All of the above — 1 per cent.[8]

❏ Another 1986 survey, of CEOs of the "Fortune 500," showed that only 6,4 per cent of them saw long-term planning or strategy as one of their top ten objectives; only 3,9 per cent included quality improvement as an important competitive weapon; and just 12 per cent of those astute managers listed customer satisfaction as their main objective.[9]

6 James C. Abbeglen and George Stalk Jr., *Kaisha: The Japanese Corporation,* Basic Books Inc., 1985
7 "The Forbes 500 Annual directory," *Forbes,* April 29, 1991
8 Frederick E. Schuster, *The Schuster Report,* John Wiley & Sons Inc., 1986
9 "Atop the Fortune 500: A Survey Of The CEO," *Fortune,* 28 April 1986

❏ A 1987 report in the British glossy *Business* noted that two-thirds of firms in the U.K. believed they were not very good at marketing. Two-thirds didn't use market research. Two-thirds didn't have a systematic process for launching new products. Two-thirds didn't train their sales people. And two-thirds of British managing directors had no significant sales or marketing experience.[10]

❏ A 1987 study by the European Strategic Marketing Institute, across the Atlantic at INSEAD in Paris, found executives in 128 companies "more or less agreed that the top three issues they face are: coping with product quality and follow-up service; continuously assessing their customers' changing characteristics; and creating a marketing culture that spreads throughout their company."[11]

❏ When chief executives of the 1 000 biggest industrial firms in the U.S. were asked in 1988 what drove growth and profit, 57,2 per cent mentioned customer relations (financial planning came in second, at 57 per cent). Yet when asked to name the most important sources of *future* growth and profit, they ranked new product planning and development first (36,8 per cent), followed by financial planning (27,8 per cent); research and development (25,7 per cent); production/manufacturing (22,9 per cent); and customer relations (10 per cent). And when asked how they spend their time now, and where they expect to spend it in the future, financial planning won hands down, with customer relations in fifth spot both times.[12]

10 Tony McBurnie, "Britain's Two-thirds Syndrome," *Business*, October 1987
11 "European Marketing Gets A Promotion," *The Economist*, 7 November, 1987
12 Richard T. Hise and Stephen W. McDaniel, "American Competitiveness And The CEO — Who's Minding The Shop?" *Sloan Management Review*, Vol. 29, No.,2, Winter 1988

❏ A massive 1991 *Harvard Business Review* World Leadership
Survey asked managers to rank the three most important
reasons for their success. Of the Americans, 52 per cent put
customer service first, with product quality ranked second
by 40 percent, and technology voted third by 36 per cent.
Of the Japanese respondents, 54 per cent ranked product
development tops, with 41 per cent voting for management
and 36 per cent for product quality.[13]

What all of these studies seem to indicate is a distinct shift in
corporate thinking. Customer satisfaction is gradually edging
up as a concern. If Japanese managers were there first, others
are getting there with a vengeance. More and more firms today
see customers in a very different light than they did just a few
short years ago. Increasing numbers of them are busting a gut
to deliver better products and services — and to delight their
customers while they do it.

**What this means, of course, is that levels of customer
attention have begun to converge, and will continue to
do so. Staking a claim to a share of your customer's
mind will get harder and harder.**

The Harvard study tells us something else, too. Just because
Japanese executives didn't mention customer service doesn't
mean they aren't fanatical about it. But perhaps it's already in
their blood. They're already boning up on those other areas —
product development, management, and product quality —
that underpin it and ensure it. Hopefully, western managers
will show equal commitment to their own priorities.

13 Rosabeth Moss Kanter, "Transcending business boundaries: 12,000
    world managers view change," *Harvard Business Review*, May-June 1991

Beware of believing your own propaganda

True, some firms do deliver truly miraculous service. Yet the vast majority have a long way to go. Unfortunately, these laggards don't know what kind of trouble they're in.

Far too many managers seem to think they're doing O.K. in the customer satisfaction area. Almost every chief executive I talk to swears blind that his organization does an absolutely terrific job of it. (Or if it doesn't, that's the fault of just a few recalcitrant people. Nothing that can't be fixed with a little work "on their attitudes!")

A recent study in the U.S. showed that 83 per cent of senior executives believed their customers were "satisfied" or "very satisfied" and that they only lost about 5 per cent of their customers each year. But just how accurate was their view? While 81 per cent of them said they "monitored" customer satisfaction, 42 per cent didn't use surveys, 62 per cent didn't use customer comment or complaint cards, 70 per cent didn't have customer service or public affairs departments, and 83 per cent didn't have toll-free lines![14]

There's an important lesson here. Beware of believing your own propaganda. The only person who really knows when your service is great is the customer. Get as many hard facts as possible about your performance. Be clear about what you're measuring, and do it methodically. Don't rely on gut feel or vague opinions — particularly those of your sales or service people who like to think they're doing pretty well, and are unlikely to tell you when they're not.

Good service is as rare as hen's teeth. It's perfectly normal to get less than you expect. Too many companies have had an easy ride for too long. Customers don't demand high enough standards, and don't complain loudly enough when they're

14 Survey by Sandy Corporation, Troy, Michigan, reported in "Facts About Customer Satisfaction," *Training*, June 1989

not satisfied. Also, competition in many industries is still not fierce enough to really grab managers' attention.

In just the last few years, a number of companies have seized customer service as their key theme. Many have made strenuous efforts in this area, with a good deal of success. But few organizations can claim to have "cracked the problem," and most still have a long way to go. Every great story you hear about a particular firm is immediately squashed by someone else's lousy experience.

Not a game for amateurs

The lessons are clear. I've made the point before and I'll make it many times again: success in the marketplace is everybody's business. You don't create and keep customers by dabbling at it. Being world class is not a game for amateurs. You've got to give it everything.

No matter what business you're in, Stew Leonard's lessons and the "iceberg factor" can work for you. (Or perhaps your competitors are using these strategies against you, right now!) So you need a step-by-step approach to building an integrated, well-rounded attack plan, and to making superior quality of everything a reality in your firm.

CHAPTER FIVE
POWER TO THE PEOPLE!

World class customer service is possible only with world class human relations inside the organization.

In many firms, sub-standard performance can be blamed on people at low levels and out at the edges who just aren't up to the job. They lack skills, they have the wrong attitudes, and their manner simply doesn't endear them to customers. These problems all need attention. A lot can be done to rectify them.

But before you point a finger at employees, be sure that's where the problem lies. In many firms the real failure is a failure of management. As the saying goes, "When a fish is rotten, the head stinks too."

In all the work I've done helping firms improve their service, I've never come across a group of employees who resisted the idea. Yes, there might have been a few individuals who paid lip service to it because management had told them to get on with it, or because of peer pressure. But most really wanted to make it happen.

In almost every employee workshop, however, participants have been intensely sceptical of management's commitment to either the concept or the process. Managers' behaviour has conditioned people to expect the worst.

Try treating them like adults

The business literature is full of evidence that treating employees well translates directly into extra profit. The so-called

115

"human relations" school of management theory has been around for half a century, and participative management is all the rage. But most managers are still stuck with the mechanistic traditions of Fayol and Taylor.

In his 1960 book *The Human Side of Enterprise*, Douglas McGregor noted that management behaviour is driven by managers' "assumptions about human nature and human behaviour." According to McGregor, these assumptions fell into two broad categories, which he labelled "Theory X" and "Theory Y."

If the concept is simplistic, it underlines the essential point that we create our own self-fulfilling prophecies. What we expect from people is generally what we get. The surest way to promote constructive, creative, cooperative behaviour is to believe that it's natural, and to act accordingly. In other words, to treat people like adults, to share information with them, to trust them — and to *empower* them.

Most of us lose out badly when it comes to tapping our people power. So we don't do nearly as well as we might in creating and keeping customers, and thus in building market share and profits.

Somewhere in virtually any company you'll probably find one or both of these statements:

"The customer is king."

"Our people are our most important asset."

These thoughts look great on plaques or posters, and sound wonderful in the annual report or a glossy brochure. They're the stuff of speeches and videos, of advertising campaigns and company banquets. I know of no company that does not like to utter them — nor do I know of many where they reflect the truth.

I've already shown what things look like from the customer's point of view. Employees don't fare much better. Despite the Hawthorne experiment and Douglas McGregor, despite *The One Minute Manager, In Search of Excellence, Theory Z*, and all the other nostrums, gurus, and best-sellers available to us, the lot of the average employee is a sorry one. Just listen to some typical views:

> "My boss treats me like a child. He refuses to give me enough responsibility, and shows very little trust."

> "They say they want you to show initiative; when you do, they complain that you're not following procedure."

> "They say they want ideas, but when you speak up nothing happens. Your suggestions just disappear."

If you think your company is different, think again. Or better still, talk to some of your people. And pay attention to what they really say, not just to what you want to *hear* them say. I work with the most successful companies in many fields. In one after another, I find the same distressing gap between what the CEO says happens, and what actually does go on. In fact, the situation is so serious, and the malady so widespread, that I feel comfortable with this promise:

> **No matter how well you're doing now, by any measure you care to apply, your company is sitting on a pile of unrealized profits. You can tap them and gain an invincible competitive edge if you focus on developing your two most precious "invisible assets": your people and your customers.**

Communications crashes

Virtually every senior executive complains of his company's "communications problem." Down the line, people cite this as the No. 1 reason for sub-standard performance.

Communication in the workplace is difficult for many reasons. But it's needlessly complicated — and *avoided* — by executives who could easily turn it to their advantage.

One reason communication is generally so poor is that managers focus on *how* to do it before they've decided *what* to say. They consider media and the mode of delivery before message content. They worry over questions like, "Should we hold a meeting, or publish a newsletter?" ... "What languages should we use?" . . . "Will briefing groups be better than quality circles?"

Putting these issues first is like trying to create an ad campaign for a product that hasn't been invented. It's an impossible task. On the other hand, when you know who your audience is and what you want them to know, think, feel, and believe, it's relatively easy deciding how to get your sales pitch across.

Explain the facts of life

What should people know? What should you communicate?

As a matter of the most urgent priority, every person in your company should be exposed to a wide-ranging, comprehensive, and frank presentation on your firm's competitive standing. Most people don't have any idea of how tough things are in the new business arena, or why their firms must change. They don't understand that there's no security in the modern marketplace, or that they personally must re-think everything they know about business.

Such a presentation should include:

❑ Changes in the world business arena and in the local economy, and their probable impact on your firm.
❑ Competitive trends — i.e., how companies worldwide are shaping up to meet the new realities.
❑ Competitors' performance.
❑ New demographics and psychographics.
❑ Customer buying behaviour, and how it's changing.
❑ Why quality, productivity, and superior customer service are vital.

❑ Your company's performance to date (with facts and figures. This is no time for secrets!)
❑ Your future strategy.
❑ The role of each employee in making it happen.
❑ What's in it for him or her (and it better be more than a pat on the back!)

This broad-brush picture should (*a*) motivate your people — through challenge, the promise of reward, or even fear; and (*b*) prepare them for change.

But that's just a beginning. To perform effectively, people need more information — and a continuous flow of it — than ever before. They need facts about customers, information about new techniques, and feedback from the marketplace. They need to know your company's strategy, and they need to know what other departments around them are doing.

Communication is the cornerstone of corporate performance, but many firms will never get it right. Their people have just never talked to each other. Managers stay in their offices and issue orders via memo or messenger. There are lots of secrets. Things are shared on a "need to know" basis.

So face up to it before you read any further: if you're not prepared to open up and to involve everyone, you might as well stop right here. Your firm will never be a great place to work. You'll never deliver world class service. Your organization will die.

The need for a tailored delivery system

Your front line people might be absolute charmers. They might be enthusiastic, imaginative, and ever-willing to go that extra mile for your customers. But ultimately they are "prisoners of the system." They can excel only if they have the right tools, training, information, resources, and support. And they will excel only if they're treated as responsible, competent adults . . . if they're allowed to make decisions, take risks, and make mistakes . . . and if they're given meaningful rewards.

When you entrust someone with your company's image, they deserve a lot of attention. (Your business future hinges on it!) They must be *empowered* to meet and exceed your customer's expectations. So your entire business system must be tailored to, and driven by, your customer's needs.

Examples:

1. McDonald's has become the world's most famous hamburger marketer by focusing on value, quality, and service. It takes just a couple of minutes for the McDonald's team to fulfil an order. Service is polite but impersonal. Every staff member is highly trained to perform carefully defined tasks. There's no guesswork in the kitchen. Suppliers work to tight schedules and very clear quality standards. Items on the McDonald's menu are pretty basic; you can "personalize" your order with a dash of ketchup or some fries or salad, but not much else.

2. The Four Seasons is regularly rated one of New York's top restaurants. The food is superb, the cellar is excellent, and the service is personal and attentive. It's the place to be seen. Guests are greeted by name. Every dish is prepared on demand. If you want your fillet medium-rare, or your grilled lobster decorated with a light shrimp sauce, all you have to do is ask. As a customer, you have virtually limitless options. You have a lot of say in what finally appears on your plate. The bill is as "customized" as the experience.

Both McDonald's and the Four Seasons understand their customers, and have created a system for satisfying them. McDonald's customers don't expect frills or special touches; Four Seasons clientele do. You wouldn't meet an associate for a "power lunch" at McDonald's; just walking in the door of the Four Seasons is a success statement.

These organizations are essentially in the same business — providing meals — but the specific needs of their customers define their "products" very differently. So their delivery systems are totally different. Every aspect of what they do and how they do it is tailored to the buyer they do it for.

They are situated in different locations, and their premises look very different. Each has a proven way of buying ingredients and preparing meals. Their service levels are like chalk and cheese. Their prices confirm that each is offering its own brand of value.

> **Firms fail in the marketplace when they design inappropriate business systems, or when they get stuck with one that worked in a different time and place. They succeed when they become stars at doing what they have to do for their particular customers.**

What comes first

To make winning with the customer a way of life in your firm, you should obviously review everything you do that falls under the heading of "marketing." In other words:

❑ How you define your customer.
❑ How you design and produce your products or services.
❑ How you package, price, and promote them.
❑ Distribution channels and methods.
❑ Sales activities and selling methods.
❑ After-sales support (installation, instruction, repair, warranties and guarantees, etc.)

These issues add up to the familiar "4 Ps" of the marketing mix: Product, Price, Place, and Promotion. But while this is the obvious place to start, it's not the whole picture. "Creating and keeping a customer" is not just a marketing function. It involves the entire organization, and everyone must play a part.

It also demands the input and support of *external stakeholders*, so the way they're managed needs attention.

To win the battle for customers, then, you need to review and revise all of the following factors:

❏ Your total business strategy.
❏ Your organization's structure.
❏ Its policies and procedures.
❏ Leadership.
❏ Your management style.
❏ Supervisors' skills.
❏ The employee information system.
❏ Technology.
❏ Training.
❏ Job definitions and performance evaluations.
❏ Your reward system.
❏ How you hire, promote, and retire (or fire) people.
❏ The physical arrangements in your firm.
❏ Symbols and signals (communication).

To help you work through this complex process, I've developed a tool that identifies the key issues (Figure 5-1). I call it the "opportunity map" because it highlights the many ways in which you can sharpen up.

The opportunity map shows how all the key factors hang together. It guides you through the improvement process, breaking it into clear chunks. It shows that the central issue in world class performance is your customers' perceptions of your performance, and while the behaviour of front line people has a major impact on those perceptions, real improvement demands that you do many things differently and better.

Favourable customer perceptions are created when your front line people act in a creative, responsive way, supporting or surpassing any promotional claims you might have made. But for that to happen, the entire business needs a rethink. Total corporate wellness must be your aim.

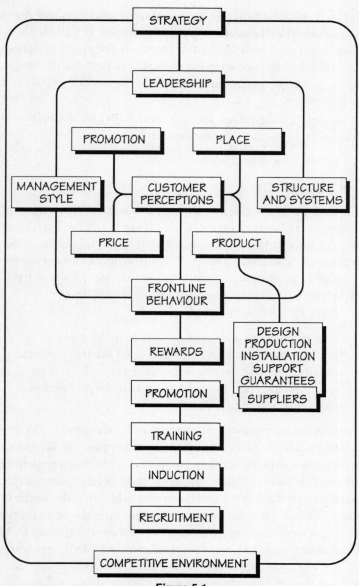

Figure 5-1
The Opportunity Map

In the chapters ahead, you'll find countless ideas and about 60 checklists and questionnaires to help you get there. Share them with your colleagues, refer to them daily, and use them in your internal discussions or workshops. By the time you get to the last page, you should be well on the way to world class performance.

Right now, however, let's get busy with an exercise that'll have a rapid impact on your bottom line.

Let's talk profits

Capitalism is a western idea, yet ironically, many western managers balk at the profit motive. They don't the like pressure it puts on them. They resent shareholders' demands for increasing dividends. They use "quarteritis" as an excuse for their poor performance, pointing enviously to Japanese firms which typically take a much longer view of things.

Peter Drucker once noted,

"The purpose of a business is not to make a profit. . . . Rather a business exists and gets paid for its economic contribution. Its purpose is to create a customer. A business therefore has two and only two, basic functions: marketing and innovation."[1]

Profit is the *scorecard* of performance in the western world. The profit requirement is not about to disappear. If anything, managers will be under even greater pressure to improve their financial results in the future. What they need to learn is that making a profit is not a zero-sum game. Meeting the needs of shareholders need not be at odds with doing the right things the right way. Nor does it necessarily take anything away from employees — or from any other stakeholders. On the contrary,

---

1   Peter Drucker, *Management: Tasks, Responsibilities, Practices*, William Heinemann, 1977

the profit motive focuses the mind wonderfully on the real priorities of business.

In recent years, managers have become increasingly aware that success hinges on their carefully balancing the interests of a host of individuals, groups, and external organizations. They watch the relentless rise of Japanese firms, which apparently put the interests of their employees above all others. They feel obliged to be "socially responsible," and to invest time and money in "good works."

The pressures are bound to grow. They'll make business decisions more difficult. However, we'd do well to remember that companies and their managers survive when they make a profit, and they die when they don't. When a company is profitable, it can afford to create jobs, to train people, to pay them well, and to get involved in wider community issues.

Improved profits also lead to better stock market ratings. This, in turn, triggers other spinoffs. As Professor Alfred Rappaport of Northwestern University's J.L. Kellogg Graduate School of Management reminds us, "Enlightened managers and public officials recognise that increases in stock prices reflect improvement in competitiveness — an issue that affects everyone with a stake in the company — or the economy."[2]

The only way to make long-term profits is through customers. The only way to grow profits is to give customers more for their money. Superior customer service is thus not just a good idea; it's the very life-blood of business.

As I have pointed out in other writings, there are five fundamental realities everyone in business needs to understand:

❏ Creating value for investors is the No.1 objective.

2   Alfred Rappaport, "Let's Let Business Be Business," *The New York Times*, February 4, 1990

❑ Creating customers is the No.1 priority.
❑ Constant innovation has to be the No.1 strategy.
❑ Quality and productivity have to be the No.1
   operational concerns.
❑ Communication is the No.1 way to create superior
   performance.

Perhaps if more managers paid more attention to these facts,
they'd perform better. An analysis of 363 U.S. companies from
1978 to 1987 shows just how much room there is to improve.
Only 38 of those firms — about 10 per cent — earned their cost
of capital each year during the survey period. Forty three
didn't earn their cost of capital at all in that time, and *231 —
64 per cent of the total — didn't make it for five or more years![3]*

Four ways to increase profits

Profit is a very revealing measure of business performance. It
tells how well you've done important things. To most people
in a firm, however, it's means very little. It's not an objective
they can relate to. They don't understand how their day-to-
day activities impact on the bottom line, nor do they particularly care. Even with all the evidence that profit-sharing is a
powerful motivator, most people still get fixed hourly, daily,
weekly, or monthly pay cheques. Very few are paid for results
(especially American and British CEOs, whose pay is often in
inverse proportion to the profits they produce!)

**Somehow, then, the importance of profit must be
brought closer to home. Individuals must understand
how it's created, and their role in delivering it. They
must be given a sense of participation, a feeling that
they can make a difference.**

3   Michael Farmer, "Pumping Profit," *Management Today*, June 1989

If you were to ask a group of employees for ideas on how to improve your profits, they'd probably flail around looking for answers. But there are essentially four ways to do it:

1. Sell more products.
2. Sell them faster (speed up your stock turn).
3. Sell them at higher prices.
4. Cut your costs.

A marginal improvement in any of these areas will yield huge returns; a major improvement will transform your bottom line. So one exercise I often give clients is to draw four columns on a sheet of paper, and get them to list ideas under each heading. It's an easy task, and most managers would say they're doing these things already, but I've never seen a company where enough imagination has gone into them.

Here's what you might discover if you and your team spent a little time on this project:

1. Sell more units

Increasing market share is every manager's dream. But too often, they try to make it happen by doing more of what got them where they are. They think that a little more effort, more money, or more time will do the trick. In some cases it might, but usually a new strategy will give a bigger payoff.

Think about some of these ideas:

- ❏ Redesign your product (better looks, fewer parts).
- ❏ Make your packaging more user-friendly, environmentally-friendly, and attractive.
- ❏ Find new distribution channels.
- ❏ Change your sales presentation — or change your sales force!
- ❏ Put your secretaries to work finding new prospects.
- ❏ Restructure your reward package.
- ❏ Change your advertising.
- ❏ Try new media — e.g. direct response.

❏ Introduce a special offer, cut prices, offer a discount for volume purchases, etc., etc.

Pretty obvious, aren't they? Well, what else can you do that's not so obvious?

2. Sell them at higher prices

As I'll show later, most companies short-change themselves by selling too cheaply. Their own sales people discount them to death. To earn their keep, they virtually give away their products.

Often, this is unnecessary. Price is just one buying criterion, and seldom the most important one, so getting more for your goods or services is usually easier than you think. Many of the above steps could help. The key is to enhance your customer's perception of the value he's getting, so he's willing to pay more for it.

Ideas for action:

❏ "Unbundle" your price by listing *all* the features and benefits your product offers.
❏ Re-focus customers' attention on features they might have missed.
❏ Create a dramatic new presentation to demonstrate the value of the service you wrap around your product.
❏ Spell out to your people the margin you expect from every sale, and get them to mentally focus on selling up rather than down.

3. Speed up your stock turn

The surest way to do this is to make your product more attractive, so customers can't wait to get it away from you. All of the actions you take to sell more units will help. But in addition:

❏ Make just-in-time purchasing a policy, not an option with just a few of your suppliers.
❏ Make quality your suppliers' problem — i.e. insist on zero defects in the stuff that arrives at your door.
❏ Change your stock mix (more of the fast-moving items, fewer of the slow-moving ones).
❏ Sharpen up your forecasting, and shorten your horizons.
❏ Manufacture to order.
❏ Announce a sale to get your stock levels down to an affordable level fast.

Above all, aim to do *everything* faster. Cut the slack out of your business system. Simplify processes. Eliminate paperwork. And learn to respond faster to your customers.

As forecasting techniques, technology, and delivery logistics improve, the best competitors are slicing huge chunks of time out of their entire systems. If you don't enter this race fast, you'll never catch up!

4. Cut costs

The surest way to cut costs effectively is to zero-base everything. In other words, to ask, "If we started from scratch right now, what's the least we'd spend to satisfy our customers and to stay ahead of the competition?"

Looking outside of your business forces you to focus on doing the right things, the right way, right first time, right on time, right every time. When you drive quality up, you drive costs down.

Most firms can save a fortune in a crunch. So create an artificial crisis. Put your team under real pressure, and see what cuts they make. Then ask them to go another round. Watch for the people they "can't do without" or the equipment they "must have." There are always some of these passengers and luggage you can't afford if you're going to become world class.

Other suggestions:

❑ Switch some of your fixed costs for variable costs by sub-contracting tasks from every department.

❑ When people leave, ask, "Do we need to do this job at all?"

❑ Reinvent vacant jobs that must be done, or combine them with others.

❑ Enforce a one-page memo rule (if it works in a company as big as Procter & Gamble, it can work for you!)

❑ Ban memos and long meetings with too many people.

❑ Buy office supplies just in time — i.e., when you need them — not "just in case."

❑ Cut the frills — fancy offices, furniture, executive dining rooms, club memberships, etc.

❑ Cut subscriptions to "nice to have" publications.

When you cut costs, be sure to cut fat, not muscle. But force people to justify what they spend. It's all to easy for a manager to argue that he absolutely has to belong to the country club, subscribe to a foreign newspaper, or give his secretary a fancier laser printer. But all too often these needs can be shot down in flames. And all too often everyone knows where money is being wasted.

Like it not, managers are going to have to adapt themselves to a harsh new set of rules. The perks of the past will have to go for two reasons: (1) If you don't set the right example, no one will do their bit to cut costs; and (2) the symbols of success all too often are *symbols of difference:* they set people apart, they suggest that one person is worthier than another, and they just plain irritate those who don't get them.

Cost-cutting is obviously an exercise to save money. But equally important, it's a way to focus people's attention on what really counts.

Customer focus makes it happen

As I explained it, the objective of this simple exercise was to increase your profits. But quite clearly, the best way to do that is to *sharpen your focus on customers*, and become more creative about how you deal with them.

The only way to do really well in terms of those four objectives is to step outside of your business, into your customers' shoes, and then work back into your business system. Taking people through this thinking process is a quick way to show them just how important customers are. It also shows them how profits are created, it underlines their role in the profit-making process, and it helps them set meaningful objectives for themselves. But most important of all, it gets the improvement process going in the most practical way.

Who should be involved in this exercise? *Everybody,* of course. It's a challenge to salesmen and secretaries, to scientists and supervisors. Improvement teams should include accountants and engineers, doormen, janitors, and drivers — and anyone else you pay. From now on, expect your people to turn up . . . *think* . . . and *light up your customers' lives!*

CHAPTER SIX

THE ENDLESS JOURNEY

No firm can ever say, "O.K., we're world class, so now we can relax." This is not like climbing a mountain. You don't get to the top, stick your flag in the snow, and go home. You keep climbing!

Becoming world class is a journey, not a destination. It's not a task with a neat ending. You can't put it behind you in a couple of weeks or maybe even over the next year. When managers start talking about customer care "programmes" or "projects," you can bet they're going to fail.

The business arena is changing so fast, and so dramatically, that no company can survive and thrive if it continues to do what made it successful yesterday. Nor is it ever safe to assume that you're far enough ahead of your competitors.

Customers continually change their buying behaviour. Competitors race to match those new needs. Society imposes new rules, new constraints, new values.

No matter how well you're doing today, you have to change — and change *fast* and *continually* — if you're serious about retaining your current market position, let alone moving ahead. A constant stream of new ideas is essential. It's virtually impossible to defend the status quo.

No secrets

Competitors get detailed information on 70 per cent of most new products within a year of development. They're not shy to copy new ideas — even patented ones — because it costs one-third less than starting from scratch and innovating themselves, and it's three times faster. And as technology continues to improve, and information diffuses ever faster, breakthrough ideas will be increasingly hard to protect.

Nor are *processes* easy to conceal from your enemy. Competitors sooner or later learn up to 90 per cent of how a firm does things — and it's usually sooner rather than later.[1] So as unique as your pool of know-how might be today, and as sharp as your skills might be, the competitive advantage they give you now will simply not last. They'll keep you ahead for a fleeting moment only, and if you don't move on your competition will move out front.

High-tech turmoil

Let's turn to Page 6 of *The Wall Street Journal* of May 6, 1991, to see what's going on in the high-tech market. Here are the main stories:

❑ "Software makers' once-peaceful world is rocked as price wars are launched."
❑ "AT&T, Tele-Communications and US West plan a joint test of new video series."
❑ "Convex to unveil upgrades and supercomputer series."
❑ "Tandy expected to introduce multimedia PCs."

The personal computer industry highlights the challenges facing virtually every organization today. Once-ignorant and nervous customers are now experts, and know precisely what they want. The field is crowded with competitors, and brand

---

1   Pankaj Ghemawat, "Sustainable Advantage," *Harvard Business Review*, September-October 1986

names offer little or no protection against "clones." There have been almost no major innovations since 1985. Price wars force every player to continually drive down costs to keep margins respectable.

Just recently, Intel, the leading computer chip maker, launched a cut-price version of its model 486 chip. The next day, 12 computer manufacturers announced PCs based on the chip![2]

When Compaq Computer Corp. came under pressure from some 50 smaller competitors, and cut prices on its laptop computers, Toshiba hit back with discounts of 19–33 per cent.[3]

The same things are happening in apparel, consumer electronics (where some products can expect to survive just six months), sports equipment, toys, beauty products, and fast-moving consumer goods.

World class companies never stop reinventing themselves. they continually test new products and explore new markets. They continually change the way they do business — not just *what* they do, but *how* they do it as well. They regard both success and failure as stepping stones to the future. They experiment, they take risks, they change direction with the speed of light.

Will this strategy keep working?

One company that has managed to stay ahead by staying loose is San Jose-based Conner Peripherals, a disk drive manufacturer. Sales shot from a record of $113 million in 1987 to $1

2 "PC firms are roiled by change as clones gain on brand names," *The Wall Street Journal*, May 17–18, 1991
3 "Toshiba unit slashes prices of laptop and notebook PCs," *The Wall Street Journal*, May 6, 1991

billion in just four years, making it one of the fastest-growing major manufacturers in America. Here are some of its secrets:

1. Conner has defined its market with rare precision: manufacturers of fast desktop units and of portable PCs that take drives up to 3½ inches wide. (Which just happen to be the two fastest-growing segments of the computer market).
2. Its products are all made to order, and premium-priced.
3. Its business system is capable of rapid, non-stop adjustments. The firm is in constant flux, responding instantly to the changing pulse of its customers. It fights bureaucracy tooth and nail. Flexibility is a trademark.
4. Keeping capital spend low is "practically religion" to CEO Finis Conner. (He gets $7,17 in sales from every dollar invested in plant and equipment, while Seagate Technology, a key competitor, manages just $3,59.) Factory space is leased. Conner designs products, and then buys most of its components and sub-assemblies from outside suppliers. Final assembly is done in Singapore, where 4 500 workers churn out disk drives 24 hours a day.[4]
5. Conner's business system embraces not just the people, processes, and policies within its walls, but also its entire network of stakeholders: suppliers, customers, and the rest. Every part of the system is forever on trial for its life. It either adds value or gets dropped.

So far so good. But will Conner stay ahead? Not easily. And certainly not by sticking to yesterday's strategies.

Consider just one fact. Conner launches four new products a year — an effort that *Fortune* magazine lauded as exceptional in an August 1990 article. But even as the story appeared, Seagate struck back with 14 new products, and within six

4   Andrew Kupfer, "America's Fastest Growing Company," *Fortune*,
    August 13, 1990

months had upgraded half of them. In the same period, Seagate cut its prices of 40-megabyte 3½-inch drives in half.[5]

Many old-style managers would frown at Finnis Conner's ideas about management. But he's a hell of an operator, and he knows that change is the name of the game. What he's doing is not all that unusual today. Tomorrow, it'll be the norm. The day after, it'll be obsolete.

The drive to be different

Young companies are driven by innovation. Good ideas get them going, and keep them alive. There's no "status quo" to preserve, so anything goes. Nor does any individual have the exclusive right to produce fresh ideas. Everyone is expected to think about his or her chunk of the business, and about wider issues too. Many people enjoy the thrill of seeing their ideas turned into action.

As firms age, however, they become culture-bound. People learn "how things work around here." Systems are needed to get things under control, but often they take on a life of their own. More effort goes into keeping them as they are than asking why they exist at all. Hardly any thought goes into reinventing them so they're really appropriate.

In young organizations, innovation is taken for granted. In older ones, it often becomes another "flavour of the month" — a fad to be driven by the human resources department or a project to be run in one part of the firm, for just a short time.

However, like customer satisfaction, innovation is not a "part-time" activity. It's not something that's good for one firm, but not needed in another. It cannot be delegated to an individual or a department, and you cannot turn it on or off at will.

5 "Conner's drive is getting a bit gummed up," *Business Week*, April 29, 1991

Seven kinds of change

Every firm exists in a complex world. One useful way to analyze this arena is to see it as a set of "macro environments": (1) economic, (2) political/legal, (3) social, and (4) technological. Within this framework are (5) competitors, and (6) customers. The company itself (7) is a "micro environment."

Each of these arenas changes constantly. Nothing stays the same. So to survive and grow, every organization must make change a way of life. Transformation and renewal must be ongoing objectives.

Yet because it's human nature to resist change, and to seek stability, organizations and individuals, products, processes, and systems all have life cycles.

Let's say you launch a new product in 1970. It "fits" the world into which you sell it. Sales go up and up. But sooner or later, things slow down. Your product passes through the "maturity" phase, and into "decline."

Why does this happen? Quite simply, because the world of 1970 doesn't stay with you through the 1980s and into the 1990s. It changes, so your product no longer fits. Yesterday's big winner become today's slouch and tomorrow's loser.

There are basically two ways to deal with this problem. One is to reinvent the product as demand peaks, so a new and improved version picks up on the momentum of the original and keeps sales tracking upward. Another is to aim for a continuous stream of small improvements.

Motor manufacturers use both strategies. From time to time — usually every five to ten years — they launch a totally new model. But they also make enough annual changes to satisfy customers' demands for newness. Some of these short-term changes are relatively minor: a new colour range, different body trim, sexier hubcaps, and so on. Others might be more significant: a bigger engine, better braking, or air-conditioning as standard rather than an option.

Major improvements — "big-bang" changes or quantum leaps — are important in any industry. They radically alter the bases of competition. The first-mover gains an invaluable advantage.

But incremental improvements may be even more important, depending on the state of competition in an industry, and the rate of change. What's more, continuous small experiments and improvements often trigger the big ones.

For these reasons, most firms need a new attitude towards innovation. They need to spread the word that it's not just a top management task, or something the folks in R&D do during working hours. Just as you and I as individuals have to change to grow, so does a company. Just as we need to risk the past to create the future, so does the firm.

When success leads to failure

Innovation is often pushed to the back burner at exactly the time it's most needed — that is, when we become successful. For it's then that we think we have the formula. And we easily fool ourselves that just doing more of what made us famous will keep us on top in future.

Innovation doesn't happen on its own. Quite the opposite is true. Without steady pressure, it dies.

The tough question is, precisely when should you change something that's working? Well, there's no easy formula. Of course, if a product or process is working well you want to milk it for all it's worth. There's always the danger, though, that you'll stay with it for too long. Many a company has gone out of business because its managers fell in love with their cash cows.

All change involves risk. Big-bang changes involve the greatest risk, because they demand big commitments. Often, they require a firm to invest a lot of money for a long time, undergo a major reorganization, or write off a comfortable way of doing things.

Smaller changes are easier to digest. One reason Japanese firms have been so successful is that they concentrate not just on being first with the best new idea, but on being *fastest* to modify their first idea . . . and their second . . . and so on.

> If customer service is a strange new idea for many firms, it's not one they can rely on for long. Those that make promises about their customer relations make themselves especially vulnerable to competitive attack. Constant innovation is the only way to keep ahead.

The end of "generic strategies"

During the 1980s, conventional wisdom in strategy circles said that to win in the marketplace, companies should choose between two "generic" strategies:

1. Cost leadership (which may or may not mean competing as the *price* leader).
2. Differentiation (otherwise known as "perceived value," or what we'll call "performance" later in this book).[6]

For most companies, this clear choice of a strategy makes a lot of sense. It forces them to make tough trade-offs, to be sure of what they must do well, and then to design a business system with as little slack in it as possible. By choosing one strategy or the other, and by working hard to implement it, they focus their resources on specific targets; and hopefully they do it better than competitors who spread themselves too thinly.

When Trust Houses Forte Hotels, Britain's top hotel group, was restructured in early 1991, its name was changed to "Forte," and its 350 U.K. hotels were grouped under three "brands" — Travelodge, Post House, and Crest — each with

---

6   Michael E. Porter, *Competitive Strategy*, The Free Press, 1980

its own identity, and each offering different "value." Accor, a French hotel group, segments its market in a similar way: its Sofitel "brand" offers luxury accommodation in city centres; Novitel caters to business travellers, so it's located near airports and motorways; Ibis is a two-star family operation; and Formula One is a low-price, no-frills chain.[7]

Obviously different guests want different things. No hotel can satisfy them all. By being clear about who they want to attract, these groups can tailor their services most appropriately. Costs can be allocated effectively in everything from their buildings to the quality of towels in their rooms, from advertising to teaspoons.

The greater the competition in any market, the more essential it is to select specific targets, to customize your offerings to each slice, and to attack each with an appropriate strategy. If you sell a single product, you can focus your resources on it. If you sell a range, you can allocate resources where they're needed most, and you can make it very tough for the opposition to get a toehold in the market; also, you can sell up or down, and cross-selling is a real possibility.

There's a danger, though, in assuming that your strategic options are limited — that you must adopt one "generic" strategy in each target market, and either be the lowest-cost competitor or offer the most added-value.

Like so many things that sound right, there's always someone to challenge them, to turn conventional wisdom upside down. It's not just strategies that change, but *concepts of strategy*. And a danger in this fast-changing world is that organizations lock themselves into a way of thinking which becomes obsolete.

They develop a strategic logic which they assume is the same for their competitors. They kid themselves that there's

7   David Churchill, "Facing The Realities of Recession," *Financial Times*, May 8, 1991

"one best way" to compete, and that they've found it. They build one strength at the expense of others. They stop learning, and they repeat what made them famous in a different time. When they wake up, they find that competitors, not bound by the same logic, have "broken the rules" and are playing a different kind of game.

My favourite cartoonist, Gary Larson, illustrates the point with his usual wit and insight. In the midst of an Indian attack on their fort, one cowboy says to another, "Hey, they're lighting their arrows! Can they do that?" The bad news is, *of course* they can. The bastards can do *anything*!

The best competitors position themselves clearly, but then they rapidly build new advantages. They see both cost and value as opportunities, and they avoid getting caught in an "either-or" trap.

New ways to sell supercomputers

Not long ago, Cray Research was committed to a differentiation strategy with its top-end, $30 million supercomputers. The firm was the pioneer in that field, and was unchallenged. There was no question of building an "entry level" machine at a lower price. But, as is now usual in so many business battles, competition suddenly emerged from various quarters. Convex and Alliant attacked in the U.S.; Fujitsu, Hitachi, and NEC from Japan; Parsys and Meiko from the U.K.; Parsytec from Germany. They came in under the umbrella offered by Cray, invested heavily in development, and launched computers that offer colossal power at a comparatively modest price. (Parsytec's latest offering is 400 times more powerful than it needs to be to be to qualify as a "supercomputer"!) Cray was forced to respond with a strategy that addressed both cost and value. In 1990 the firm started shipping the Y-MP2E, a $3,3 million midrange supercomputer. Its line-up now starts at about $300 000. And, says CEO John Rollwagen, "We must do more to make our products cheaper."[8]

Computer buyers have learned that a product's launch price will dive by 30–60 per cent or even more in the first year. IBM's RISC System-6000 550 hit the market as a $130 000 "minisupercomputer" in late 1990. When Hewlett-Packard attacked with lower-priced "workstations" a few months later, IBM was forced to respond. And respond it did — by repositioning its system as a "technical workstation" and slashing the price to $52 000![9]

Airline offers take off

Or take the airline industry. Deregulation and soaring numbers of passengers made it a real bun fight over the past decade. (And the impact of the Gulf War on tourism has made things even worse!) Cut prices and frequent flyer bonuses have become the norm. Every airline promises the best customer service. Passengers get hot towels, gifts, travel socks, toilet bags, glossy magazines. The crew — both on the ground and in the air — go out of their way to be nice.

Every airline's seats are the widest . . . their food's the best . . . their wine comes from the most famous private cellars. Movies are shown in all sections, but some airlines now offer first class passengers hand-held video machines and a choice of up to 100 films. I recently phoned home from 20 000 feet above New England, charging the call to my American Express card.

The problem is, every airline offers the same goodies. Their market research has told them what customers want: wide seats, good food, free drinks, on-time arrivals and departures,

8 "Convex wants to be a full-fledged heavyweight," *Business Week*, April 22, 1991
9 Loise Kehoe, "IBM cuts its computer workstation prices by up to 60%," *Financial Times*, May 8, 1991

attentive service, safety, and so on. So their ads all sell these benefits. And as fast as one airline introduces a new twist, the others catch up and pass it. Today's surprise is tomorrow's ho-hum standard. More value must always be on offer.

Travellers are bombarded with bigger and better deals. TWA offers gift cheques . . . Pan Am offers to refund the full price of a first class Trans-Atlantic ticket if you're not happy . . . Virgin Atlantic sends a limosine to fetch Upper Class passengers anywhere in the United Kingdom . . . British Airways gives away every seat on all its flights on a single day. . . .

When SAS was first repositioned as the airline of choice for business travellers in 1980, CEO Jan Carlzon took out first-class cabins and launched his EuroClass business-class service. Passengers got wider seats and special attention from the minute they boarded. But as he says, "The metal tube we are flying them around in limits the possibilities of service. Are you going to feed them vodka and caviar until they vomit?" So he started doing more for them on the ground: faster check-ins, EuroClass lounges, computers, and fax machines. And more recently, he's aimed to become a full-service travel broker: SAS is linked to 131 hotels around the world (it actually runs 25 of them), and in 1989 bought 40 per cent of the plush Intercontinental chain for $500 million.[10]

Aircraft manufacturers, too, are drawn into the customer-satisfying process. The hold of the new A-340 airliner from Airbus Industrie, due for delivery in 1992, will carry standard cargo containers fitted out as bedrooms. Each will have five beds, air-conditioning, a refrigerator and bar, and an entertainment system. Quips The Economist, "Frequent long-distance travellers might eventually buy their own containers. These passengers could then be loaded, along with the rest of the freight, while fast asleep on their monogrammed pillows."

10 Kenneth Labich, "An Airline That Soars On Service," Fortune, December 31, 1991

Who'll own the luxury car market?

If these examples don't prove the point, take a look at the auto industry. Car buyers who pay the full sticker price in the U.S. are hard to find. (Even Japanese manufacturers have been forced to slash prices.) Most dealers offer incredible incentives, including overseas trips, rebates of up to $5 000, interest-free loans, and free accessories.

Or watch the stunning success of Toyota's Lexus or Nissan's Infiniti. Both these luxury sedans were launched in the U.S. in late 1989, to compete with the likes of Mercedes-Benz, BMW, and Audi. They offer a host of innovations, and sell at prices way below the competition.

The Lexus came to market at about $35 000 — compared to $63 000 for a Mercedes 420SEL. The Infiniti hit the road at $38 000, yet is such a remarkable vehicle that one industry expert said he couldn't understand how it sold for less than $58 000. (By July 1990, Toyota's luxury division was ahead of both Mercedes-Benz and BMW in the American market. Mercedes snatched the lead back in August, but the game is on!)

Fight on all fronts

What all these examples show is that both careful positioning and continual learning are essential. You have to know exactly who your customer is, so (a) you can reach and attract him most effectively, and (b) you can develop a product and a business system that will satisfy him better than the competition can do. But then you have to keep moving and improving.

In today's no-holds-barred business arena, yesterday's strategy is about as valuable as yesterday's product. Not long ago, when management experts talked about "portfolio strategies," they meant the mix of businesses or industries that a company competed in. (Remember the glory days of "stars," "cash cows," "question marks," and "dogs?") Now, they mean the mix of things it does to build competitive advantage.

As Harvard Business School professor Christopher Bartlett says in an interview in *The McKinsey Quarterly*, "Simplifying global competition to a decision to be low cost or differentiated ignores the reality that today's competitive battles demand a portfolio of strategic capabilities."[11] So while world class firms do focus their efforts, and always do a few things exceptionally well, the secret of their success is often hard to pin down. They're single-minded — about relentlessly raising the standards of everything they do!

Value up, costs (and prices) down — there's just no escaping this formula in the new arena. The MIT study referred to earlier put it this way:

> "The best of the niche producers set objectives for quality and product differentiation, but they also mount an intensive effort to reduce costs and establish competitive prices. Successful mass producers recognize that price competitiveness must be matched by attention to quality and service, and indeed, they stress quality of design and production engineering as a means of reducing manufacturing costs."[12]

You might decide to be the low-cost competitor in your industry, and for a while at least that might give you a real advantage. Or you may choose to deliver high value-added products and services, and to carve out a niche in the upper end of the market. With few exceptions, neither course will give you a sustainable advantage. Sooner or later, a competitor is likely to appear who isn't stuck with your strategic logic. If your

11 Amir Mahini, "Facing up to complexity: an interview with Christopher Bartlett," *The McKinsey Quarterly*, Spring 1990
12 Michael L. Dertouzos, Richard K. Letser, Robert M. Solow, and the MIT Commission on Productivity, *Made In America*, The MIT Press, 1989

organization stays slavishly devoted to one concept of success, you'll be in real trouble.

The trends I've talked about presage a new business climate. Whole industries are in upheaval. Managing the changes will be a colossal challenge. It'll require risky changes in the way companies compete. Above all, it'll demand that managers continuously re-examine their assumptions about what leads to business success.

CHAPTER SEVEN

An Obsession with Quality

There was a time when quality was a fad. For some companies it still is. (Most managers "place quality third," says quality guru Philip Crosby — after controlling costs and keeping production on schedule.[1]) And most efforts to improve quality end in failure.

There was a time when managers could ask themselves, "Should we think about quality *or* price?" But the time for such questions is now past. "The best formula for any company that wants to be successful in the 1990s," says Joe Cappo, publisher of *Advertising Age*, "is to marry the perception of product quality image with a fair price."[2]

Any company that sees quality as a fad, or quality and price as mutually exclusive, is in deep trouble. Today they're two sides of the same coin. Cheap and shoddy are a recipe for failure. The new credo is quality *and* price.

Quality is everybody's business. It permeates everything a firm is and does. In world class organizations it's a way of life rather than merely a short-term project that can be started and stopped at will. It's a central issue in creating and keeping customers.

1 Francesca Lunzer, "Does Your Car Have A Fan Belt?" *Forbes,* December 3, 1984
2 Joe Cappo, "Cornerstones for the future," *Advertising Age,* November 13, 1989

"There's no great mystery to satisfying your customers," says Lee Iacocca in a Chrysler advertisement. "Build them a quality product and treat them with respect. It's that simple."

Yes, it is that simple. But getting there isn't easy. Just look at the American motor industry's performance, as one glaring example.

A recent list of "Top 10 Trouble-Free Cars" from J.D. Power & Associates featured seven Japanese cars and two Germans (Mercedes-Benz and BMW). Buick was the only American vehicle.

Increasing competitive clutter means that customers' quality standards are raised each day. At the same time, manufacturers and providers of services are ratcheting up their performance through a host of measures. A lot of managers think they'll succeed by brushing up here and there — a kind of covering the cracks exercise, if you will. But far greater efforts are necessary. A beautifully-produced brochure entitled "Quality is no fluke," from Zanders Feinpapiere, the German paper company, says it like this:

"Quality? Quality? A term said to stand for excellence in a product or for dependable and professional workmanship. No wonder the word is so ubiquitous: who would dare admit a lack of quality in his own efforts? But just try defining it — in a product like paper, for example, let alone the quality of a company. . . . Can you see quality in its staff or management? Is it shown in the balance sheet? Is being the market leader a mark of quality? Is it mirrored in the utility of a firm's products, or in its outlets, its award-winning ads? Maybe quality has something to do with maintaining a certain standard for a certain period? Or did some Board meeting have to resolve: "Let there be quality!" . . . and there was? Obviously, quality has many facets and can hardly be summed up in a couple of sentences. Quality is the sum of many qualities."

Japanese firms understand all this extremely well. The best of them live by a strict quality code. They view quality as a philosophy rather than a technique. They know that quality is as much a *learning process* as it is a matter of organization, technique, or technology. They take a holistic approach to improvement, and neatly balance both short-term and long-term objectives. Quality is an integral part of their strategies. According to Professor David Garvin of the Harvard Business School, Japanese companies deliver superior quality and reliability through "a carefully orchestrated campaign of micro and macro policies, top management involvement, and shop-floor activities. Little has been left to chance."[3]

Ironically, the Japanese firms whose quality standards now set the pace learned from American experts such as W. Edwards Deming, Joseph Juran, and Arnold Feigenbaum. An article in the *Sloan Management Review* reminds us that continuous improvement programmes have been "America's most successful export to Japan."[4] But whereas Japanese managers listened and learned, and put quality principles into practice 30 or 40 years ago, managers in the West just went about their business as usual.

At least, that was the case until about ten years ago. Then along came a veritable flood of business books which all got managers thinking about the real potential in their rusty charges.

The timing was perfect. The world was just coming out of a long period of recession, and Reagan and Thatcher were about to do their stuff. Suddenly, quality was seen to be an important issue that went beyond inspecting things after they were badly made.

3   David A. Garvin, *Managing Quality*, The Free Press, 1988
4   Dean M. Schroeder and Alan G. Robinson, "America's most successful export to Japan: Continuous improvement programs," *Sloan Management Review*, Spring 1991, Volume 32, No. 3

What does your customer expect?

Quality is not just a product issue. It applies to everything you do, and to the way you do everything. It applies to services, systems, and processes just as much as to products.

Managers who jumped aboard the "excellence" bandwagon had nothing by which to measure themselves. "Excellence" was just a vague ideal which looked good in ads or annual reports, and hopefully roused the troops to action. Quality, on the other hand, is measurable. Customers know what it is. They set the standards, and if you ask them what they expect, they'll tell you. *Customer definitions of "value" drive every business decision, every business activity.*

External customers are out there daily in the shopping place. They're bombarded with new offerings. They're making choices all the time. They have a fine sense of what's good, bad, or just plain indifferent. Ultimately, they decide which products will survive and which will die.

Internal customers, too, are expert in knowing what they need. If a machinist asks for a part to be delivered by a certain time, in a certain way, there's probably a good reason — so that's the way to deliver it. If a manager says he wants the financial accounts on his desk by the fifth of the month, and presented in a particular way — do it. These people are customers. Their view is the one that counts.

You can do a job to your own highest standards, but if your internal customer is unhappy, you're in trouble. So starting right now, make sure you know precisely what your customers want and need. And don't guess. Go *ask* them!

There's profit in quality

Superior quality translates directly into profits. It triggers a stream of benefits that add up to a competitive advantage. It has a direct and very powerful impact on costs, sales, prices, and return on investment.

When customers believe they're getting value for money, they buy more *and* they're prepared to pay more. As volumes rise, and quality improves, unit costs fall. (According to the experience curve, they fall by 15–35 per cent each time there's a cumulative doubling of volume.) Prices can then be cut to encourage more buyers, or the savings can be used to fund R&D, extra advertising, or sales force incentives. Or prices can be *raised*. Either route means bigger profits.

According to the well-known PIMS database, companies that deliver superior perceived quality get a lot in return:

❑ Stronger customer loyalty.
❑ More repeat purchases.
❑ Higher price without the loss of market share.
❑ Lower marketing costs.
❑ Bigger market share.[5]

But to earn these benefits, quality must be built into the product from the start, and enhanced step by step; it cannot be *inspected* in afterwards. (And the customer should never be the inspector!) Likewise, maximum productivity must be squeezed from each step of every process as it occurs. It cannot be an afterthought.

There are plenty of complex quality "formulas." There's a seemingly endless array of courses and systems to improve quality. Yet as always, a few fundamentals need attention. The logic of quality is undeniable: *the customer is its judge and the employee is its creator.*

5   Robert D. Buzzell and Bradley T. Gale, *The PIMS Principles*, The Free Press, 1987

Quality logic

Elsewhere I have talked about "quality logic."[6] Here it is again, as a reminder.

1. Quality is a satisfied customer's *perception* of the value offered by a product or service.
2. Customers change and demand new satisfactions, and competitors improve their offerings, so quality is an ongoing process of change and improvement from the customer's point of view.
3. Quality is an attitude . . . a learning experience . . . a process, not a programme.
4. Quality is created through:
   • Awareness (of the need).
   • Analysis (of what customers want).
   • Action (throughout the organization).
   • Assessment (review and feedback).
5. To be quality performers, people must know:
   • 'What to do' (objective).
   • 'Why to do it' (context).
   • 'How to do it' (method).
   • 'How well to do it' (standards).
   • 'How well they're doing' (results).[7]

What it all comes down to is making sure that people know those five things: (1) what to do, (2) why to do it, (3) how to do it, (4) how well to do it, and (5) how well they're doing. This seems quite obvious, yet the fact is:

❑ Most people in most companies don't know precisely what is expected of them. They don't know their company's vision or mission, they don't understand its strategy, and they don't know their own roles. So when they get to work in the morning they get busy doing the wrong things.

6   Anthony D. Manning, *The New Age Strategist*, Southern Books, 1988
7   Ibid.

❏ Most people in most companies don't understand the impact of their performance. They don't know what competitive pressures their firm faces, nor do they know what their colleagues expect of them. They don't know how important it is to do the right things, the right way, right first time, every time.

❏ Most people have had far too little training, so they cannot do their jobs properly, and they certainly can't fill in for anyone else. They waste an awful amount of time and energy trying to figure out the best way to do their jobs, and they make lots of costly mistakes.

❏ Most people don't work to clear standards. They don't have objectives — and they certainly haven't had a say in setting them. Thus it's impossible to measure their performance except in the most subjective way.

❏ Most people get little or no feedback — or mostly *negative* feedback. Too many managers "manage by exception" — they stay away until things go wrong, then they're quick to criticize or even punish.

In addition to these glaring quality killers, another three factors deserve a look:

❏ Most people in most companies are paid in ways that cause them to do the wrong things quite badly, to do as little as possible, and to use their initiative as seldom as possible.

❏ Most people in most companies are treated as immature and irresponsible. They're not given the information they need to perform. They're not asked for ideas.

❏ Most people in most companies don't trust too many of their colleagues, so they spend inordinate amounts of time in KYA ("Cover Your Ass") activities. The memo is a favourite weapon. Politics is rife. Teamwork is a rare commodity.

Quality logic can work miracles for your business if only you'll take advantage of it. Make sure your people know what they need to know, and they'll give you an unbeatable competitive edge.

Communicating the critical messages is not a stop-start process. There's a lot to be said for the "internal marketing" of all the concepts in this book, but the task should never be reduced to slogans on buttons, badges, and T-shirts. And tools such as quality circles, "green areas" (a Nissan idea), and suggestion schemes must be part of a holistic, system-wide approach.

Best of breed

As I've shown, a growing number of aggressive marketers in virtually every industry have stopped debating whether to compete on the basis of price or performance. And they've stopped questioning the wisdom of focus or niche marketing. Now they attack both cost and differentiation at the same time, and they carefully slice up their customer bases into smaller, clearer targets.

To satisfy new market segments, the best competitors aim to do everything better and faster. They know there's no such thing as the "average customer," even in a global marketplace. As Ted Levitt says, "The more powerfully homogenizing and relentlessly globalized the world's communications and commerce get, the more varied its products and more numerous its consuming segments seem to become." [8]

The new "killer competitors" understand that yesterday's standards are obsolete and tomorrow's will last for only the briefest moment. They're totally committed to both driving down costs and to driving up quality — and to doing it even

8   Theodore Levitt, "The Pluralization of Consumption," *Harvard Business Review*, May-June 1988

before customers ask. And they never stop raising their standards, by benchmarking themselves against the best.

Instead of setting their own internal standards of performance, these firms look outwards, at the "super stars." They
break their operations into functional chunks — R&D, design,
manufacturing, marketing, etc. — and send teams out to learn
who's best in each area, and how they got so good. The result
is a set of standards that really stretch everyone to the limits,
plus a whole lot of valuable insights from the world's best
players.

In 1983, Toyota chairman Eiji Toyoda challenged his engineers to create "the best car in the world." The design specs
were awesome: the new sedan was to carry four people at 150
m.p.h. in quiet, comfort, and safety. Chief engineer Ichiro
Suzuki made it clear from the start that "compromise was
unacceptable." When the first 32-valve aluminium block V-8
engine guzzled too much petrol, he had it stripped down, part
by part, and improved to meet his target. He sent 20 engineers
to visit U.S. dealers and run focus groups. And he set up
"Flagship Quality" committees to watch progress on every
component. Six years and $500 million later, the Lexus went
on sale.

Xerox Corporation once dominated the world copier market. It was the hot growth company of the 1960s and early
1970s. But like so many other firms that think they've found
the secret of success, Xerox got fat and happy — and hit the
skids. Minolta, Ricoh, Nashua, Canon, Mita, and others suddenly appeared on the copier scene, and tore away great
chunks of market share.

"We were arrogant enough to think that no one could do
anything better than we could," vice-chairman William F.
Glavin told *Business Week*. "We didn't have anyone to learn
from."

The surprising thing was that it took Xerox so long to see
it was in trouble. Only in 1980 did management discover that

the company's Japanese competitors enjoyed a 40–50 per cent cost advantage. The bureaucracy had burgeoned; decision-making was slow; the company dealt with 5 000 suppliers.

Becoming competitive again required drastic measures. Some 15 000 jobs were cut in 1982–83. The ratio of support staff to factory workers was 4,5 to 1 in 1979–80, but rapidly fell to 0,7 to 1. Where once each service manager controlled 13 representatives, they looked after only 18 by 1987. Small teams cut the labour component of a new machine by around 40 per cent.[9]

An important factor in Xerox's comeback was its determination to be best in every aspect of the copier business. Each manager was given the goal of becoming the world leader in what he did. Every component was analyzed against the best, and new standards were set. Competitors' performance in every process was examined, and Xerox aimed even higher.

Look beyond the obvious

Watching your direct competitors is a real turn-on, but is not enough on its own.

Companies that practice benchmarking watch *any other firm* that can teach them something. They "unbundle" themselves department by department, function by function, and look outside for role models. Then they aim to be "best in their class" in every way.

And they watch not just the "hard," easy-to-measure things, but also take into account the more elusive "soft" factors that impact on performance in a particular area. The quality of leadership, management style, systems, policies, and procedures, "attitude," the organizational climate, relationships with customers and suppliers — all have a bearing.

9   "Culture Shock At Xerox," *Business Week*, June 22, 1987

ICL sharpened its distribution methods by looking not just outside its own walls, but beyond the computer industry — at Marks and Spencer, the retailer. Xerox doesn't just keep an eye on other copier manufacturers, but also on L.L. Bean (the mail order clothing company), American Express, Florida Power and Light Co., and Toyota. As an executive explained, "At first glance, the companies have little in common. But each performs at least one job also done by Xerox — and, in Xerox's judgement, does it better than anyone else."[10]

To identify top performers in various functions, Xerox managers attended conferences, talked to consultants, and scanned trade publications, annual reports, and other company literature for "statements of pride."[11]

Benchmarking stretches minds

Benchmarking is about standards. But it goes much further than that. It's really about a mental attitude, an obsession with winning, a relentless drive to be best. And above all, it's about urgency — improvement *now*.

When firms use their own standards as a starting point for improvement, they seldom achieve more than marginal changes. They "know" what's possible. Their "personal best" is all they've experienced.

When they expose themselves to "best-of-breed" performers, however, order-of-magnitude change becomes possible. In the early 1980s, for example, Ford decided to cut the cost of its North American accounts payable department. Management estimated that by eliminating some tasks and putting in new computer systems, it could cut staff from 500 to 400. The

10 "The Benchmark Method: What Xerox Asks Toyota," *International Herald Tribune*, April 26, 1990
11 Frances Gaither Tucker, Seymour M. Zivan, and Robert C. Camp, "How To Measure Yourself Against The Best, *Harvard Business Review*, January-February 1987

20 per cent saving looked great until Ford looked at Mazda —
and discovered that in the Japanese firm the same task was
handled by just *five* people. After adjusting for the relative size
of the two organizations, Ford decided that its accounts
payable department was five times bigger than it should be. It
set — and achieved — a new target of a 75 per cent cut in staff.[12]

In a McKinsey Award-winning article in the May-June
1989 issue of the *Harvard Business Review*, Gary Hamel and C.K.
Prahalad observe that companies that became global leaders
in the past 20 years often had ambitions out of all proportion
to their resources and capabilities. They became successful by
creating *"an obsession with winning at all levels of the organization,"* by learning from their mistakes, and through
astonishing persistence in improving everything. (My ita-
lics.)[13]

Adds Harvard strategy expert Michael Porter: "Rivalry
among domestic firms often goes beyond the purely economic
and can become emotional and even personal. . . . Domestic
rivals fight not only for market share but for people, technical
breakthroughs, and, more generally, 'bragging rights.'"[14]

The payoff from this new attitude is little short of
astonishing. A McKinsey study showed that the best manufacturers get new products to market 2 1/2 times faster than
average, and at half the cost. Motorola quality expert Richard
Buetow says, "Best-in-class companies have error rates 500 to
1 000 times lower than average."[15]

12 Michael Hammer, Reengineering work: don't automate, obliterate,"
    Harvard Business Review, July-August 1990
13 Gary Hamel and C.K. Prahalad, "Strategic Intent," *Harvard Business
    Review*, May-June 1989
14 Michael E. Porter, *The Competitive Advantage of Nations*, The Free Press,
    1990
15 "First find your bench," *The Economist*, May 11, 1991

Quality and productivity come from outside

Quality and productivity are, like customers, moving targets. The standards get higher every day. Every firm doesn't use the Japanese term *kaizen* — "do it 100 per cent well today, and do it better tomorrow" — but more and more of them act that way.

There's a real possibility, however, that many efforts to push productivity up will in fact push it down. That between now and the year 2000 many firms will become less productive, less competitive — and less *profitable* than they are today.

The reason is simple: too often, efforts at productivity improvement are aimed the wrong way. Managers focus on what happens *inside* their companies, and ignore or misinterpret what happens outside. Thus, over time, their people learn to do the wrong things with great skill and energy.

The problem doesn't end there. These managers rely on an incomplete set of measurements to show how well they're doing. They record capacity utilization, the use of raw materials, reject rates, downtime, absenteeism, and so on. Their careful observations tell them everything except the most important thing: *what value the customer wants, how the customer's needs are changing, and how well the company is perceived to satisfy those needs.*

> Of course, it is necessary to pay attention to what goes on inside a firm. Marketplace performance hinges on many internal activities. But results are created *outside*, by satisfying customers, and all efforts should be focused on that goal.

Unfortunately, the term "productivity" conjures up images of "dark satanic mills," long production lines, specialised tasks, noise, and heat — in other words, largely unpleasant processes and rote procedures. So it's quite natural to think first of these activities when thinking of productivity improvement. But that's putting the cart before the horse.

The fact is, like quality, *productivity is a companywide issue. And productivity doesn't create customers; customers drive productivity!*

You daren't stand still

A "generic" strategy might be just right for you. But before you get hooked on the idea, take another hard look at the realities. Ask yourself these questions:

❑ Are you up against "best of breed" competitors?

❑ Are *you* aiming to be "best of breed?"

❑ Can you win by aiming to be either the low-cost producer or the differentiator? (In other words, through a one-or-the-other strategy?)

❑ What are you doing to build on your key skills? . . . To continuously improve on your own internal standards? . . . To reinvent your strategy even when it appears to be working well?

It's no longer good enough to match your competitors in terms of cost and quality. That might make you feel safe, but it won't guarantee your survival, let alone that you might win. They're a moving target, and it's lethal to assume that they'll keep doing what you see them do today.

Like a "SWOT" analysis, benchmarking gives you a snapshot of the present rather than a video movie of the future. It rates you against the present performance of present players — not against tomorrow's champions. So while it's a useful start, it's not a complete answer.

Benchmarking is a learning tool. It's too valuable to be used from time to time.

"Strategies based on imitation are transparent to competitors who have already mastered them," say Hamel and Prahalad. "Moreover, successful competitors rarely stand still."[16]

In the short run, you might do well by offering the lowest prices or the best performance. Longer term, you probably have to work on both simultaneously. This calls for a dynamic approach to strategy.

> **Everything you do must be revised before it runs out of steam — not after. The moment at which a strategy appears most successful is the moment at which it's most at risk; and that's when you should re-shape it. The renewal process never stops.**

---

16 "Strategic Intent," Gary Hamel and C.K. Prahalad, *Harvard Business Review,*" May-June 1989

CHAPTER EIGHT

PRINCIPLES OF WORLD CLASS SERVICE

Most of us have been brought up to know the "Golden Rule": Treat others as you'd like them to treat you. But in business it makes sense to do quite the opposite. In other words, to treat others as *they'd* like to be treated.

The fact is, each of us is special and different. We all have our own tastes, our own likes and dislikes, our own hopes and fears, wants and needs, dreams, and ambitions.

This means that there's no such thing as an "average" customer. Every person who buys anything is unique. Even in this age of globalization we must think about our customers' *differences* as well as their similarities.

For the moment, however, let's focus on the similarities. Let's look at the common factors that almost all customers seek when they buy products and services.

1. Their expectations must be met.
2. They want to be treated with respect.
3. They want to be heard.
4. They want to feel that you're on their side.
5. They want information.

1. Their expectations must be met.

Customer expectations set the standard for customer service. Marketers have a great deal of influence over those expectations. Yet so often they create dreadful problems of credibility for themselves, by making unrealistic promises.

This is an easy trap to fall into. As competition increases, it becomes harder and harder to set yourself apart from the crowd. Differentiation begins with the underlying product idea, and it's enhanced all the way through the value chain. According to Ted Levitt, every product has a range of possibilities:

❏ The "generic product" is the basic "thing" you sell.
❏ The "expected product" meets the customer's basic expectations.
❏ The "augmented product" offers more than he needs or expects.
❏ The "potential product" embraces everything you can possibly do to get and keep him.[1]

Aggressive marketers spend a fortune shaping customers' expectations. They make bold advertising promises. They publish glossy annual reports and costly brochures. They build impressive head offices. They deck their people in snappy uniforms. And public relations consultants get their executives wide exposure in the media.

All this causes customers and potential customers to expect a certain standard of performance. But more often than not, the merchandise doesn't live up to the window dressing. From the very first contact you know that what you expect is not what you'll get.

There's no one to blame for this but the company's own management. If you can't keep a promise, don't make it. Building trust takes time and costs money. Destroying it takes just a moment, and can be done by anyone.

2. They want to be treated with respect.

Customers don't expect you to go down on your knees before them, but they do like to be treated with warmth and de-

1   Theodore Levitt, *The Marketing Imagination,* The Free Press, 1983

ference. This means a welcoming smile, politeness, concern for what they want, and a clear signal that solving their problem is your priority.

All too often, front line people talk down to customers, and act as though they've been interrupted in some really important task. This, despite the fact that the customer might be wealthier, more powerful, or more influential than even the *owner* of the business.

Customers should be addressed by name whenever possible, or as "Sir" or "Madam" if you don't know their names. And they should be made to feel important even when they make a minor purchase.

3. They want to be heard.

Successful sales people know that listening is their most powerful lever. So they pay a lot of attention to what customers say. In fact, the new wisdom in selling is that probing questions are a lot more effective than slick answers. The objective of a first client meeting should often be only to secure a *second* meeting. The best way to convert a one-time buyer into a long-term partner is to listen, listen, listen.

The reason is evident: when you let the customer speak, he (a) describes most clearly what he wants, and (b) becomes your partner (a "prosumer") in meeting his own needs.

Listening is especially important when things go wrong. A key cause of customer dissatisfaction is that "nobody listens." When people pay good money for something and they're not happy, they're entitled to a little air time. You might be able to anticipate what they're going to say, and you might have other things to do, but you score points when you let them spell out precisely how they feel.

4. They want to feel that you're on their side.

When you buy something, there's nothing worse than the feeling that you've got to wrestle it away from the supplier.

It's equally frustrating to feel that vendors are in opposition to you.

The most fruitful supplier-customer relationships are win-win *partnerships*. All parties gain through them. They're created when sales people go out of their way to establish their customers' needs, to deliver, and to follow through.

Many sales people fall into the trap of taking sides — either against their customer or *against* their own company.

In the first case, they bust a gut to prove that they and their company are right and the customer is wrong.

In the second, they criticize their firm in front of their customers, or they cause havoc by making unreasonable demands of their own team-mates.

Every employee needs to understand two things. Firstly, that he or she *is the company* in the eyes of customers. Customers deal with the individual before them, not with a faceless corporation. Secondly, employees must acknowledge that their job is to *build relationships* between the company and its customers. This means that they're a critical link in the marketing process, and their role is always a diplomatic one.

5. They want information.

In this information-rich world, customers need help to (a) make sensible buying decisions, and (b) to be able to use products or services properly. Yet front line people don't know enough about their companies, their products, or their services to give customers professional help.

This means that they're seldom as effective as they might be. It also means that customers far too often buy loads of features that they can never really use.

I recently bought a fax machine which was delivered while I was out. The salesman showed my daughter how to load documents. Then he left, and I've never heard from him since. The machine has a 32-page manual and a great bunch of features. There are probably many things it could do for me, if only I knew how. But I'm too busy to read the manual or to figure out how the damned thing works. So all the effort that went into producing it is wasted.

Whatever I paid for that sophisticated fax machine, it is, in reality, worth much less to me than the purchase price. And when I need another piece of office equipment, I'll almost certainly shop around. I have no relationship at all with the supplier who had my ear, and I don't care if I never see that firm again.

The basic principles of superior service

Business is a subject that gets complicated very easily. Yet there are some very basic basics to staying in business and making a profit.

Principle no.1:
Everything you do must drive value up, costs down.

As we saw in Chapter 6, world class companies have moved beyond "generic" strategies. Even if you still do aim to compete on the basis of either low cost or differentiation, every person in your organization must focus on two goals:

1. Drive value to the customer *up*.
2. Drive your own costs *down* (Figure 8-1).

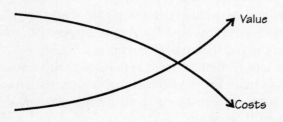

Figure 8-1
The new strategic secret

This isn't a one-time project; it must be worked at over and over again, over time. Continuous improvement in these two areas must be the goal.

Many managers immediately react to this suggestion by saying, "That's impossible. Value costs money. If you want to drive value up, you have to spend more." But as the following examples show, value — *differentiation* in the customer's mind — comes from doing the right thing, the right way, right first time, and right on time. Lower costs come the same way. So virtually every company would do a whole lot better if everyone burned those two words — value and costs — into their minds.

Examples:

❏ Not long ago, I took my car to be serviced. I asked the workshop manager to check the brakes and steam clean the engine at the same time. When I went back that evening, the car wouldn't start. I called the manager; he called two mechanics. They spent 20 minutes blowing the steam out of the engine. In effect, *they were donating their profits back to me.* I got 40 minutes of their expensive time, absolutely free. My perception of their delivered value fell, their costs soared.

But that wasn't the end. As I drove away, I noticed that while my brakes worked, I now had a bad wheel-wobble. And whereas previously a factory fault had caused the car to pull gently to the left, it now pulled sharply right.

So back I went the next day. Again, my perception of their value fell, and their costs went up.

The saga continued. I had to return five times before the job was right. Every visit cost that service station money, and every one made me more determined never to do business there again.

❏ A new restaurant recently opened near my home. Friends recommended it, so I decided to take a business guest there for dinner. I phoned to book a table, and at the same time made sure they had a liquor licence.

My guest arrived a little late at my house, so I called to tell the restaurant we'd be there at eight-fifteen instead of eight sharp. I didn't have to, but I thought that was the courteous thing to do. However, when we arrived and I gave my name to the owner, he snapped, "You're late. You were booked for eight."

"I know," I said, "but I did phone and tell you."

"Well," he said, in an offhand manner, "you're lucky. We've still got your table."

After that good fortune it was downhill all the way. My guest and I both had to send our soup back three times to be warmed. The wine list was almost non-existent. The service was appalling.

Like the service station in the first example, this restaurant will never see me again. From the time I walked in their front door, they systematically destroyed my perception of value, and they also drove their own costs up by having to do things over.

These two examples show how easy it is to get the basics back to front (Figure 8-2). And how people throughout the value chain literally steal their company's profits (Figure 8-3). They underline how vital it is that every team member get his or her part of the job right first time. Which leads us to the second basic principle of business life.

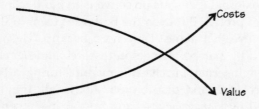

Figure 8-2
How most firms fail

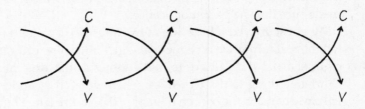

Figure 8-3
How employees "steal" profits

Principle No.2: Customer care is everybody's business.

Customer care must be a companywide obsession. Everyone must get involved. It's not something that only the sales team needs to know about. It's not what you teach service people so they don't screw up the sale. It's not a short-term project, not a quick-fix, not a conference theme.

Customer care is a way of life.

It's an attitude. A habit. A never-ending quest to go a little further, try a little harder, and improve a little more.

Customer care isn't first-aid for bleeding profits. It's not an idea you can pick up and drop, or a project you can think about when real work slows down.

Customer care *is* real work. It's hard work. And it's unnatural for most companies, so it must literally be forced down their throats.

A commitment to customer care forces organizations to have an external focus. Its objective is to build sales, market share, and profits. But even the best sales team in the world can't achieve that alone. They need backup. They must be supported by star performers in research and development, design, engineering, purchasing, manufacturing, administration, secretarial, and distribution. Above all, they must be supported by *management* — and by a management system that makes quality performance possible.

Every link in the value chain is important. Total teamwork is an absolute necessity. The complete business system must be designed to exceed customers' expectations.

Principle No.3: Top management must make it happen

Superior service starts with top-management commitment. It must be driven through the organization from the top down. People at lower levels might draw attention to the need for better service, and might even get the ball rolling in their own area, but sooner or later the CEO must get involved. And he must get involved with a vengeance, and not just put his thumbprint to someone else's programme.

In many companies I've worked with, the initial call has come from someone below CEO level: a divisional manager, a human resources manager or the marketing department. But I've discovered the hard way that frustration and failure are inevitable if the top man doesn't become the key player.

For any company to create a genuine customer focus, a huge change is necessary. For many it's more of a quantum leap. Corporate priorities are always a reflection of a company's leadership.

Changing direction is never easy. Changing it from the bottom is impossible. If the boss believes that customers come first, and lives by that belief, people soon catch his drift. If, on the other hand, he's more concerned about manufacturing or finance or some other function, and if by his actions he so much as suggests that customers are incidental to the real business of business, everyone will follow his lead.

The CEO is a powerful role model. His first priority must be to drive a customer consciousness deep through every fibre of the firm. He must talk about customers, he must talk *to* customers, and he must reinforce the message over and over again.

When Jan Carlzon took over as president of SAS in 1981, the company was about to lose $20 million after 17 profitable years. A year later it earned $54 million. During the turn-around, says Carlzon, "I spent exactly half of my working hours 'out in the field' talking to SAS people."[2]

Roger Smith, former chairman of General Motors, didn't put the same effort into talking to his people, and admits it was a serious mistake.

"I sure wish I'd done a better job of communicating with GM people," he said in a *Fortune* interview. "I'd do that differently a second time around and make sure they understood my vision for the company. Then they would have known why I was tearing the place up, taking out whole divisions, changing our whole production structure. If people understand the *why*, they'll work at it."[3]

Like everyone else, the CEO must recognize the existence of both internal and external customers. He must lead the way in creating a climate for high performance, in providing the structure and systems which make it possible, and in giving people the support they need to make it happen. There's just no substitute for his visible, vocal presence. Stand-ins and other "second-hand" forms of communication never carry the same weight.

Principle No.4: Superior customer service takes a total on-slaught.

From time to time a helpful salesperson restores your faith in business. He or she goes the extra mile to give you exactly what you want, and to make you feel good.

But no firm can be successful over the long run if it relies on exceptional individual performers. Even the most enter-

2   Jan Carlzon, 1987
3   "The U.S. must do as GM has done," *Fortune*, February 13, 1989

prising front-liner is ultimately a reflection of the total organization.

Customer service is a process that must be *managed*. The way you treat people inside your organization determines the way they, in turn, treat outsiders.

Customer service cannot be delegated. To make it a reality, and to make it a way of life in your firm, it must be driven in several ways.

It begins with a revolution in management thinking and behaviour. Then it must be monitored, measured, encouraged, and publicized. People must be trained to create value for customers. They must be given information, resources, and support. And they must be sensibly rewarded.

When you get great service from a company, you may be sure that management is the reason. It never just happens by itself — and certainly not over the long run.

For this reason any attempt to make your company customer-driven must involve a hard look at the way you and your fellow managers do things. Your style, your priorities, the things you talk about, and the way you treat customers, all send powerful signals to your team.

In industry after industry today, companies work so hard, on so many fronts at once, it's difficult to keep track of the improvements. No competitor can hope to stay abreast by doing just one or even a few things better. Continuous improvement of everything is essential. Total, ongoing change must become a way of life.

Superior service is not a miracle cure

Superior customer service is a big job. Success comes through an uncompromising quest for quality in the products you offer and in the way you deliver them. The best front line training in the world, and the best customer care "packages" or programmes, will have no more than a marginal impact if you don't fix the underlying basics first.

> **Winning with the customer is a complex process. For most companies it requires a total review of everything they do — and an ongoing commitment to change and continuous improvement. The customer is a moving target. Competitors are more innovative and more aggressive than ever. And as tough as things might be today, they're bound to get even more challenging tomorrow.**

To become a world class competitor is a big task, but don't let that put you off. The key to success is action. The long journey is begun with one small step. Make the bigger picture clear to your team, but at the same time, put them under intense pressure to do some small things differently and better fast. Their experience of victory will be a powerful incentive to reach for even greater heights.

PART II

STRATEGIC MIND,
STRATEGIC MUSCLE

CHAPTER NINE

THE STRATEGY PROCESS

If you're serious about becoming a world class competitor, the time to begin talking about it is when you talk about your overall business strategy.

This is necessary because:

1. Superior customer service is *the* focal business issue, the factor that drives every decision and action. Customers determine the thrusts a firm will make. The total business system and all operations, policies, and procedures support those thrusts.

2. To be competitive over time, you have to deliver unique value to your customers. This demands the continuous, rapid improvement of everything. But the effort must be focused: it is more important to do one thing especially well than many things quite well.

3. When people are involved in strategic debates, when information is widely and openly shared with them, they learn, they grow — and they are able to make more creative, more insightful contributions.

4. Trust underpins superior customer service. A lack of trust undermines it. Involving people in the whole process of strategic thinking and action is a powerful way to earn their trust and their commitment.

Industry logic

Every industry has its own "strategic logic." Over time, competitors identify the same key factors of success. They measure

179

the same things. They watch each other and mimic each other, so they start behaving in similar ways. They form associations and their representatives meet, share ideas, and agree on what "the industry" should say in public.

Industry logic is shaped by the environment, by the experience of competing firms, and by cooperation and collusion between them. Markets tend to be stable when they're growing fast, when there are relatively few competitors, and when competitors are of a similar size and capability. They become turbulent and unattractive when growth slows and many competitors of different sizes and with different capabilities battle for a slice of the cake.

While conditions are reasonably stable, competitors tend to behave in a similar way. When the environment turns hostile, however, the rules go out the window. When war breaks out companies cut prices, add value, and adopt new methods of manufacturing, sales, or distribution.

For a time, these activities squeeze margins. The industry becomes unattractive, so potential entrants stay out and some incumbents get out. Then there's a shakeout, followed by consolidation of the industry with just a few strong competitors. In some cases, one or more weak competitors will be tolerated, to avoid charges of monopolistic practice.

This pattern is now visible in the computer industry, in airlines, in heavy engineering, consumer electronics, and automobiles. In each case, it's not just the rules of the game that are changing, but the game itself. To keep playing, companies must rethink their logic and reinvent themselves.

❏ What is the strategic logic that drives competition in your industry?
❏ What impact does it have on your team's thinking?
❏ What has happened that could have changed it in the past three years?
❏ Do any of your competitors appear to be driven by a different understanding of your industry's logic?

❑ What different performance measures might give you an edge?

❑ Is your industry involvement as constructive as you once thought it was?

Corporate logic

Just as industries develop a strategic logic, so do companies. They learn what works, they make assumptions about new realities, and they adopt a mindset which drives their decisions.

A company's strategic logic tends to be *implicit* rather than *explicit*. Managers seldom consciously discuss what makes their firm successful. They also seldom agree on what gives them an advantage. If you asked them about it individually, one might say, "Our marketing," another would say, "Quality," and a third would say, "Our people." Or they might argue about the importance of low costs, of sharpening up on distribution, or of the need to invest heavily in brand-building. If they agreed on just one important factor, they could single-mindedly work at it. Back in the mid-1980s, Coca-Cola marketing executives decided to home in on three issues: acceptability, availability, and affordability. Scientists at Japan's Sharp Corp. are racing for world leadership in liquid-crystal displays (LCDs), because the technology shrinks personal computers into laptops and palmtops, and the sales potential of these tiny portables could take the Japanese computer industry past that of the U.S. by 1992. Trans Atlantic airlines vie for landing rights at London's Heathrow Airport, because it's the gateway to Britain and an important link to many European destinations.

Over time, of course, a firm's key factors of success will change. Today's high value-added product is tomorrow's commodity. Today's hot fashion item is ho-hum a year from now, or perhaps even a month from now. Today's big winner is tomorrow's big loser.

So in addition to agreeing on their strategic logic, executives need to constantly review it. Some things they do will siphon resources into activities with a low payoff or no payoff. Others will have a long life and will give the biggest rewards; these activities and projects must become priorities, and money and minds must be poured into them. This is how invisible assets are built. And this is how future competitiveness is assured.

❑ What is your firm's strategic logic?
❑ Do all your people agree?
❑ What shaped it?
❑ What new factors dictate that it should change now?
❑ What would the impact be if you changed?
❑ What would you have to do to change?

A firm's strategic logic is a product of its past. It is shaped by all the factors that shape its industry's logic. But two other issues warrant special attention, as they both impact on a firm's logic and are impacted by it. Firstly, there's the "corporate attitude," which is, in turn, a product of the employees' attitudes — and particularly the leader's attitude. Then there's the company's unique capability — its special skill or core competence (Figure 9-1).

Attitude is perhaps the most under-rated cause of competitive success or failure. "For a large organization to be effective," says Richard Tanner Pascale, author of *Managing on the Edge*, "it must be simple. For a large organization to be simple, its people must have self-confidence and intellectual self-assurance."[1]

---

1   Richard Tanner Pascale, *Managing On The Edge*, Viking Penguin Inc., 1990

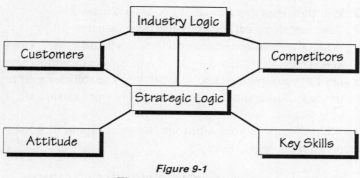

Figure 9-1
The strategic interface

Firms that are consistently aggressive in the marketplace don't get that way overnight. They've fought the odds for years. They've learned that limited resources are less of a handicap than limited ambition.

When managers in less successful companies talk of "changing people's attitudes," they're usually looking for a quick fix. What they should do is work on those attitudes every moment of every day.

Similarly, they should work consistently on building their key skills. They should avoid being sidetracked by novelty or news. Their resources should be focused on the few vital strengths that will put them ahead of their competition, and keep them there.

If you pay attention to these two weapons — attitude and capability — you'll give your firm a real shot at being world class. If you don't, you'll never get there.

❑ Do people who come into contact with your firm immediately feel, "This is a company with 'attitude?'"

❑ Do you and your team have dreams out of proportion to your resources?

❑ Do all your people really want to kill your competition?

❑ Do they love winning, and hate losing?

❏ Will they bust a gut to satisfy your customers?
❏ Can they shrug off setbacks and even disasters?
❏ When they make mistakes, do they learn and grow — and keep going?
❏ Do all your people know what key capabilities you're trying to build, and do they deliberately work towards that objective?
❏ What impact do your attitudes and your capabilities have on your strategic logic?

Strategy is a product of human minds. It emerges partly through rigorous analysis and clear, creative thinking, and mostly from aggressive, single-minded action and fast learning. In the past, more attention has been paid to up-front planning, and too little to the ongoing entrepreneurial process.

Tools for strategists

In many companies, discussions about strategy are largely ineffective. They don't focus on key issues, they don't encourage lateral thinking, and they don't address all the factors which influence performance.

One reason is that managers fail to agree on the language they're going to use. Aristotle said, "If you would converse with me, define your terms." Managers should follow his advice. They use different words to describe the same issues, or the same words to describe different issues. Concepts such as *strategy, vision* and *mission* are often bandied about as if they were one and the same, when in fact they're each quite different.

Equally, managers talk about ideas such as *corporate culture* and *values* with a great deal of fervour and to little positive effect. These become topics of conversation, themes for conferences, the stuff of wall plaques and posters — and a rod for managers' backs.

It's horrifying to think how much time managers must have wasted in recent years, crafting sexy mission statements and philosophies. Potentially powerful business tools have been reduced to the level of fads. A lot of motherhood has spewed forth. In most cases, the impact on profits has probably been zero or worse.

The conceptual tools you need to create and implement effective strategy must meet two tests:

1. They should help you *think* more effectively about what you do, and why.
2. They should help you *communicate* your organization's priorities.

If the terms you use don't pass, stop using them. Sort out misunderstandings at this stage, and you'll find that progress is easier down the line.

Designing the future

What precisely is "strategy?" Is it a mission statement? A "SWOT" analysis? An action plan, or a planning process? A grand attack, or a tactical strike?

In fact, it's all of these and none of these. There are many ways to define strategy, but as usual it's best to keep things simple. So my definition says:

> **Strategy is the process of thinking through what today's business is and what tomorrow's business should be, and then getting there.**

Or, to put it slightly differently:

> **Strategy is the creation of "fit" between an organization and its environment over time.**

When I use the word "fit," it's not to describe a static condition, a state of perfection, or a goal. What it suggests, rather, is

learning, development, and evolution in harmony with the
world around you.

In theory, managers plan for the future in a systematic,
structured way. At a fixed point in time, they scan the environment to get a fix on the state of the economy and the
socio-political situation . . . they look at what customers are
buying and at how competitors are acting . . . and they check
technological trends. Thus armed, they look inside their own
organizations to get a sense of their preparedness for the
challenges ahead. Then, on the basis of this "scan" (often called
a "SWOT" analysis — strengths, weaknesses, opportunities,
threats), they choose a course of action — what to do, how to
do it, and so forth. Finally, with their plan neatly bound and a
budget attached, they begin acting it out.

In real life, however, things are a lot different. The process
is altogether more messy. Most plans aren't worth the paper
they're written on. The thinking that goes into them is neither
rigorous nor imaginative, and the end result is wasted time,
frustration, and piles of plastic folders that become a company
joke.

Plans become outmoded virtually as soon as they're com-
pleted. Everything around the company — and often a great
deal *inside*, too — changes immediately and continuously. The
environment becomes hostile. The fit between the firm and its
world becomes uncomfortable. The gap starts to widen between where management aimed and where they actually go.
This is why corporate (and product) life cycles occur. It's also
why companies (as well as individuals and even *countries*)
come and go.

> Strategic planning is a useful exercise, but in the real
> world strategic *plans* have a very short shelf life. In fact,
> most of them wind up on the shelf. Planning becomes
> a calendar-driven task, a paper chase, and a distraction
> from "real work."

Strategic planning is not strategic management. Creating a plan is not the same as *living* it. Planning has value, but the best plan in the world is worth nothing until it becomes action. The objective of planning should never be a plan, but rather, new insights, a point of view, an attitude, a posture, a way of thinking. Above all, it's about exercising your corporate mind and stretching your corporate imagination.

Planning is thus not a one-time activity with a neat beginning and ending. It's a *learning* process. It needs to be managed over time. It must be ongoing (or "seamless"), and it needs the input, involvement, and commitment of many people throughout the organization.

The building blocks

Strategy has five building blocks (Figure 9-2). Each has a specific purpose and encourages a particular kind of analysis, creativity, and action. They all mean quite different things, though they're all locked together.

In designing your corporate future, the essential task is to think about your purpose and how you might achieve it. In other words: Where do you want to go? How can you get there? What must your priorities be? What "rules" should guide you and your people?

These issues are framed by five key business concepts: (1) vision, (2) mission, (3) values, (4) objectives, and (5) action plans. Here's what they mean and how they stack up:

Vision

"Where we're going" . . . "Our dream of the future."

Mission

"The business we're in" . . . "The task we set ourselves" . . . "The game we play and how we play it."

Values

"What counts around here" . . . "What we pay special attention to" . . . "The rules' we live by."

Objectives

"What we want to achieve, by when, at what cost."

Action plans

"How we'll make it happen."

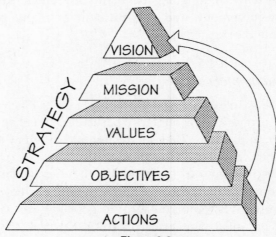

Figure 9-2
Building blocks of strategy

Since strategy is about learning, this is not a simple top-down process. It's "circular": an exercise in experimentation, feedback and readjustment. As you work down through the strategy "pyramid," thoughts and ideas become clearer and clearer; then, as you act and monitor your results, new possibilities surface.

In recent years, many managers have eagerly grasped at notions such as vision and mission in the vain hope that they might offer some panacea for their problems. This is ridiculous. There are no simple "solutions" in business. Worse, by doing it, these executives trap themselves and kill creative thinking and entrepreneurial action.

> **The best strategists are opportunists. They understand the role of chance and luck in business. They place themselves in the most likely path of opportunities, and seize them when they appear. If they use a formal planning process, it's to increase the odds in their favour.**

"I'm no guru," says GE chairman Jack Welch. "I'm not here to predict the world. I'm here to be sure I've got a company that is strong enough to respond to whatever happens."[2]

Woody Allen once said that nine-tenths of success in life was "turning up." A good strategy will help you "turn up" more often than your competitors. Think about it this way, and maybe you'll avoid the trap of planning for a guaranteed future.

Where are we headed?

If I were to say to you, "We're going on a journey, and I want you to take care of the food," what would you do? As a good leader I've delegated a key task. You have all the freedom in the world to manage it as you see fit. Or do you?

What would you bring? A tin of beans? A *case* of beans? A few sandwiches? Half an ox? And what about equipment and utensils? Should you bring pots and pans, a fridge and stove, or what?

A lot of what passes as delegation is no more than *dumping*. Leaders give their people vague instructions which are open

2   Ronald Henkoff, "How to plan for 1995," *Fortune,* December 31, 1990

to endless interpretations. Deliberately or otherwise, they set them up to fail.

In the simple case above, you'd have to be 100 per cent lucky to get your job right. You don't know how long the journey will be, what kind of terrain it'll cover, what the weather will be like, how many people to feed. You can't make a single sensible resourcing decision. You have to rely on guesswork. Your chances of failure are far better than your chances of success.

Most people in most organizations want to do a good job. They're also capable of far bigger things than their bosses ever know. They under-perform because they have no sense of purpose or direction. The boss urges them to run faster, but he doesn't tell them where to; so they run in circles. Each individual picks a direction, and does his or her own thing.

The problem extends through all levels. As Christopher Bartlett and Sumantra Ghoshal say in *Managing Across Borders*, "In any complex organization, the main difficulty in obtaining individual commitment to an overall purpose is the limited perspectives and parochial interests of managers in key positions."[3] Myopia and turf wars kill team performance. And once managers disagree on direction, confusion quickly spreads.

Not long ago I was on a corporate jet with six directors of a major company. We were on our way to a weekend strategy retreat. The managing director had gone to see a new factory, and was on another plane.

I asked them, "What's the most useful thing we can achieve this weekend?" As one man, they said, "Find out where this damned company is going!"

Typically, they assumed that someone, somewhere knew the answer. They further assumed that the MD would be that

3   Christopher A. Bartlett and Sumantra Ghoshal, *Managing Across Borders*, Harvard Business School Press, 1989

person. But they were wrong. When we got into the meeting, we discovered that he didn't know either. The company had become "fat and happy." Founded many years earlier, it existed in a reasonably benevolent environment, and now it was a juggernaut rolling along as a result of sheer momentum. There were problems with the unions, problems with customers, and profits were going nowhere. Managers had become more and more autocratic. Even the smallest decisions were delegated upwards.

> **World class performance is possible only when every person in a firm is empowered to deliver it. Customers are dazzled by initiative, creativity, energy, and responsiveness — qualities that all too easily suppressed. Setting them free begins, paradoxically, with clear, unambiguous focus. When the leader says, *"That's* the hill we're going to take." When the organization is driven not by its past success or its present size, but by total commitment to a stretching goal.**

A corporate vision statement provides both direction and "stretch." It points to "the hill." Who can be in any doubt about the intent of "Kill Yamaha!" (Honda), Let's beat Xerox!" (Canon), "Beat Matsushita Whatever" (Sony), or "Encircle Caterpillar!" (Komatsu)? Which worker in Nissan's factory at Sunderland in the U.K. can be confused about his purpose in life when a huge sign proclaims, "Best in the world"? And who in GE aims for anything else, when chairman Jack Welch says that the firm must be No. 1 or No. 2 in every industry in which it competes?

The Bible tells us, "When there is no vision, the people perish." Henry David Thoreau saw the compelling "pull" in vision when he wrote:

"If one advances confidently in the direction of his dreams, and endeavours to live the life he has imagined, he will meet with a success unexpected in common hours."

Vision describes where you imagine your company to be some time in the future. It might talk profits, turnover, market share, or position relative to a competitor; equally, it might include statements about your human resources practices, your stance on social responsibility, or your aims in terms of the environment. It's possibly idealistic and maybe imprecise, but it must give people a sense of purpose, and therefore where they should aim their efforts. When they hear it or read it they should know *"where we're going."*

Examples:

❑ "To be the biggest computer company."
❑ "To be the leading supplier of heavy trucks."
❑ "To be the most profitable supermarket chain."
❑ "To be a key player in entertainment, leisure, and food."
❑ "To be a place where people can reach their true potential."

If the idea of corporate vision is not attractive right now, or if you're loath to commit yourself to a goal that might change in the not-too-distant future, consider the alternative.

Vision has been a "soft" issue in the past. The vision statement in many organizations might just as well not exist. Publicizing your vision does expose you to questions and debate — and even to criticism. But business performance hinges in large part upon subtleties and nuances, on dreams and on inspiration.

Arriving at an effective vision statement is seldom easy. Writing one that you can live with over time is a task that needs imagination and attention. When you start work on it, keep in mind this piece of graffiti from the wall of the Sorbonne in Paris:

"BE REALISTIC: ATTEMPT THE IMPOSSIBLE!"

What *business* are we in?

The most fundamental question in strategy is: what business are we in? The way you define your business can make all the difference between success and failure. It determines where you'll compete, and how you'll do it.

Everything else flows from the "product-market decision." Every objective, every action plan, every system, policy, and procedure, depends on it. The shape of your company, the people you hire, the location you choose for your office and factories, the machinery you invest in — all follow the decision about who your customer is.

Kenichi Ohmae, managing director of the Tokyo office of McKinsey and Co., the giant consulting firm, puts it like this:

> "First comes painstaking attention to the needs of customers. First comes close analysis of a company's real degrees of freedom in responding to those needs. First comes the willingness to rethink, fundamentally, what products are and what they do, as well how best to organize the business system that designs, builds, and markets them."[4]

In his classic 1960 *Harvard Business Review* article, "Marketing Myopia," Theodore Levitt warned companies against defining themselves too narrowly. Every organization must "learn to think of itself not as producing goods or services" he said, "but as *buying customers*, as doing the things that will make people *want* to do business with it." He argued that Hollywood film makers would have been less affected by television if they'd understood that they were in the entertainment business, and that buggy whip makers would have survived if they'd seen that they were actually in the transport business.

---

4   Kenichi Ohmae, "Getting Back To Strategy," *Harvard Business Review*, November-December 1988

Defining your products and markets is not easy. It demands tough choices. And it's complicated by a third factor: *how* you will compete.

Competitive advantage doesn't come from knowing what you'll sell to whom, but rather from doing key things in a unique way. This capability usually takes time to build. Then, since it seldom gives you an edge for long, you have to continually re-create it.

From "driving forces" to "core competence"

Two well-known American management consultants, Benjamin Tregoe and John Zimmerman, suggest that there are nine "driving forces" which (*a*) influenced past decisions, and (*b*) give an organization "the basis for defining its future product and market scope." They are:

❑ Products offered.
❑ Market needs.
❑ Technology.
❑ Production capability.
❑ Method of sale.
❑ Method of distribution.
❑ Natural resources.
❑ Size/growth.
❑ Return/profit.[5]

These "driving forces" underpin the company's strategic logic and shape virtually every decision. As we saw earlier, some firms make their strategic choices from a consistent base. Everyone agrees that a unique technology, for example, is the firm's greatest strength; product/market decisions are taken which exploit that strength, and all efforts are directed at improving and adding to the technology for future battles.

---

5 Benjamin B. Tregoe & John W. Zimmerman, *Top Management Strategy*, Simon and Schuster 1980

In other companies, however, people in various areas have different perceptions of which "driving force" is most important. One person thinks that the product line is sacrosanct; another sees the distribution system as the key to success; a third is hell-bent on growth at all costs. The result, inevitably, is confusion and a lack of commitment to building any one of them. But as experts at the Harvard Business School note, a company can only create a sustainable competitive advantage when it's efforts are "directed not toward opportunistic deal making, but rather toward the development of specific organizational competencies and relationships that are difficult for competitors to match over the long term."[6]

C.K. Prahalad and Gary Hamel argue that one reason for the success of many Japanese companies is the effort they make to develop and exploit their "core competence." "In the short run," they say, "a company's competitiveness derives from the price/performance attributes of current products." But in the long run, it comes from the "ability to build, at lower cost and more speedily than competitors, the core competencies that spawn unanticipated products."[7]

❏ Honda has spent years learning to design and build engines and power trains. Now, it exploits this expertise in lawnmowers, pumps, motorcycles, and motor cars.

❏ Casio uses its knowledge of microprocessors and material science in tiny calculators, digital watches, and pocket TVs.

❏ Sanyo is applying its know-how in "soft energy products" — rechargeable batteries and solar cells — into environmentally-friendly refrigerators and air conditioners, and roof tiles that generate 2,5 watts of electricity each.

6 Robert H. Hayes, Steven C. Wheelwright, and Kim B. Clark, *Dynamic Manufacturing,* The Free Press 1988
7 C.K. Prahalad and Gary Hamel, "The Core Competence of the Corporation," *Harvard Business Review,* May-June 1990

❑ Sony has expanded its interests from private entertainment via audio and video equipment, to mass entertainment under the umbrella of U.S.-based Sony Software
   Corp. which owns CBS Records and Columbia Pictures.
   The firm is now looking at building a number of "Sony-
   land" theme parks to compete with Disneyland and
   Universal Studios in Southern California, and worldwide
   expansion is on the cards.
❑ Firms such as Ford, GE, and Marks and Spencer have
   exploited their cash, their brand names, and their huge
   customer bases to build powerful finance companies that
   now compete head-on with banks.

By continually beefing up their key skills, these companies are
able to apply them across a portfolio of products and customers. If they choose, they can continually redefine their businesses. Understanding their strengths, they can spend time
imagining products and services that don't exist. This puts
their future firmly in their own hands, as they don't have to
wait for customers to decide what's next. It also gives them a
head start over competitors who follow customers rather than
show them the way.

> Having built specific skills, it's tempting to exploit
> them in many areas. It's easy to forget to "stick to your
> knitting." So here's another of those management para-
> doxes: While there's always the danger that managers
> may be blinkered by their industry logic, they do need
> a deep understanding of that industry to succeed in it.
> Mastering a technology or a skill is seldom enough.

Think through what you do particularly well today, and what
you should excel at tomorrow. You have to be great at something. It's virtually impossible to be both a brilliant ballerina
and a star football player. The particular skill or strength you
develop will determine what products you can sell, to what

customers. It'll also put distance between you and your enemies.

But then match your strengths to industries and customers you already understand, or can learn about fast. Your "better mousetrap" will only bring the profits you expect if you can sell it against competitors who know the territory.

Writing your mission statement

Mission is clearly quite different to vision. It's more specific, more precise, and more prescriptive (though you'd never think so, considering the way many are written!)

Whereas vision describes an end goal or a future state, mission defines your company's business, and spells out what you'll do to succeed in that business. It's a statement of intent and gives a broad-brush picture of your strategy. It describes the task you and your people aim to perform. When your people hear it or read it they should know *"what to do."*

Many firms today have mission statements because it's "the thing to do." Managers aren't sure what they should include, or what to leave out. They start off simply, and express themselves in reasonably concrete fashion, but then they get carried away and their writer's block disappears. The words flow. Philosophy creeps in. The result is pure motherhood. You could take the mission statements of any number of companies, across virtually every industry, switch the names — and not notice any difference.

Before you sit down to work on your mission statement, it's worth reminding yourself yet again why you're doing it at all. On their own, mission statements never got anyone to do anything. But the exercise of crafting one does focus minds.

To define your business, and thus write a meaningful mission statement, you have to answer three seemingly simple questions. Each deserves far more thought than might at first appear necessary.

1. Who is our customer?
2. What "value" will we offer? (Products, services, benefits.)
3. How will we do it? (What key skills will we develop and exploit? What technology will we use? What kind of business system will we design?) (Figure 9-3.)

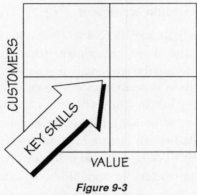

Figure 9-3
Defining the business

Examples:

"We develop low price personal computers for small businesses, and distribute them through independent retailers."

"We provide scientific software to universities, through a dedicated network of sales specialists."

"We build the toughest trucks in the world. Our investment in research, our advanced manufacturing capability, and our concern for our people make quality our distinct advantage."

"We make luxury soap for beautiful women, and we sell it through upmarket stores."

Some companies will be able to answer those three questions quite easily. Others will find it far more difficult. But it's vital that you work through them carefully, for many decisions flow from the answers.

At first glance, all the questions look deceptively simple, so when you tackle them, beware of being superficial. And accept that the answers demand real commitment, for business success usually depends on persistence over the long haul rather than a series of quick hits.

Here are some issues to think about as you work through the process:

❑ When you pick your particular customers, can you really be better than anyone at satisfying them?
❑ Is the target meaningful in terms of size, growth, profitability, and "bragging rights," and what you might learn from it?
❑ Can you progress from your initial customer base by adding new products and services or new customers?
❑ If you invest heavily in a key skill, will it bring the returns you expect?
❑ Will competitors be able to copy or nullify your advantage soon, or will you have the field to yourself for a reasonable time?

Why the mission statement is so vital

To see why the mission is so important, consider this example:

A firm which is part of a conglomerate has four divisions which operate in a single industry. They serve different markets with different products. The industry is very cyclical, and profits bob up and down with the economy.

To iron out the results, management decides to invest in an industry which is less cyclical. They buy a very profitable company in a totally different industry. It performs extremely well, and the group's profits are more even.

But then there's a switch in chief executives. The new
man is under pressure from his holding company to
deliver better profits. He has three options: (1) he can try
to squeeze more profit out of the companies he owns; (2)
he can invest in other businesses in the same industry; or
(3) he can venture outside of his industry.

His holding company doesn't want him to build a conglomerate. *He* doesn't want a conglomerate. But since he
already has one "outsider" in his organization, why not
another? And if that's the decision, where does he begin?
After all, if his intention is to get a smooth and predictable return, and if he's already in one unrelated industry,
why not more?

If the core business is, say, chemicals, and the first extra
company is in tyres, what should this executive buy
next? A meat pie factory? A retail store? Something in
abrasives? Or, what the hell, why not buy them *all* and
sell his original core business? After all, he did start the
shopping spree to make more money!

Without some kind of game plan the choices are endless.
Without clear criteria there are no boundaries. Without a
carefully thought through view of what business he's in, the
man is more likely to make a bad decision than a good one.

The mission statement helps solve problems like this one.
It forces managers to think hard about what they do, and why.
It also addresses the "how," so it makes them think about
matching opportunities and resources.

Most importantly, however, *a well thought out mission statement focuses attention on customers, on the value you offer them, and
on the way you do it.*

By structuring your mission statement in the way I've
suggested, you say, loudly and clearly, that customers drive
your business decisions. The words you finally choose should
underline this view.

Platitudes won't do. High-sounding phrases and lofty prose are a waste of time. The mission statement should be lean and specific, practical and clear. It should tell people quickly and unambiguously "what we do around here." No less, and no more.

But be sure that it actually *tells* them. A survey by British accounting firm Peat Marwick McLintock showed that while 80 per cent of companies have a mission statement, only 2 per cent of them distribute it to all their staff. "The fact that the majority of companies do not communicate them to their staff makes a complete nonsense of the idea," says the consultant who did the study.[8] Hear, hear!

8   *Eurobusiness,* June 1989

Chapter Ten

What Counts Around Here?

In the same way that the mission tells "what we do around here," *values* tell *"what counts around here."* They're the underlying beliefs or principles that guide people's behaviour.

Values indicate which issues should get attention, and which should be ignored. They're a kind of checklist for making decisions, and they're an important yardstick of performance. Clear values give people a code of behaviour. On the other hand, when values aren't clearly spelled out, people have to continually work out whether they're doing the right things in the right way. Each person is likely to judge the same situation differently.

Values are "propaganda." If they're going to be useful, they must be explicit and as objective as possible. Yet most company value statements are loaded with subjective words like "integrity," "respect," and "dignity." These sound good but cannot be managed or measured. This makes it very difficult to either communicate their importance or make them a reality in the workplace.

So this is where I depart sharply from much current thinking. This is where I use the term "values" differently than some would like. This is where I put them to work as *a logical extension of the vision and mission, as a foundation for both, and as a link between them and the company's objectives and action plan.*

The "7 Cs": framework for a corporate mind-set

My approach promotes as "values" those factors which directly impact on the firm's *profits*. There are seven of them, and they can be managed, measured, improved, and objectively discussed. They are: Customers, Competition, Challenges, Cooperation, Creativity, Costs, and Communication (Figure 10-1).

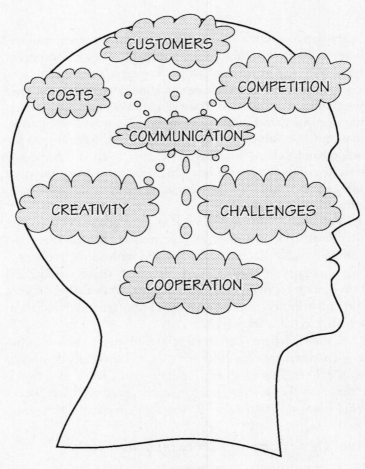

Figure 10-1
The "7 Cs": mindset of the world class company

With remarkable consistency, studies of corporate effectiveness underline the importance of the "7 Cs." Researchers might not always use the words I've used, but the ideas are the same. I've simply captured them in an easy-to-remember framework. Here's why the "7 Cs" are important:

No.1 Customers

Winning companies put customers first. Their people all understand the overriding importance of customers, and every employee is made to feel part of the value-creating process. They all have a role to play and a contribution to make, and management drives home this message in every possible way. So customer satisfaction is top-of-mind throughout the organization. It's talked about, thought about, and acted out. Marketing is everybody's business.

No.2 Competition

Winning companies want to be No. 1. Market share is a key measure of their success. But so are "bragging rights." These firms are driven by a deep desire to be the very best in all they do. Winning is vitally important to them so they fight aggressively for every inch of territory. Their ambitions are often out of all proportion to their resources. They watch their competitors, they analyze competitors' performance, and they never stop looking for ways to gain an edge.

These firms accept that there's a lot of truth in the old admonition, "Know thyself." But they know that looking inward isn't enough in this dog-eat-dog business world.

As Sun Tzu once said, "If you know the enemy and know yourself, in a hundred battles you will never be in peril. When you are ignorant of the enemy and know yourself, your chances of winning or losing are equal. If ignorant of both your enemy and yourself, you are certain in every battle to be in peril."

World class companies go to endless lengths to build their competitive capability. They measure themselves by the best, and they continually strive to raise their standards. They celebrate exceptional achievement, they encourage mavericks, and they never stop learning.

No.3 Challenges

World class companies are stimulating, demanding, challenging. They give people an environment in which they can experiment, stretch themselves, and test their limits. Today's great achievement becomes the starting point for tomorrow's new effort. Success is celebrated, but even the most spectacular achievement is treated as just a stepping stone to the future rather than the destination itself.

Novelist Tom Wolfe said it perfectly in *The Right Stuff*, his book about America's space heroes:

> "A career in flying was like climbing one of those ancient Babylonian pyramids made up of a dizzy progression of steps and ledges; a ziggurat, a pyramid extraordinarily high and steep; and the idea was to prove at every foot of the way up that pyramid that you were one of the elected and anointed ones who had *the right stuff* and could move higher and higher and even — ultimately, God willing, one day — that you might be able to join that special few at the very top, that elite who had the capacity to bring tears to men's eyes, the very Brotherhood of the Right Stuff itself."[1]

In these organizations, every person is part of the renewal process. Their energy and ingenuity are seen as a key invisible asset. They're encouraged to aim higher than they ever dreamed was possible, to strive for goals that will keep them awake at night, and to believe in their own ability.

1   Tom Wolfe, *The Right Stuff*, Farrar Straus & Giroux, 1979

Leaders of world class companies know that our complex environment provides an endless flow of opportunities, and that people must be given responsibility for dealing with them. So they expose people to the larger issues of the day . . . they demand breakthrough answers . . . and they support their bold performers through thick and thin.

What's more, these organizations are designed to induce a dynamic tension between the present and future, between current achievement and what might be possible. So their systems, their policies and procedures, their structure and their style all empower people to excel. If you've got "the right stuff" here, life is a ball; if you haven't, find another job!

No.4 Cooperation

The shrinking world makes companies inter-dependent. World class managers know that their success is not won in isolation. Strategic alliances are essential, even for the most localised of operations.

Teamwork is thus an essential factor in any organization's success. When people cooperate with each other, one plus one equals three. *Synergy!* But there's an important caveat: you don't want everyone agreeing with one another about everything. While it might be sensible to manage by consensus, beware of situations where all dissent is squashed, where people are too polite to each other, and where ideas are not rigorously debated.

Differences should be encouraged. Healthy conflict brings out the best in teams. People need to know that when they express an idea or make a presentation they'd better be prepared to defend their views. They should have done their homework, thought through alternative options, and have the data they need to defend themselves.

Too many management meetings are a total waste of time because the participants behave like pussy cats. They're too darned polite to each other, for fear of offending a colleague or a friend. Result: poor performance is tolerated, lousy decisions get slipped through, shoddy thinking is O.K.

Teamwork is important not just *inside* the firm, but equally important, with *external* stakeholders. All of them need to know the company's objectives and as much of its strategy as possible. They should also get regular reports on its performance.

The most important relationship is obviously with customers. Supplier ties also need special attention. But don't forget financiers, licensing authorities, government, the local community, etc. There's a complex network of people "out there" who influence your firm's direction and its performance. All of them must be brought "on side" and into a win-win relationship with your firm.

No.5 Creativity

World class companies know that it's not enough to continually create new products or to improve old ones; *new ways of doing business* are just as important. So they continually push their people to think . . . to dream . . . to experiment . . . to ask, "What if?" Creative thinking is a way of life in these companies. Learning is a key goal. Good ideas are actively sought, carefully analysed, tested, and supported.

But you can't stop at thinking; *action* is all important. Ideas must be translated into work, and must result in some sort of change. Innovation occurs when new concepts are funded and developed, when they're refined and integrated into products or processes.

Some meaningful changes occur as quantum leaps; others are small, incremental improvements. Both must be encouraged.

Advances come from many formal structures: quality circles, project teams, "blue-sky" sessions, "skunk works" and R&D labs. But they also come from casual chats in the passage . . . from a lone worker's sudden flash of insight . . . from unexpected successes, and from unexpected failures. In other words, while creativity can be managed to a fair degree, good ideas cannot be decreed. The best that managers can do is create an environment in which serendipity has a chance.

No.6 Costs

World class companies focus their investments on value-adding activities. They go for growth but they're ruthless about waste. They zero-base everything, asking, "Does this activity add cost or value?" If it doesn't make a difference to customers, they think twice about incurring it.

To drive the message home, they drive financial responsibility way down the line. People at all levels in all functions often control their own budgets. This has two important effects: (1) it helps them understand the economics of the firm, and (2) it puts power where it's most effective.

The CEO or the financial director has a broad overview of how much gets spent, and on what. But finer details are best left to individuals who actually use funds. It's possible, for example, to set a transport budget up in head office, but people who drive vehicles make that budget realistic or not. Similarly, while management might impose a budget for cleaning materials, the cleaner knows best how many brooms, brushes, or cloths to buy. And the cleaner will use them wisely or waste them.

In too many firms, budgets become the starting point for planning. Last year's spend is used as the base for this year's. As a result, many items sneak through from one budget period to the next, without anyone questioning why they're there at all.

One client of mine discovered how easily this happens when they enlisted teams of volunteers to review their costs. Small groups were formed with people from various levels in various departments. In one meeting, the telephone bill was examined. A low-level secretary asked, "Why do we spend so much on directory listings?" Answer: because nobody had ever asked the question before. As the company had grown, more and more numbers had been listed. The bill came through each year, the finance chief signed it, and that was that. After the team review, though, the firm saved a fortune by halving its listings.

Cost-cutting should be an ongoing exercise. There's always a way to pare expenses. But beware of falling into an "after-the-event" trap. Once money has been committed — to employees, plant and equipment, or exciting new projects — pulling the plug can be extremely painful.

The best way to manage costs is up front. It should be an everyday discipline. As with all these activities, everybody should be part of the process.

No.7 Communication

Communication underpins all the other "Cs," and holds them together. People need to know "what's important around here." They need to know what concerns top management. They need to know the company's strategy, and their own role in it. They need to know that they can create and share ideas — and that their ideas count. Above all, they need to know that when they speak, someone is *listening!*

This framework makes life easier

The "7 Cs" separate world class companies from the rest. Of course, "Customers" are on top, and that's where they should be in your people's minds; but every one of the "Cs" is of crucial importance. All must be managed if you want to deliver superior service.

(Try leaving one out, to see what I mean! Can you really perform if you ignore your *competition* . . . if you don't *challenge* your team . . . if you don't foster *cooperation* with all your stakeholders, both inside and outside your firm . . . if you don't encourage and reward *creativity* . . . if you don't manage *costs* carefully . . . or if *communication* is poor?)

I've worked with many companies to "customize" the "7 Cs." The more I use them to spur thinking and debate, the more value I discover in them.

Their usefulness has been particularly evident when I've watched executives try to spell out their values *without* a framework. Usually they flounder around, not sure where to begin, how to progress, or what to say.

The "7 Cs" help managers home in on the few critical factors which underpin performance. They help them develop a holistic picture of the organization: its health, its strengths and weaknesses, and its priorities.

And perhaps most important of all, they help communication. When executives complain that communication is bad in their organization, I ask, "What do you want to talk about?" This usually throws them. They've thought about the "how," not the "what." In fact, their communication would be extremely healthy if they simply made an effort to talk about the first six "Cs": customers, competition, challenges, cooperation, creativity, and costs.

You might be uncomfortable talking about these "7 Cs" as values. By all means call them something else: driving forces, key activities or whatever. But treat them as fundamental beliefs. And use them to make winning with your customer a reality.

What to say in your statement of values

A written statement of values provides a kind of road map for behaviour. When you put pen to paper, remember that your objective is to focus attention on the few things that will make a positive difference to your business results. Whatever you say, and however you say it, your people must be able to live out these beliefs on a minute-by-minute basis.

The "7 Cs" provide an umbrella for many key ideas. Here are some thought-starters. Be sure to emphasize those issues that are most relevant to your particular circumstances and needs.

1. Customers

- ❏ We act as their partners.
- ❏ We are committed to their success.
- ❏ We help them add value for *their* customers by continually improving our quality and productivity.
- ❏ We go out of our way to understand their needs.
- ❏ We keep promises.
- ❏ We keep them informed in good times and bad.
- ❏ We respond fast to their requests.
- ❏ We build relationships with them at all levels.

2. Competition

- ❏ We watch our competitors carefully, but we make our own decisions.
- ❏ We aim to be winners . . . not followers.
- ❏ We learn from them.
- ❏ We act fast to stay ahead of them.
- ❏ We try to anticipate their future moves.
- ❏ We cooperate with them, but we do not collude with them.
- ❏ We treat them with respect, and we refrain from publicly criticizing them.

3. Challenges

❏ We give them the biggest possible assignments.

❏ We give all our people equal opportunities to grow.

❏ We give them the information, resources, and support they need to be winners.

❏ We plan their careers with them.

❏ We give them the training, education, and development they need to be all they can be.

❏ We promote them on the basis of performance, not the length of their service.

❏ We adapt our structure, systems, policies, and procedures to support our people, not the other way around.

4. Cooperation

❏ We encourage win-win relationships, both inside our organization and outside, with all our stakeholders.

❏ We tolerate conflicting ideas.

❏ We acknowledge and accept differences in race, religion, language, and political belief.

❏ We value diversity in our workforce.

❏ We encourage our people to share ideas, to break down barriers, and to support each other.

❏ We go out of our way to make sure the right people are in the right jobs.

❏ We don't allow friendships to get in the way of performance.

❏ We don't tolerate politics.

5. Creativity

❏ We believe that "there is always a better way."

❏ We expect our people to reinvent their jobs — not just our products or services.

❏ We regularly and systematically challenge all our assumptions, beliefs, and behaviours.

❑ We have a disciplined way of gathering, reviewing, testing, and rewarding new ideas.

❑ We respond fast to suggestions — and we tell people what's happening to their ideas.

❑ We expect people to make mistakes, and we allow them to fail.

6. Costs

❑ We zero-base everything.

❑ We push the budgeting process as far down the line as possible, so people are responsible for their own costs.

❑ We make all our stakeholders partners in our cost-control effort.

❑ We systematically look for new ways to design our products and services to cut the cost of providing them.

❑ We give our people regular feedback on how costs are being managed.

❑ We aren't penny-pinchers; though we watch costs carefully, we also invest for the future.

❑ We share savings with the people who make them.

7. Communication

❑ We involve as many people as possible in developing our strategy.

❑ We go out of our way to keep them informed about what we're doing, why, and how it affects them.

❑ We give them regular, open briefings on our performance.

❑ We give them honest feedback on their personal performance.

❑ We work hard to create a climate of trust, in which they feel they can be honest with their superiors.

❑ We encourage them to ask tough questions.

❑ We own up to mistakes.

Setting meaningful objectives

Objectives are the targets you aim for. They describe "What we want to achieve, by when." They should be ambitious, specific, measurable — and attainable.

Setting effective objectives is a balancing act. On the one hand, you want to change people's sense of possibilities; on the other, you want them to succeed, not fail.

Many of the companies I've worked with have dramatically improved their results by simply aiming higher. Hiroyuki Itami, professor of management at Hitotsubashi University, suggests that objectives should be "destabilizing," so they introduce creative tension into the business.[2] One challenge I often throw down in management workshops is to say, "O.K., let's scrap all previous objectives and action plans, and be 20 per cent more ambitious. Can we do it?... and what must we do to reach *that* target?"

At first, most people balk at reaching that far ahead of where they were aiming. But when they do buy into the exercise, and when they do rethink their action plans, it's surprising how often the new targets are achieved.

That said, a word of caution is necessary. Beware of shooting for ridiculous goals. Don't try to coerce people into achievements that everyone knows are impossible. Objectives should motivate people, not paralyse them.

Top managers often put people under unreasonable pressure to raise their sights and deliver more than they did last year, last quarter, or whenever. Deals are struck which bear little or no relation to reality. The failure that follows is not a performance problem so much as a fault in the way objectives were set.

2   Hiroyuki Itami, *Mobilizing Invisible Assets*, Harvard University Press, 1987

Since they are, in essence, a contract between the employer and the employee, objectives should be set *with* people, not *for* them. The individual who must meet objectives should "own" those objectives and feel a deep need to achieve them.

Naturally, objectives are needed in areas such as marketing, finance, productivity, quality, and customer service. But it pays to also describe what you intend achieving in support of your seven core values. This ensures that you "cover all bases," and it includes the "7 Cs" in your appraisal process.

At the beginning of a year, you can ask people to tell you what they'll do to make those values live. At the end, you can ask, "So how did you do?" This keeps the "7 Cs" top of mind. It shows that you're serious about them. And it shows that you expect people to go way past paying lip service to them — and to actively support them.

How many objectives should you have?

There's a lot of truth in the old adage, "Too many objectives is no objectives." People get into a dreadful bind and end up with "wish lists" when they try to do everything. One manager told me that planning made no sense for him, because he had too much to do. When I asked how many objectives he had, he pulled out his time management diary to show me; there were 37 things on the page!

"Which are the priorities?" I asked.

"They're all important," he said. "I've got to do them all."

Well, that was clearly impossible. So I had him boil the list down to five things he had to achieve in the next five years to take him towards his vision, and another five things to do in year one.

Choosing those few five-year and one-year objectives wasn't easy. He'd taken on too much, but was reluctant to give anything up. But when he took the plunge, he found that it wasn't actually so hard to delegate many of the other tasks or to drop them altogether.

Motto of the story: pick the few things that will really make the big difference in your life, and go for them with all you've got. If someone else wants to fool around with the issues that won't bring important results, let them get on with it.

You only live once. Aim to be great at something!

Keep your action plan brief

Action plans highlight priorities. They tell people, *"This is how we'll reach our objectives."*

Just like most lists of objectives, however, most action plans are too long and too vague. They often include a lot of stuff that won't do much to move the company forward.

So once again, be specific. Indicate target dates and who'll be responsible for each activity. And be brutal. Cut the number to the bone. Remember the 80/20 law, and pick the few things that will make the most difference. If you don't, you'll wind up with a list of priorities which gets longer every day. Your agenda will be "hijacked" by someone else.

A good rule is to ask yourself, before you do anything at all, "Will doing this move me closer to my objective, or further away?" If it won't get you closer, do something that will.

Finally, to be sure that your actions become results, start work on them immediately. Put pressure on the whole business system to make progress fast. Force change. Reward people for trying even if they screw up; and make life terribly uncomfortable for those who don't try — but don't make a difference either.

Cascade this thinking

The framework I've described achieves the two important goals of helping you think through your strategy, and telling your team about it.

Ideally, a group of senior managers should work through this thinking process first, to define the strategy. Then the same process should be repeated at other levels — cascading all the way down to work teams or even individuals.

I'm often asked, "Can different parts of the organization have their own vision and mission, or must they all have the same one?"

The answer is self-evident: while the entire organization must work towards the same larger purpose, each division, department, business unit or work team will obviously have its own vision, mission, objectives, and action plan.

The Finance department will want to achieve certain things, and will set about it in a certain way; Marketing will have another goal; Manufacturing yet another. This is fine, as long as they all pull in the same direction and contribute harmoniously to the greater good of the organization.

The one factor that doesn't change is the values. These stay consistent from top to bottom of the organization. The "7 Cs" are basic success factors which apply equally to everyone, so they must be acted out by everyone.

Each unit is free to think as creatively as possible about its purpose and its methods. The core values lend consistency to the task. Among other advantages, this makes communication easy because everyone uses the same language, focuses on the same key issues, and measures the same things.

Making the planning process work

In many companies, planning has become a major task with a life of its own. It ties up people, computers, and copiers for a ridiculous amount of time. It's complicated by sophisticated methods and models. And the final planning book that emerges is shoved on the shelf until the next round. (One group of managers recently told me that they don't even bother to change the content of those binders; they just change the date on the cover!)

The value of planning lies not just in the plans that are produced, but also in the discipline of having to think about your business in a structured way, and in *the thinking process itself*. (Remember George Bernard Shaw's comment: "Most people never think more than two or three times a year. I have made an international reputation for myself by thinking two or three times a week." And Einstein once said, "The trouble with people is they just don't think!")

It probably makes sense for the top management team to take time out to work on a plan. But the process shouldn't be tied to budgeting or become a once-a-year escape. In a turbulent world plans quickly become obsolete. Ongoing, continuous dialogue should be the objective.

The first rule of effective planning is: *keep it simple*. General Electric Co. chairman Jack Welch runs the world's tenth largest company, and employs 300 000 people. He wants GE to be first or second in every market it serves. By insisting that his managers boil their plans down to just one page, he forces them to think ahead, but he also enables them to move fast when opportunities crop up.

The second rule of effective planning is: *be disciplined*.

When things are too loose, nothing gets done. The gap between vision and action just never closes.

There's another problem too. When managers from various parts of a company — different functions, divisions, branches, business units — meet to talk strategy, they all try to reinvent the wheel. Each one has a vague idea of what should go into his presentation. Each emphasizes something different. There's no focus. Important issues are likely to be overlooked.

Things flow much more smoothly and effectively, and time is used far more productively, when the whole team uses the same framework for thinking about and talking about the business. It makes sense to give each manager a checklist such as the following one, and ask them to build their presentation around it. This ensures that all relevant issues are addressed, all key questions are answered, and everyone knows where the conversation is headed.

Use the checklist to create a "strategy briefing book." Send it to managers before they start work on their plans. Include relevant background data that will help them in their thinking. Also include a section for "the numbers."

Planning checklist

1. *Executive summary.* A 1-page overview of where you've come from, and where you're going. Include your past year's performance, the current state of your business, the outlook for next year, issues that will impact your performance in the next three years, and your priorities. This summary has two purposes: first, it forces you think, to focus your ideas, to get down to the real nuts and bolts. Second, it gives your colleagues a quick look at your chunk of the business.

2. *What is your present strategy — vision, mission, objectives, action plan — and how well has it worked?* What got you where you are? What have you achieved? How satisfied are you?

3. *What assumptions was it based on?* When you wrote that plan, what did you expect would happen inside the company? What did you see happening outside — i.e., what would customers, competitors, and other stakeholders do? What economic, social, political-legal or technological changes

did you predict? Looking back always teaches you something (if only that assumptions will be wrong!)

4. *How have those assumptions changed?* What has changed so far? What *might* change, inside and outside your business unit?

5. *What are your strengths and weaknesses?* How do you stack up against the competition? How powerful are you relative to your suppliers? How much leverage do you have against other stakeholders? Can you deliver the value your customers expect? What invisible assets do you have? What do you do especially well? What do you do especially badly? (Remember when you weigh yourself against competitors that you're looking at a moment in time; what you get is a snapshot, when what you need is a moving picture. Nor do you gain any insight into your competitors' underlying intentions.)

6. *What opportunities and threats lie ahead?* List them. Rank them by their likelihood, their probability, and their impact on your organization.

7. *What internal/external issues will have most impact on your business?* Externally, you might face an aggressive move by a competitor, political upheaval, or a legal development. Internally, you might foresee industrial unrest, machine breakdowns, or the resignation of key people; or you may be installing a new computer, commissioning a new plant, or launching a new product. Consider positive as well as negative changes. There will always be some surprises, but often events will send strong signals way in advance.

8. *What are your key factors of success?* What are the few things you *must* do to survive and thrive? In every business there are one or two things that make the critical difference. They're either not evident at first glance, or they're so obvious that they're taken for granted and no one thinks about them.

9. *What is your new strategy — vision, mission, objectives, action plan?*

10. *How will you reinforce your core values?* How will you make the "7 Cs" live in your company or your part of the organization? It's not essential to include this question, but by doing so you concentrate attention on your values and signal their importance. When they're discussed in every major get-together, they soon become top-of-mind throughout the firm.

This framework increases the productivity of strategy workshops or retreats because it forces managers to prepare well. It also takes a lot of heat out of the process because they don't waste time wondering what the hell you meant by "strategy" or how they should put their presentation together to impress you. Instead, they all start "on the same page," they know precisely what you expect, and after the meeting they know precisely what to attend to.

The first time you use this framework, don't worry about Questions 2–3. You possibly haven't defined your vision, mission or values yet. But the work you put into them now will naturally become the basis for your second effort.

Who to involve

Traditionally, strategy has been the prerogative of a few people at the top. It has fitted neatly with the concept of deeply layered, hierarchical organization. Most people have been doers rather than thinkers, and never got to see the strategic plan, let alone work on it. Most plans became no more than a record of good intentions.

Today, it makes sense to push planning out of the executive suite, and down the line. Here's why:

1. In this rapidly changing world, it's essential to have many eyes and ears scanning the environment. Top management cannot possibly stay in touch with everything that's going

on. Many important facts and feelings will simply never reach them. Vital trends will escape them.

2. There's just not time to refer every move back to the top. People everywhere must be empowered to respond to change. The process must be managed by the people closest to the factors that trigger the need for change.

3. Strategy is formulated continuously by the things people pay attention to. The prices they offer, the deals they strike, and the choices they make all change the firm's direction, if only a bit at a time. When they know where top management is trying to go, they're less likely to choose the wrong course.

4. We need to harness more thinking power — and there's just no doubt at all that most people could contribute much more to their companies if only they were given the chance.

By weaving strategy more deeply into the organization, overall effectiveness is greatly enhanced. When people are "counted in" and involved in important thought processes, they're far more likely to be committed. A sense of ownership encourages positive, cooperative action.

This is uncharted territory for most managers. They've been brought up to keep strategy quiet, to talk about it in hushed tones and behind closed doors.

But you simply cannot empower people if you don't involve them. You can't do it without giving them information. And you won't do it if you don't trust them.

One of my clients started sharing everything with his people (except salaries.) It had an incredible effect. Suddenly everyone became part of his team. Good ideas popped up all over the place. Results began to improve. In less than a year, he doubled his profits.

CHAPTER ELEVEN

"WHO IS OUR CUSTOMER?"

The first question any manager must answer is, "Who is our customer?" That's the issue that underpins all strategy, and the one that trips up so many efforts to become world class. The question is central to the mission statement, yet seldom gets the thought it merits.

On the surface the answer is easy. Managers have a feel for who they sell to, they "know" who their customers are, and they reply, "Everyone!" But this is almost never true.

There's no such thing as an "average" customer. No single product or service can satisfy every buyer. And many buying decisions involve a number of people, not just the obvious customer. Take butter, for example:

❑ A supermarket sells it.
❑ Journalists publish recipes which promote it.
❑ A housewife buys it.
❑ Her husband eats it.
❑ The family doctor warns him to avoid it.

Who is "the customer?" Who should the butter marketer's messages be aimed at? The obvious answer is the housewife, with her family a close second. But the other influencers can't be ignored.

Marketing costs are rising fast, and the risks of failure are enormous. No company has unlimited resources. So it's vital to identify the few customers who are most important to the business, and to focus on them. But you also have to identify the other stakeholders who will influence your core customer, and you have to keep some resources in reserve to earn their votes.

❑ Some hotels target specific markets but most need a mix of guests. They fill their rooms with both holidaymakers and businessmen, so they have to sell themselves to these individuals as well as to secretaries, travel agents, airlines, incentive specialists, conference organisers, and tour operators. And they have to get plenty of media coverage to build their image, so journalists are a key audience too.

❑ One estimate suggests that American kids have a say in around $150 billion worth of "family purchases": food, electronic goods, and the like.[1] If you want to sell to mothers, you've got to get past these junior "gatekeepers."

❑ Tyre manufacturers make the fattest profits from replacement sales to motorists. But they compete viciously on price to sell their main brands as original equipment to motor manufacturers. The reason: experience shows that car owners replace worn tyres with the same brand.

Of course, some messages do "leak" from one target to others. Media can be deliberately chosen to make sure there is some overlap. But beware of trying to be all things to all people. The more specific you can be in matching messages and audiences, the better.

Customers start wanting to do business with you when you get under their skin, learn to think like they do, and respond with lightning speed to their demands. Or, better still, when you *anticipate* their future demands. They want different things, and they want to be feel special. So aim to reach them one at a time, and if your message spills over and reaches other important audiences, consider that a bonus.

1 Patricia Sellers, "The ABC's of marketing to kids," *Fortune,* May 8, 1989

Think global, act local

Some commodity products do satisfy a wide range of customers — a "mass market." Hence the current preoccupation with "global marketing."

The idea of selling the same product across countries and cultures has great appeal. In theory at least, the cost savings — in R&D, engineering, manufacturing, and marketing — are substantial.

But the most successful global marketers recognize the importance of treating their customers as individuals. Even if they aim at a mass market, they concentrate on "making one sale, one customer at a time." They think global but act local — or "glocalise," as the Japanese put it.

"Pattern" advertising for such products as Coca-Cola, Camel cigarettes or Pirelli tyres might be centrally produced for a worldwide audience, but local country managers choose whether to use it or how to modify it. And while signs at a World Cup soccer match might build brand awareness for Agip, Daiwoo, Mitsubishi, Apple Computer, or ICI, these firms all know that sales are made to *individuals*, not *audiences*. They're made one at a time. And getting awareness is just one small aspect of creating a customer.

Many companies have learned to their cost that the idea of "one sight, one sound, one sell" is seldom practical or advisable. They're learning fast that since value is a customer perception, they have to know their customers intimately if they're to be competitive in a world of endless choices. They're learning to precisely tailor the way they do business in various markets. "Demassification" is no longer a distant possibility or even an option; it's here, and it's a must.

French housewives like top-loading washing machines; British women prefer front-loaders. German women want high-speed spin-dryers; Italians are happy with slower speeds. In Spain, breakfast is not a "meal occasion." To sell in France, yoghurt must be "live." Americans use credit cards far

more often than Germans or Italians. Tyres must cope with
different road conditions in the Alps than in Africa. Different
countries have different environmental and advertising laws,
different packaging requirements, different distribution systems, different electric plugs, and different tastes in chocolate.

Brands across borders

Customer tastes in the global village are converging in many
ways. Rising incomes mean that customers can afford more
than ever before. Movies, TV shows, and sponsored sports
events are seen by audiences of hundreds of millions worldwide. Brands such as Ford, Cartier, Rolex, Sony, Benneton,
Marlboro, Levis, Royal Dalton, Liz Claiborn, and Ralph
Lauren have broad appeal in many countries. But at the same
time, markets are fragmenting and the people within them are
becoming more different and more demanding.

If a product appeals to a particular group of customers in
one country today, it might well find eager buyers in other
countries, too. So effective segmentation doesn't mean you
must confine yourself to one geographic area. Rather, *seek out
targets with common characteristics on a global basis*. This can give
you the scale and scope you need to become "best of breed"
in any particular market. Multi-country marketing might
generate enough revenue to allow you to automate a plant,
shift production offshore, fund a new R&D initiative, or sponsor a sports event that will be get worldwide TV coverage.
Above all, the experience you gain in one country can help you
rapidly improve everywhere.

You can't reach an audience of "everyone"

On the surface, many marketers appear to beam their messages at "everyone." But for *effectiveness*, they slice their markets

up as finely as possible, take sensitive account of nuances, and speak to customers on a one-to-one basis.

❏ Coca-Cola appeals to young and old alike, so it would be tempting for the marketing department to aim at everyone. In fact, the main brand targets people in the 18 — 24 age group. And the Atlanta-based beverage giant's other brands each have their own niches. Even Coke, with all its marketing muscle, can't afford to be all things to all people.

❏ A new Polaroid camera, the Cool Cam, is designed for "tweens" who are 9-to-14 years old. Delta Air Lines' "Delta Fantastic Flyers Program" recruits passengers who are between 2 and 12. Crest For Kids and Colgate Junior are toothpastes for youngsters.[2]

❏ Buick aims at 60-year-olds with a high school education and a white collar salary.

❏ A $2 million Detroit firm called Hotel Doctor provides medical care to guests in 113 Detroit hotels.[3]

❏ Medco Containment Services Inc. of Fair Lawn New Jersey sells $1,3 billion a year worth of maintenance medication drugs to patients who need regular dosages for ailments such as abnormal blood pressure, arthritis or diabetes.[4]

❏ Progressive Corp., a Cleveland-based auto insurer, has become one of the most profitable firms in its field by selling to clients that other companies reject.[5]

❏ Los Angeles-based 1st Business Bank serves "midsized" companies (annual sales $3 to $100 million), and takes on just ten to 15 new accounts each month. "Some people collect antique cars or trophy real estate," says Chairman Robert Kummer Jr. "We're collectors of fine companies."[6]

2   Patricia Sellers, "The ABC's of marketing to kids," *Fortune,* May 8, 1989
3   Howard Rudnitsky, "Drugs by mail," *Forbes,* April 15, 1991
4   *Forbes,* ibid.
5   Sylvia Nasar, "Hard road ahead for auto insurers," *Fortune,* May 8, 1989
6   "Niche player," *Forbes,* April 1, 1991

❑ The personal stereo market is flooded with options, but Sanyo's SPT1000 Sportable is designed especially for health nuts. A cassette player and AM/FM radio, it also has a pedometer to calculate distance and lap speed, and can be set for three exercise modes: walking, speed walking, and jogging.[7]

The tighter you can target your marketing efforts, the more successful you're likely to be. The closer you get to your individual customer, the more profit that customer is likely to mean to you. The more information you can gather about a customer, the better your chances of a lengthy relationship. But as buying behaviour, values, and demands constantly shift, keeping up is hard work. Competitive activity makes it all the more difficult.

Start with simple differences

There are many ways to segment a market. The starting point is to look *outside* of your company at the two key parameters of customer type and customer needs. Then, if you need to slice your market more finely, you might look *inwards* at your business system, and consider such factors as your method of sale, the channels you use, and your financing and support policies. Segmentation is not just about *who* you aim at, but also *how* you focus your efforts. Seen like this, there's an almost infinite number of options. But remember, there's also a trade-off between cost and effectiveness.

Segmentation can become a complicated intellectual exercise. Once that happens, people lose sight of the original objective, and it becomes impossible to easily describe target audiences to employees who must attack them. So keep the process simple. Start with the most critical information, and

7   Stephanie Losee, "Jogger's companion," *Fortune*, June 3, 1991

see what that tells you. If it doesn't give you a narrow enough target, add a few more factors. Say, for example, you sell a product used by men. That's half the world's population — far too big. So you might decide that they should be:

❑ English speakers
❑ 25 — 40 years old
❑ Married
❑ College graduates
❑ Home owners
❑ A/B income group.

If that doesn't give you an accurate enough description, you could narrow your focus further by aiming at people who:

❑ Play golf
❑ Travelled overseas in the past year
❑ Have two children
❑ Spent at least $6 000 on personal entertainment in the past year
❑ Visit the cinema regularly.

Demographics and psychographics

Whatever you sell, you need information which essentially falls into two categories: *demographics* and *psychographics*.

Demographic data provide the starting point in most segmentation efforts. This is the "hard" stuff which defines customers by facts such as:

❑ Age and life-cycle stage
❑ Sex
❑ Race
❑ Education
❑ Disposable income
❑ Occupation

❑ Geographic location
❑ Product consumption (type, volume, value).

The other type of information — the "soft" psychographic detail — rounds out the profile of your customers. It often gets far less attention than demographic data because it seems less tangible and less specific, and it's not always easy to get. But it's just as meaningful as "the numbers" — if not more so.
    Psychographic facts include:

❑ Brand awareness and loyalty
❑ Importance of image or status
❑ Lifestyle (leisure activities, hobbies, social habits, etc.)
❑ Values
❑ Product consumption
❑ Aspirations.

Demographic data give you a broad-brush picture of your market. Psychographic insights let you home in on ever-narrower targets, precisely describe customers and their perceptions of value, and create sharply-focused messages.

> **Demographic data describe *markets*. Psychographics describe *people* within those markets (outdoors types, stamp collectors, music lovers, "greens," "yuppies," etc.)**

Segmentation sharpens your sense of opportunity

Sony is super-sensitive to market signals, and ever-alert to the emergence of new segments. Its My First Sony range of electronic products was introduced when it saw the astonishing buying power of kids, and recognized that luring them early could make them customers for life.
    Volkswagen and Societe Suisse Microelectronique & d'Horologie SA, makers of the best-selling Swatch watch, are

collaborating to produce a "cheery, environmentally safe and inexpensive city car for two people and two cases of beer."[8] They're taking advantage of the fact that both of their highly visible brand names suggest trendiness, quality, and affordability — just as many customers start shying away from conspicuous, costly consumption.

Noting the importance of nostalgia and consumers' desire for good old-fashioned value, McDonald's is testing "the cafe of the 90's" in Hartsville, Tennessee. The Golden Arch Cafe serves old-fashioned Coke floats, Salisbury steak platters and lasagne (and of course, if you insist on burgers and fries, they're also on the menu — but the Big Mac branding has disappeared).

Alert to consumers' concern for the environment, Procter & Gamble has launched refill packages for cleaning products. "Enviro-paks" containing Liquid Tide detergent, Ivory dishwashing liquid, and Mr Clean household cleaner were tested in Canada, and are now rolling out in the American market. At the same time, Unilever is looking at two-in-one products such as combination detergent/fabric softeners and concentrated cleaners that need less packaging and create less waste.

What all these examples show is that tomorrow's market opportunities are emerging right under your nose, right now. The signals may be faint, but they are there.

Over time, the information you gather about your customers will become a valuable asset to your firm. As you add to it, you'll be able to continually improve the way you approach, attract, and serve target your market.

8   "'Swatch' maker, VW think time is right for a new small car," *The Wall Street Journal Europe*, July 5–6, 1991

Industrial buyers are human, too

One might argue that both demographic and psychographic information are essential if you sell to consumer markets, but that industrial markets can be segmented on the basis of demographics alone. But industrial markets are made up of people, just like consumer goods markets. Companies don't buy computers or mining equipment; *individuals* within them do. They shop for products, test them, specify them, use them, and recommend them. They sign purchasing orders, and they sign cheques to pay you.

Your ability to deliver world class customer satisfaction increases to the degree that you treat every customer, in whatever market, as a unique individual. Knowing your customer's name, address or age is one thing; but when you also know his wife's name, how many children he has, what beer he drinks, how often he plays golf, and what he likes to read, you dramatically improve your ability to grab his attention. (See the Appendices for checklists to help you through this process.)

The 80/20 rule

The 80/20 rule suggests that 80 per cent of your customers will give you just 20 per cent of your results, while the other 20 per cent of customers will account for 80 per cent of results.

Think about your customer base as a source of future profits. It includes today's customers, tomorrow's customers, and a reservoir of others who may become interesting. Each group presents a different opportunity. By ranking them, you can define your priorities, tailor your strategy, and allocate resources most effectively.

Customers won't all yield equal sales, so they don't all deserve equal attention. So in addition to the above steps, you should separate "key" customers from "non-key" customers in each group. These are the ones who need the most time and attention.

But don't forget the rest. It's all too easy to get bogged down with meeting the needs of your present customers, and it's tempting to think that today's relationships will last forever. That's a dangerous view, and no way to grow a business. Sooner or later you'll need new income. And in most industries, creating customers doesn't happen overnight. It always takes longer than you think, and it always costs more than you budget for.

It naturally makes sense to pay most attention to the most valuable 20 per cent of customers — in other words, today's key customers. After all, they're the ones who provide your income in the here and now. The question is, how do you identify them?

The most obvious criterion is the income they give you, but this is invariably a mistake. Other factors are equally important, and may even count for more. Some of the factors which put customers into the key customer category are these:

❑ They should want or need the products/services that you provide.

❑ They should operate in an area of the market that's important to your future.

❑ Their market segment should be growing, and should have significant growth potential.

❑ They should really want to become your company's long-term partner.

❑ They should be prepared to share confidential information with you.

❑ They should want a mutually rewarding relationship with you.

❑ You should be able to learn from them, and improve the way you do business as a result of the relationship.

❏ If possible, they should be leaders in their field — i.e., their reputation should benefit your company.
❏ They should contribute meaningfully to your profits.

Deciding what special treatment to give key customers begins with your knowledge and understanding of them. You also need to know what your competitors are doing for them now, and what they might do in the future.

This information is all very valuable. Over time it becomes an invisible asset on which you can't put a price. So your senior people are likely to argue, "If it's worth so much, we'd better keep it under wraps!"

The problem with this thinking is that the prospecting process becomes self-defeating. Secrecy immediately cuts into your ability to serve your customers. It also destroys trust. A "need to know" policy builds barriers between those who "need to know" and those who aren't allowed to.

Everyone in your organization should have the information they need to surprise your customers. This means that every employee needs to understand the over-riding importance of customers. And everyone who has anything to do with your key customers should know why they're special, and what you do differently for them. It's tough enough trying to create and keep customers when everything's going for you; turning your own team against you just makes no sense at all!

Information gathering

Quality customer information helps you get ahead and stay ahead of your competitors. It must be gathered assiduously, kept within easy reach, and added to all the time.

Getting the right information about your customers — and enough of it — is often a lot easier than it seems. But to do it well, you need a structured and disciplined process which is carefully designed and properly managed. And all of your people should be empowered to act as your eyes and ears in the marketplace.

Many firms sit on a pile of useful information, and don't even know it. The chairman plays golf with his counterpart in the customer company, so he has one view; a salesman meets with people at another level, so he knows something else; service technicians, credit controllers, and others all gain different insights. Unfortunately, all this information remains dispersed, as it tends to stay largely with the person who gets it first. It's seldom systematically shared, analysed, and stored. It remains, in a sense, the "property" of various individuals — some of whom will sooner or later leave the firm. What should be a growing asset is wasted.

To get around this problem, you need some way for people to "dump" information as they get it. Regular sales meetings are an obvious opportunity, but usually are used for other things. Sales reports should always require new *insights,* not just hard historic facts. By holding a regular weekly meeting (early Monday mornings or last thing on Fridays is probably best), you could quickly make talking about customers a habit. One firm I work with has developed a simple computer programme that lets staff members report on any contact they have with customers: what was said, what was agreed, next moves, etc. Anyone who's about to see a customer just has to call up the information on screen to have a really useful picture of the relationship.

Obvious sources of customer information include:

❑ Sales records.
❑ Market research.
❑ Newspapers and trade journals.
❑ Trade shows and exhibitions.
❑ Conferences and seminars.
❑ Annual reports.
❑ Customers' advertising and promotional materials.

Each of these sources must be carefully tapped for early warnings of change. Sales records should be regularly analyzed. It's a good idea to appoint specific staff members to scan the news, and to circulate a summary of what's hot. By developing close relationships with journalists, you not only get early warnings of trends and key events, but also a better chance of positive media coverage when you need it. Whenever possible, you and your team should attend trade shows and conferences, to "network" with customers, competitors, and others in the know.

From time to time, you might need to commission formal surveys to learn more about your customers and your prospects. Focus group discussions might throw up all sorts of ideas. But don't overlook the faint signals that are often detected in other ways. (For example, a chance remark in a pub or at an industry get-together could be invaluable.)

Key customers are themselves a vital source of market information. Asking them about their plans and their needs has two positive results: on the one hand, it gives you exactly what you need, straight from the horse's mouth; on the other, it helps cement your relationship with them. Nothing creates a bond like shared information. When customers have opened up to you, it's hard for them to walk away.

Getting the right information

To manage your customers effectively, you need three kinds of information about them:

1. *Basic facts.* Names and addresses, phone and fax numbers; key executives; financial rating. This information can be obtained up front, and is usually quite easy to keep up to date.

2. *Performance data.* Key activities — i.e., products made/sold and markets served, competitive standing, pricing,

policies, R&D investment, what they buy and how they buy, etc.

3. *Contact records.* These should describe all contacts — phone calls, personal meetings, letters, etc. Record the names of those involved, what got said and done, what was agreed, next moves. Also spell out action plans for future contacts, and ideas to work on or debate.

This information must be systematically collected and stored. It must be easily available to the people who use it, so they can rapidly check on the current status of your key account relationships, and so they can update your databank.

These records provide a living picture of everything that occurs between you and your customer. They form the basis of your entire key account management programme.

What about other customers?

While key customers should get the very best attention, others cannot be ignored. They talk about the service they get from you, so they affect your reputation. They might one day become key customers themselves. And they're often the source of the innovations which will change the course of your industry.

In a perfect world, your account management strategy would keep all customers equally satisfied. But trade-offs are always necessary. You simply can't give every customer the same bundle of benefits. Key customers must come first.

What can you do to make all the others feel loved and cherished?

The answer lies in a critical re-examination of the way you stay in touch with them. In a careful analysis of all the communications techniques available to you, and in a judicious mix of methods. Your objective should be a new strategy which:

1. Cuts the cost of each contact.
2. Keeps up a *perceived* level of contact.

The first step is to draw a clear line between contacts *you* initiate and those that *customers* initiate. Then, to further divide these two groups according to the reason for the contact.

Some reasons for your calls will be to:

❏ Introduce yourself, and arrange meetings.
❏ Provide information.
❏ Confirm delivery details.
❏ Report on new developments.
❏ Advise of price/specification changes.
❏ Remind the customer that you still exist.

On the other hand, customers will contact you to:

❏ Place orders.
❏ Check on deliveries or invoices.
❏ Call for service
❏ Ask for information, support or advice.
❏ Complain.
❏ Lodge guarantee/warranty claims.

When you initiate contact, you have many options. You can "mix and match" messages and media to suit your budget, your strategy, and the precise needs of each customer.

For example, to keep costs down you might make fewer, better planned visits. You might phone instead of calling in person (and you might have more of your lower level people make the contact). Or you might stay in touch through letters, mailshots, or copies of interesting articles.

To keep up the perceived level of contact, you might sensibly combine two or more of these means of communication.

Customer "A" could warrant two personal visits a month, plus at least four phone calls and two personal letters, while customer "B" could be kept happy with only one visit, two phone calls, and a weekly mailshot.

When customers take the initiative

Life isn't quite so simple when customers call you (or call *on* you.) You have less control over the whole process. They choose the time; they set the agenda; they fire the opening salvo.

The only way to regain some measure of control is to ensure that whoever manages the "moment of truth" at your end is trained and equipped to cope. If one of your selling points is that every customer deals with a particular sales person, account executive or service representative, these people should be well versed in the ways of your firm. They should also know who else they can call on for help, and they should be empowered to make quick decisions for which there may be no guidelines in the policy manual.

It might help to separate incoming calls into various categories at your switchboard. This puts a special burden on the operator, but ensures that customer calls will quickly be routed to specialists.

Once the connection is made, your staff should go out of their way to make every customer feel equally important. However, they should beware of unduly raising customers' expectations, or of making promises that can't be kept. They should know when to bend the rules, and when to say, "No!" They must understand the need for diplomacy, but they must also be businesslike.

Most customers are quite reasonable. Those that aren't must be dealt with politely but firmly. If the value of an order doesn't justify extraordinary attention, tell your customer. If a customer buys a little but demands a lot of service, explain why you can't provide it. There are times when you simply can't afford to give every customer precisely what they want. *You* must manage the value you offer.

CHAPTER TWELVE

"WHAT 'VALUE' WILL WE OFFER?"

Once, you probably could build a better mousetrap and have customers pounding on your door. They just didn't have much choice. But in any vaguely sophisticated society, creating and keeping customers is a running battle. Success in today's trendy, fickle, and disloyal marketplace demands specific knowledge of what customers want and need, and continual innovation and improvement in the way you satisfy them. "Almost nothing lasts," says Ted Levitt, "especially if it's a good thing."

Every product is a complex bundle of benefits or satisfactions. The way you "wrap" your product in service, support, and imagery sends a powerful message. The late Malcolm S. Forbes, publisher of *Forbes* magazine, put it well:

> "In selling, your product has got to have differences that are perceived and real. You've got to fill a niche. You've got to point out the difference as a plus. It's infinitely more difficult to compete selling something that isn't better or isn't far less expensive. So you've got to have an angle, a twist, a point that differentiates you and then you've got to make the most of it."[1]

1 "Personal Selling Power," an interview, *Forbes*, July 24, 1989

Consider what happens when you buy a hamburger, and how your perceptions of "value" are affected by the way different vendors offer their products:

Supplier "A" operates a street cart. He offers cheap and convenient take-aways. You can smell his burgers grilling from a mile off, but you can't be sure about their quality, and you worry a bit about hygiene.

Supplier "B" is an international franchise with a name to protect. Service is slick and the menu is short, but at least it gives you a few alternatives.

The stock-in-trade of this business is the basic burger, but then you can add cheese or bacon . . . choose from various sauces . . . and get a side order of fries, onion rings or mushrooms.

You can also order soft drinks, tea, coffee, or hot chocolate, plus apple pie or cheesecake. And you can either sit there to eat (on a plastic chair, with plastic knife and fork) or take your meal away.

The burgers are consistently good. The company's advertising has persuaded you that the meat is pure beef, and the bun is fresh. You can see that cleanliness counts because the place is spotless, and everyone wears a neat uniform and a paper hat.

Prices here are higher than the street vendor's, but you get a different level of "performance."

Supplier "C" is a steakhouse. It's decorated in Western style, with comfortable seats and pretty checked table cloths.

There's a vast salad bar, where you help yourself. Wine and beer are available. The place is full of happy families, the sound system belts out the "Top 40," and the waitresses are attentive.

Your burger looks great on the plate, and is surrounded by a generous helping of fries and onion rings. You "customize" it further with "home made" sauces. And you end the meal with a delicious waffle and fresh cream, and a cappuccino.

Although you get a hamburger from each of these suppliers, the "value" you get from each is totally different. You feel different about each purchase. And though you might usually choose one over the others, from time to time you might switch.

"Value" is always a trade-off between price and perceived performance. But it's seldom wise to promote one at the total expense of the other. Customers buy a whole bundle of benefits in any product or service. They expect a certain minimum level of *all* of them before they part with their money.

While you might use the term "performance" to describe, say, the speed, roadholding, or braking of a motor car, it also embraces all the vehicle's other properties: the name on the bonnet, comfort, ride, service, and so on. Try selling a car which doesn't offer all these benefits!

Every customer makes the price/performance decision differently. It's influenced by both facts and feelings (logic and emotion), and both must be considered in developing sales messages.

This is often easier said than done. Customers are not always clear about why they buy something. Their obvious answers aren't necessarily true. Their underlying motivations are complex and hard to unravel.

It's not that customers deliberately want to mislead or confuse marketers. They simply are not in touch with themselves. So they often say what sounds right, or what they think you want to hear. And often what they say is not what you need to hear at all.

Is a $40 Swatch watch a cheap way to tell the time, or a powerful fashion statement? Are Banana Republic clothes bargains or the "in" thing to wear? Is a Fiat Uno an affordable way to drive, or an expression of the owner's personality? Why do travellers really fly first class? What satisfaction do people get from a particular cigarette? Why will a housewife travel miles to save on no-name-brand dishwasher and margarine, but then reach for Heinz ketchup and Lux soap, and a pack of Callard & Bowser's expensive sweets?

Information that leads to world class performance

Since customers determine the value of your product or service, it's vital that you know what criteria they use, and how they rate you and your competitors. You also need to know how your own people see your performance.

Six key items of information underpin your entire marketing effort:

1. What is "value" in your customer's mind?
2. How do you rate against your competitors?
3. What is your customer's demand pattern?
4. How well does your product's life cycle fit with your customer's buying cycle?
5. How well do you think you're doing altogether?
6. How can you improve your offering?

1. What is "value" in your customer's mind?

What do customers really buy from you? Sure, you sell fly fishing rods, but how important is the Hardy brand name? How valuable is your expert advice on fly-tying, and your reputation as a man who knows the local streams? What kind of premium might these "extras" command?

Or let's say you sell life assurance. Are you successful because you represent New England Mutual or Liberty Life, or because you've got a nice personality? Or is it because you're a tax expert. . . or because you happened to knock on a prospect's door just when he needed a new retirement plan

. . . or because you act as a broker, and you really do find the best rates for your clients?

What do your customers mean by "value" when they think of a product or service like yours? What substitutes might they buy? How easily can they switch? Why do they stay with you? If they're still buying from your competitors, why do you not have 100 per cent of their business?

Customers don't just buy "generic" products. They want far more than that. And suppliers are eager to oblige:

❑ BP sells oil and petrol, but now more than 30 service stations in Britain have mini-supermarkets on the driveway, carrying about 2 500 items. Most are open from 7 a.m. to 11 p.m. — some right around the clock.[2]

❑ In the hotly contested U.S. minivan market vehicles can cost upwards of $20 000. If you want space-age styling, Chevrolet's slant-nosed Lumina sets the pace. If you want power, GM's GMC Safari has an extra-strong 6-cylinder engine which pulls up to 6 0000 pounds. If you like camping, you'll like the way the back seats fold down to make a bed in Mazda's MPV.

❑ Sunglasses are more than just protection for the eyes — they're a fashion statement. And none so fashionable as those sleek black shades that carry the Porsche name. Designed by Ferdinand Alexander (grandson of Ferdinand Porsche) in 1978, and manufactured by Carrera, they sell at a rate of 500 000 pairs a year — at about $250 a time. (In fact, they're so popular a Brazilian firm once turned out 200 000 fake copies a year!)

❑ Women buy perfume because it smells great, right? Wrong! Although rare essences might cost as much as $35 000-$45 000 a kilo, the raw materials in a perfume

account for less than 10 per cent of its cost. Labour adds
another 10–15 per cent. The rest is pure razzmatazz.

Two classic marketing blunders underline how easy it is to
mis-read customers' views. The Ford Edsel was supposed to
be the car of every motorist's dreams. It turned out to be a dog.
"New" Coke was launched to end the Pepsi challenge once
and for all; it, too, was a disaster.

Both these short-lived products were developed in response to carefully-researched customer needs. In the case of
"new" Coke, 400 000 taste tests were conducted in the marketplace. Consumers rated the new taste ahead of both Pepsi and
"old" Coke, by margins of up to 2:1.

So what went wrong?

As so often happens, the executives responsible for both
the Edsel and "new" Coke relied on carefully-structured, me-
ticulously-controlled market surveys. They went by the numbers instead of by gut feel. They pored over research reports,
instead of getting out into the marketplace and talking personally to customers.

From the moment "new" Coke was announced, franchise
bottlers voiced their displeasure. They were close to their
customers, and instinct told them the switch was a bad move.
But the people down in Atlanta knew better.

Coca-Cola's researchers asked consumers to compare the
taste of their new product with "old" Coke and with Pepsi.
They didn't ask, "How would you feel if we replaced the
Coca-Cola you know and love, with this new product?" As
events showed, consumers hated the idea of anyone messing
with the "mother brand."

**Unfortunately, even the best thought-out question-
naire is no guarantee of success. Respondents don't
always say what they feel. Interviewer bias is often a
problem. And customers often don't know what they
might want sometime in the future — their opinions**

have little or nothing to do with what they'll really do when the time comes to spend their hard-earned money.

How the Japanese use "hands-on" research

It's unlikely that any self-respecting Japanese or South Korean marketer would have gone ahead on the basis of second- or third-hand information. They know the importance of really understanding customers as people. They use formal research, but they go to elaborate lengths to back it with informal opinions. Some of their methods:

1. *They track both "hard" and "soft" market data.* The hard stuff is measurable: shipments, inventories, actual retail sales. The soft stuff comes from personal contact with distributors and customers.

   Japanese executives at all levels call on their customers, talk with them, and ask their views. They visit trade shows, suppliers, and even competitors, armed with cameras and notebooks. They spend a great deal of time talking with their wholesalers and retailers. And they track what's happening in the distribution chain on a monthly, weekly, or even daily basis.

   They gather information assiduously, and they sift it and share it. Building a pool of knowledge about customers and competitors is a highly disciplined process, not just an exercise that's left to juniors or attended to in odd moments.

   • In late 1989, a Californian couple sued Nissan for fraud, invasion of privacy, trespassing and unfair business practices, alleging that the Japanese auto firm had planted an engineer in their home to study their lifestyle. They answered an ad seeking homes for Japanese "exchange students," and when told that none were available, took 29-year-old Mr Takashi Morimoto instead. They later discovered to their chagrin that he was actually collecting data for Nissan.[3]

- Seeing a hugely lucrative market in luxury cruises, Crystal Cruises decided to build several liners that would compete head on with the QEII and Viking Lines. Their chief designer took 16 lengthy cruises on competitors' ships to get a first-hand look at their amenities, to check their service levels, to see what entertainment they offered, and to watch passengers at play.

- At Sony's Industrial Design Centre in Park Ridge, New Jersey, designers spend hours paging through magazines, studying popular culture, and watching people go about their daily business, so they can develop products "that serve no preexisting demand" — such as the Walkman, the Watchman, and the My First Sony range.[4] Sony is just one of many Japanese firms that has located a sophisticated design facility in an important market, so that designers have a hands-on feel for what will sell there.

2. *They sample products before final production.* Real-world trials always yield a great deal of useful information. When people can see, touch, hold, smell, and taste a product, they give the best feedback.

3. *They set up consumer test centres, where people can come in off the street and try out new products.* They encourage visitors to offer critical advice, they watch how they respond to products, and they listen to what these potential customers say.

Motor manufacturers, computer companies, and appliance marketers all use this technique. They know that

3 "U.S. Couple Sues Nissan For Snooping," *International Herald Tribune,* December 910, 1989
4 Paul Kunkel, "Beat the competition," in *Competing By Design,* a special advertising supplement published by *Business Week* in 1990

R&D isn't an exclusive in-company affair; often customers have the best ideas, and a lot of innovation starts with them.

4. *They interview people who've already bought their products.* Not content to talk only to "representative samples" of possible future customers, they solicit opinions from people who already own their products or competitive products.

   They visit customers after the sale. They use ghost shoppers, satisfaction questionnaires, service and re-order records, telephone interviews, and even complaint-handling procedures, to gather information. This assures them of a flood of accurate and timely feedback.

5. *Retail sales people are involved in the research effort.* They question shoppers, or interview people by phone or by mail. Stores become, in effect, information-gathering centres. In the process, sales staff develop strong loyalty to their suppliers.

There are any number of innovative ways to get under your customers' skin. The danger is to assume you're already there. Costly marketing mistakes are made when executives believe that their own wants and needs, likes and dislikes, hopes, aspirations, and expectations are an accurate reflection of how their customers feel.

Research is always risky, and all too often provides an inaccurate picture of what's inside customers' heads. So several probes are generally more useful than just one. And "soft" methods are as important — if not *more* important in many cases — than "hard" ones.

Hence quantitative research, using carefully structured questionnaires, should wherever possible be tempered by qualitative studies such as focus group discussions, field trips, and the like. And as with every other aspect of improving the customer service process, these research efforts must be ongoing. Obsolete information is worse than useless.

Every product a survey instrument

Most companies have a very autocratic approach to marketing. Ivory-tower decisions are forced down the chain of command and out into the marketplace. This naturally takes a long time and doesn't allow for much flexibility. Nor does feedback have an immediate impact.

World class firms spend a great deal of time learning precisely what their customers want. And from the moment a product hits the market, *it's a dynamic test for the next one.* Continuous feedback leads to continuous improvement.

A great product idea is only great if the customer says so. Formal market research is one way to get customers' views, but not the only one and certainly not the most effective. So if you really want to improve your marketing effort, start working now on new ways to get more accurate, more usable, information from the front.

Ford adopted the Japanese approach for the launch of its all-new Fiesta model in Europe. The company's own test drivers racked up close to a million miles on secret tracks; in addition, some 250 cars were placed with high-mileage private and business motorists and police forces, to get their views.

The gruelling programme began months ahead of the launch. Cars were checked weekly for quality, durability, economy, and reliability. Said Alex Trotman, chairman of Ford of Europe: "By placing these cars with high-mileage, severe-duty fleet operators at the beginning of a European winter, we can quickly accumulate data that will assure the highest possible quality levels when we begin selling the new Fiesta next spring."[5]

5   John Griffiths, "Ford Selects Private Motorists To Test Fiesta Before Launch," *Financial Times*, December 5, 1988

Apple Computer involved customers during the development of its low-cost "Classic" version of the Macintosh. Their suggestions triggered key changes just months before the launch date.

Xerox's latest research efforts have involved customers and other important stakeholders right from the start of new product development. They've helped decide Xerox decide what kinds of products to make and what features to include. Many of the firm's best ideas come from outsiders.

This kind of "real time" research shouldn't be left to specialist researchers. Sometimes their help is necessary, but as a general rule, they should be called only when the firm can't generate its own intelligence. Your own people are your own best sources of information and ideas.

Deere & Co., the American farm equipment firm, had factory workers visit or phone six out of every ten customers who bought one of their combines in 1989. They learned that farmers didn't like side-mounted cabs, as they made the machines look unbalanced and spoiled their view. So the design was changed. Now the cab is in the centre.

Another team of Deere factory workers — nicknamed the "haymasters" — hit the road to promote their hay machines. They later developed a new round baler based on ideas they got from farmers.

Take advantage of the "layers of value" you offer

Customer needs and wants should be carefully tabulated and ranked. Value is always a "bundle" of satisfactions. It always includes both "hard" and "soft" factors. It's both tangible and intangible.

Exploiting customers' needs and wants begins with understanding, at the very deepest level, precisely what value means to them. This insight allows you to then focus your business system so that value is added step by step, layer by layer.

Great works of art are often only a little more decorative than lesser ones. But they are prized because every time you look at them you experience different things. And you can go back to them time and again, without tiring of them.

The charm of a Russian doll is not its cute, hand-painted face, and its tubby body, but the fact that when you open it there's a smaller one inside . . . and then another . . . and another. . . .

Chances are you have not taken advantage of the full potential of your products and services. Nor will you if you don't make the intense effort that's needed to get into the mind of your customer, and if you fail to exercise your imagination.

Ask them to complain — the feedback is invaluable!

Nobody likes criticism. It's not easy to stay silent when someone rips into you, even if you are wrong. But customer complaints are an essential element of the improvement process. They're an accurate measure of how you're doing in the real-world. And there's plenty of evidence that even the unhappiest customer can be turned around — in fact, can become a "missionary" for your firm — if he or she is handled properly. The essential steps are:

1. Listen empathically.
2. Be honest about what you can or cannot do.
3. Act fast.

Front line people take the brunt of most customer problems. They're the ones customers reach most easily. They're the ones who manage the "moment of truth." Yet far too many of them don't try to be helpful.

Some just don't have the personality or the imagination to do what's needed — particularly under pressure. That's a *hiring* issue.

Others simply can't be helpful. That might be a *training* problem. Or it might be because they don't have the information, resources, or support that they need. And that's a *management* problem.

Of course, some customer complaints just cannot be satisfactorily resolved. Some customers go out of their way to be difficult, and nothing will please them. Some can be abusive or even threatening. But more often than not, even the unhappiest customer will see reason and will put up with some inconvenience. It all hinges on how they're handled.

People buy things because they want them, not because they want to send them back or get into a fight. It's all well and good to say, "Let the buyer beware," but customers do buy in good faith and they do deserve to be treated fairly.

Use complaints to trigger the next sale

Getting complaints may not be pleasant, but it should be easy for customers to complain. First prize, of course, is for them to be able to talk directly to the person who can fix their problem. But in large or complex firms, that's not always possible.

Second prize is to make it clear to customers who they can talk to when they have difficulties. Some firms might have people whose sole task is after-sales service and complaint handling. World class companies go even further: they actively follow up every sale — in person, by phone, or by mail — to check that customers are happy. Staff who do this are highly trained, they know the ins and outs of their firms, and they're empowered to take decisions to help customers.

These companies know that the sale is never over. They understand that what a customer buys is not just a product or service that works today, but ongoing perfect performance. They use every sale as a bridge to the next one. They treat every customer as a missionary for their business. They invest in creating and keeping

customers, **not just in products or services. They know about invisible assets.**

Problem . . . or opportunity?

Getting complaints, or identifying problems is one thing; dealing with them constructively is equally important. Actions always speak louder than words.

❑ When an Iowan farmer complained that his new Deere & Co. combine wasn't quite the right shade of green, four factory reps visited him to check. They offered to repaint the machine, but he demanded a new one. So his local dealer drove him 120 miles to Deere's East Moline plant, where he was given lunch and a factory tour; then they let him choose a brand new machine.[6]

❑ When Toyota launched its $35 000 luxury Lexus LS400 sedan in the U.S. in September 1989, the objective was to steal business from Mercedes-Benz and BMW. The car embraced 300 technological innovations, and came with a four-year, 50 000-mile warranty. But within just a couple of months, Toyota had to recall more than 8 000 vehicles. In some cars, the cruise control went on running after it was switched off, and a rear brake light didn't work properly when it got hot.

Events like this are a nightmare for any auto company. Unhappy customers quickly spread the word. Once they have a problem they often go out of their way to look for more, and then become a real thorn in the company's side. Toyota faced a crisis of credibility.

But the recall was handled with consummate skill and speed. Lexus owners were given a choice: they could drive to the nearest dealership, or have the cars picked up from

6 "Deere Faces Challenge Just When Farmers Are Shopping Again," *The Wall Street Journal*, February 8, 1990

their offices or homes. When the problem was fixed the cars were washed, and the tank was filled with petrol. Many dealers also gave owners a small gift.

To look after just ten customers in Grand Rapids, Michigan, 240 kilometres from his Detroit operation, dealer Ken Meade flew in mechanics and rented workshop space, then fetched, fixed, washed, and returned the cars.[7]

Most motor manufacturers boast about their concern for customers. Most understand the lifetime value of a loyal customer. Yet their dealers seem to be on a different wavelength.

I recently sent my car for major and very costly repairs. The job was badly done, and I was furious. But I was too busy to go back to the workshop. When a young lady phoned a few days later to ask if everything was O.K., I gave her hell. She promised to talk to the service manager and get right back to me — but that was the last I heard from her.

You can choose to treat customer complaints as a problem or as an opportunity. You can handle them in a way that costs you a fortune, or you can turn them to your advantage. World class companies manage customer expectations with a great deal of care. They manage customers' experiences just as well. They don't always like what customers say, but they encourage them to speak out anyway.

How to make questionnaires effective

There are many other ways to get feedback from customers. One obvious route is to use questionnaires.

Here are ten rules for making them effective:

1. They should be readily available. Place them where customers can see them — for example, in hotel rooms, on sales or service counters, or inside product packaging.

7   S.C. Gwynne, "New Kid On The Dock," *Time*, September 17, 1990

2. Make them simple and clear. Use boxes, line drawings, or other graphics to lead the customer through them.

3. Be sure what you want to find out. Be specific about the questions you ask. Get the information you think you need, but also leave space for customers to make their own observations. Let them tick "Yes/no" boxes, circle numbers on a scale (1 — 2 — 3 — 4 — 5), circle an opinion (always agree — sometimes agree — seldom agree — disagree), or give you one-word answers. If you get more complicated, people won't take the trouble to help you.

4. Ask for positive suggestions as well as the bad news. customers feel good about helping you design your business. And remember, when they invest time in the task, they generally find it harder to switch to another supplier.

5. Give respondents the choice of signing their names or staying anonymous.

6. Complaint forms should be addressed to the CEO rather than some obscure department or faceless minion. Customers need to know they're talking to someone with real authority.

7. Make it easy for forms to be returned. Provide a prominent deposit box or a pre-addressed, pre-paid envelope.

8. Act on complaints and suggestions.

9. Be *seen* to act on them. Talk about the way you're responding. Publicize it. Make it clear you want more feedback — either positive or negative.

10. Keep in touch with customers who complain. Let them know their views are important, and that you take them seriously. Thank them for helping you. Tell them what you're doing to deal with their complaints.

How to run a focus group

Another strategy is to conduct focus group discussions, and ask for negative as well as positive views. This costs almost nothing to do, and is a great way to build relationships. In fact, it's so simple that it should be a regular habit. Just think about it: if you got ten customers together for just an hour a week, you'd hear the views of more than 500 people in the next year.

Here are some guidelines to make these sessions effective:

1. Invite people well ahead of time. A supermarket might get away with asking morning shoppers to pop back later in the day, but if your customers are senior executives they'll need a lot more notice — maybe even a few weeks. They might also need a written invitation, and a reminder by phone or fax.

2. Five to seven people is the best size for most group activities, but you might go up to ten for a session like this.

3. Some kind of incentive might be needed to get people to attend. But don't go overboard; customers are more willing to help than we expect.

4. Provide comfortable chairs. Make sure the temperature's right. Ask people not to smoke.

5. Make notes or record the session. If people have taken time out to help you, the least you can do is show them you're really listening.

6. *Listen* — don't talk! You're learning, not selling!

7. Provide refreshments. Nothing elaborate — maybe just coffee and soft drinks, and a plate of sandwiches or biscuits.

8. Don't allow interruptions. Stop all phone calls. Give customers your undivided attention in return for the time they're giving you.

9. The CEO or another senior executive should run the session. Most customers never get to see the top people, so it's a treat for them. It sends a powerful signal that you take them seriously.

10. Follow up. Stay in touch. Imagine what you'd gain if you put those 500 names onto a word processor, and popped off a letter to them once a quarter!

2. How do you rate against your competitors?

The value you offer is always relative. Customers compare goods and services continually. Any company that wants to be a winner has to pay attention to competitors as well as to customers.

Your product or service is one of many. Customers have infinite choices. "Remember that the people you address are selfish, as we all are," said copywriter Claude Hopkins. "They care nothing about your interest or your profit. They seek service for themselves." Your competitive edge arises out of a meaningful advantages in your product; not from your R&D boffins' opinions or from fanciful ideas about what customers "should" want.

> Remember, too, that much as your own efforts position your company and its products or services in the minds of customers, *you are positioned by your competitors.* What they do and what they offer shapes customers' perceptions and expectations, and becomes a yardstick by which you're measured.

For all these reasons it's important to keep your finger on the competitive pulse. You need to know who's offering what, how they're doing it, how they're likely to change, and how they might respond to your moves.

Most firms spend far too little time on systematic competitor intelligence. Very few have a budget for information-gathering, or a person responsible for that task, so it's largely left to chance. The main sources of insight are odd trade journal articles, passing comments, gossip, rumour, and the sales team's (often prejudiced and distorted) views.

These sources all have some value, but needless to say they're not enough. Nor is there one best source of information.

What you really need is many antennae monitoring the outside world on a continuous basis; a way of coordinating everything you see or hear; and a forum for analyzing and talking about it.

Competitor analysis is a task that deserves special effort and quality thinking time. Ask:

- ❑ What are our key competitors doing to take customers from us?
- ❑ Why do customers find them attractive?
- ❑ How do customers rate them against us?
- ❑ What might they offer in the future?
- ❑ What is their vision of the future — i.e., what drives them?
- ❑ What is their mission — i.e., how do they define their business?
- ❑ What are their values?
- ❑ What is their strategy?
- ❑ What key skills do they have, and what skills are they building?
- ❑ What invisible assets do they have?
- ❑ What are their greatest strengths and weaknesses?
- ❑ What opportunities and threats do they face?
- ❑ How are they financed, and how strong are they financially?
- ❑ What is their cost structure?
- ❑ How will they react to our moves?
- ❑ What will they let us get away with?

A lot of this information is easily available from public sources: competitors' advertising, their annual reports, press articles, exhibitions, and the like. In addition, distributors, customers, and other stakeholders can provide a wealth of insights. It takes time and effort to gather the stuff, but your competitiveness depends on it. The task shouldn't be left for some junior person to do in his or her spare time. It's a crucial exercise, and must be managed like any other important issue. Some information will only be available through qualitative or quantitative surveys. Some of this work can be done in-house (the way Stew Leonard or Japanese firms do it, for example), but critical facts are often only available through a structured, professional study conducted by an independent research organization.

The problem for every firm is to keep the process in perspective. There's a fine line between too much research and too little. It's easy to become paranoid about the information that comes in. When companies spend their time looking over their shoulders they're in dead trouble. Competitor information is part of the learning process, and must be leavened with judgement.

Once you have the information you need, share it throughout your organization. In most firms, too few people know enough about their market standing, their customers, or their competitors. They have little reason to strive for better performance because they don't know what they're up against. So enlist the help of as many of your people as possible in gathering the information you need, and when you've got it, involve them in using it.

Make sure that people throughout your business system know what you're up against, what competitors are doing, and how they're advancing. This information is not only useful for thinking about your own operations, but can also be highly motivating. Providing it is both educational and developmental, and essential to creative thinking.

However you depict your competitive standing, remember the K.I.S.S. principle — Keep It Simple, Stupid! Computers can be useful in drawing perception maps, for example, but it's easy to get sucked into the technology trap. Thick reports look impressive on the marketing manager's desk, but are useless until they trigger action.

When it takes too much sophistication to tell you how you rate, you probably don't. When differences are too small, they don't matter. If you can't explain, in a short sentence and words of one syllable, what makes your product special, save your breath.

3. What is your customer's demand pattern?

Customers buy at different times. It's important to understand what triggers their buying decisions, and then, where possible, to anticipate their needs.

Grocery purchases peak at month end. Fashion purchases peak at the start of each season. If you sell to retailers in these industries, you know when to make major deliveries.

If you sell parts to motor manufacturers, however, the demand pattern will be quite different. It'll probably peak early, when a new model is about to be launched, then tail off over time. Over several years, you might be required to keep up a continuous flow of small shipments at short notice — e.g., if the customer practices JIT.

The better you can match your production to your customers' buying habits, the better your service will be. At the same time, you'll keep your own costs down, because you'll be able to manage your own inventory levels more effectively.

4. How does your product life cycle fit in with your customer's buying cycle?

Just as products have life cycles, so do buyers go through fairly predictable phases. And their need for information and attention changes along the way.

In the early days of computers, for example, sellers held the whip hand: they had all the information about how the things worked, what they could do, and how to work them. But over time buyers became more expert. And since they knew precisely how computers aided them on a day-to-day basis, the balance of power shifted. Now, computer marketers face buyers who really know their stuff.

Naturally, this affects the buyers' perception of value. In the early phases, they have to pay for know-how, so price is less important than the best advice and support. Later, as they get to feel more comfortable making their own decisions, price becomes more important.

Marketers who don't keep track of these changes will sooner or later find that they're selling the wrong things the wrong way.

They might be too light on information and too ready to cut prices up front, when they hold important advantages. On the other hand, they might mis-read their customers' growing knowledge and sophistication, and persist in offering something that's no longer needed at prices that no one will pay.

5. How well are you doing altogether?

The view from inside a firm is usually quite different from that seen by outsiders. It's very easy to become complacent, to believe that your own standards are adequate, and to assume that all's well. But constant change and improvement are essential in every area of the business, and external benchmarks drive the process.

❑ How do you and your people rate your performance?

❑ What are your measures of success — and do they really tell you anything of value?

❑ How do your views compare with those of your customers? (You might kid yourselves, but you can't kid your customers!)

❑ Do you and your team agree on your strengths and weaknesses?

❑ Why are there differences of opinion?

❑ What should you do about them?

Armed with the right information, you'll be in a position to develop a customer service strategy that will deliver what your customers expect, and set you apart from your competition.

The final questions are:

❑ Where to now?
❑ What must you do close the gaps, to exceed your customers' expectations, and to keep your competitors at bay?
❑ How will you make "the improvement after next," to stay one jump ahead in the race for market share?

6. How can you improve your offering?

Most firms have infinite choices for adding value. Every step in your value chain is an opportunity to do something different and better. In the design stage, for example, you can:

❑ Include unique features.
❑ Make the product's appearance distinctive.
❑ Simplify production.
❑ Cut the number of components, to cut costs and make assembly and repair easier.
❑ Make easy add-ons possible (e.g., in a stereo system).
❑ Make the item more durable.
❑ Involve suppliers to tap their ideas, and to get them committed to quality levels and delivery arrangements.

And that's just a start. Every other stage offers the same long list of opportunities. The improvement process never ends. No matter how well you're doing today, your offering will be bettered — or made irrelevant — tomorrow. Keeping up with customers requires incredible endurance. Staying ahead of competitors takes a succession of innovative sprints.

Customers don't just buy things. They buy solutions to problems. The marketer's task is to provide unique

**solutions to problems that trouble customers today,
and to anticipate those they haven't yet thought about.**

The service package

As we've seen, competitive advantage begins with a clear definition of your product, your customers, and your key skills. Communication is an essential tool in the whole process of delivering value to your customer. People throughout your business system need to know your strategy; equally, customers need to know clearly what you offer.

Advertising man Rosser Reeves made the Unique Selling Proposition (USP) famous. But for many advertising agencies and their clients, the idea went out of fashion. With economies everywhere on a roll, and in their eagerness to break through the clutter in every medium, they took creative risks and pushed advertising to its limits. They used famous personalities, humour, and all manner of visual and verbal tricks. In the process, they obscured their promise. (Nissan's launch ads for the Infiniti, for example, featured "zen-like" photos of rocks, swirling water, and trees. They drew attention and media comment, but also a barrage of criticism from dealers. After just a few months, they were dropped in favour of a more conventional, product-oriented approach.)

As we enter the 1990s, world economic growth is slowing and competition is increasing. "Creative," soft-sell advertising is giving way to hard-sell pitches for everything from groceries to motor cars. Image ads are being dropped in favour of pitches that say, in effect, "Buy this product, and you'll get this benefit." Marketers have learned at great cost that the most effective promotional messages are simple and clear, and make one meaningful, memorable promise. The total "bundle of value" that a product offers must be reduced to an unforgettable image or a few words — "The world's best engineered car" (Mercedes-Benz); "The choice of a new generation"

(Pepsi-Cola); "The power to be your best (Apple Computer); "The world's favourite airline" (British Airways).

In the same way that products are positioned in customers' minds, a firm's employees must understand precisely what they're selling. Slogans like the ones above are not just consumer promises; they drive the competitive thrust of the entire organization. They set up customers' expectations, and they become a measure of internal performance.

A "service theme," "service strategy," or "service package" can help achieve this. In some organizations, a brief statement of intent is all that's needed; others require something far longer — perhaps even several pages of information.

The service package spells out your promise. It's a statement of all the things you'll do to satisfy your customers. Some of them will be tangible and measurable; others will be intangible and "soft."

Facts and feelings make the sale

Logic says that the hard stuff would be easier to talk about. Yet far too often, marketers skimp on facts. They underestimate customers' intelligence and their need for hard data. With complex products particularly — e.g., computers, aircraft, medical equipment, chemicals, pharmaceuticals, consulting services — there's a need for plenty of information before, during, and after the sale.

Equally, research shows that marketers underestimate the power of emotion. People buying perfume, motor cars, and holidays do so for many complex reasons. Industrial buyers, too, need "high-touch" attention. How they feel — and how you make them feel — is critical.

An effective service package, therefore, combines both facts and feelings in the way that means most to customers. It's a "contract" which goes a long way to ensuring a win-win business relationship. The tangible parts can be easily spelled

> ✓ Salesman to call at least twice a month
> ✓ Key technical executives to meet at least once a month
> ✓ Orders to be processed within two hours
> ✓ All deliveries to be completed within 24 hours of order
> ✓ Exchanges to completed within 12 hours
> ✓ Invoices to be mailed within 48 hours

Figure 12-1
Factors that might make up a service package

out (Figure 12-1); the intangible aspects have to be *lived* out. To make sure the latter happens, define as clearly as possible how you want customers to feel about their dealings with your firm. Then ask, "What must we do to trigger those feelings?" (Figure 12-2.) This way, you and your team progress from vague statements of intent to deliberate actions, and you start to manage the all-important emotional content on your customer relationships.

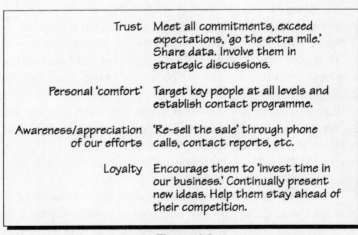

Trust	Meet all commitments, exceed expectations, 'go the extra mile.' Share data. Involve them in strategic discussions.
Personal 'comfort'	Target key people at all levels and establish contact programme.
Awareness/appreciation of our efforts	'Re-sell the sale' through phone calls, contact reports, etc.
Loyalty	Encourage them to 'invest time in our business.' Continually present new ideas. Help them stay ahead of their competition.

Figure 12-2
Making intangibles tangible

Some firms use the service package as an internal guide only. Others share it with their customers. And still others *negotiate* it with customers, to be sure they're both on the same track.

The service package can have a number of objectives, and it's important to be sure what you expect from it. Some thought starters:

❑ To help you define the value you'll offer.
❑ To help customers clarify their expectations.
❑ To negotiate with them what you'll deliver, how you'll do it, by when, and at what cost (this makes them "prosumers" and goes some way to committing them to you).
❑ To take the emotional heat out of debates about your performance, by providing an objective base for assessment.
❑ To provide a starting point for benchmarking your performance.
❑ To focus your people's attention on what really counts.
❑ To simplify and improve communication.

If your service package is purely an internal tool, you may not want to expose it to customers. To check your performance, ask, "How are we doing so far?" "Why have we got these results?" "How can we improve?" Encourage your employees to continually review the original service package, and when necessary, to re-create it.

When the service package has been negotiated with customers, the same internal reviews apply. But you also have a commitment to giving customers regular feedback on how you're doing, and asking for their opinions.

You might want to send them regular (monthly, quarterly, half-yearly) statements of performance, much the way your bank sends you a monthly statement. It's vital to keep *reminding* customers just how much you're doing for them. Products are tangible, but services are intangible and thus often invisible and quickly forgotten. Advertising agencies and PR firms send "contact reports" to their clients, ostensibly as a record of meetings, but in addition, to show how hard they're working.

Of course, all this doesn't just happen. It takes consistent discipline. It also takes a lot of time and effort up front, as systems must be put in place to ensure regular feedback on how you're doing, and baseline data must be gathered to give you a starting point.

The danger, as with any system, is that it can chew up resources, and people may switch their objective from satisfying customers to maintaining the system. Does sophisticated information technology help? "No," says a computer industry executive whose firm had tried to create a system to manage its own sales process. "The effort that goes into defining a service package, agreeing the details with customers, monitoring performance, and providing feedback to key people is just not worth the trouble."

The service package is not just something that keeps front line sales people busy. It's a potentially powerful management tool, and needs to be understood by everyone who affects your service levels. Its objectives should be clear from the start, and they should be kept in sight later.

When promotional claims change

Few companies stick with a single promotional statement over many years. Products evolve. Competitive conditions change. The business system improves. So the service package must be seen as part of the dynamic process of keeping the company and its customers in sync. It must be continually reviewed, revised, and recommunicated.

The Mercedes-Benz claim to be "the world's best-engineered car" appeals to certain buyers, and establishes a particular set of priorities within the firm. BMW's slogan, "The ultimate driving machine," sells a very different bundle of values, and focuses employees' attention on different issues. But the once-clear line between the two marques is blurring; their claims and their behaviour now overlap. Mercedes is shedding its somewhat stodgy image with a new line of state-of-the-art sports cars. BMW's latest TV commercials take Mercedes-Benz head on in the safety stakes. Over time, as the two firms compete increasingly for the same customers, their promises will converge even further. And their business systems will become more and more alike.

If Mercedes-Benz and BMW were the only two organizations competing in their segment of the market, they would theoretically reach some kind of balance some time in the future. But aggressive new competitors like Toyota and Nissan will force them to innovate even faster than they have. They will have to launch more new models, more quickly than they are able to do now. They will have to change their advertising promises and their internal performance — and thus their service packages.

CHAPTER THIRTEEN

THE WAY TO TOTAL IMPROVEMENT

Fierce competitors are out there in the jungle, changing everything at a terrifying pace, improving what they did yesterday,
developing new offerings that customers don't even know
they want.

Little wonder, then, that customers continually change
their buying habits. There's so much new and improved and
totally different to catch their attention. What's more, their
values change, their lifestyle changes, their wants and needs
change, and the way they buy changes.

Your customers might appear happy right now, but the
time will come when they'll look around. In most cases, they
have any number of options to choose from. And for most
customers switching suppliers is all too easy.

At the same time, your competitors change continually.
They launch new and different products. They spend more on
R&D. They foster partnerships with their suppliers. They
sharpen their manufacturing. They introduce new technology.
They streamline administrative procedures. They drive down
prices. And they spend more on advertising.

**Somewhere out there, right now, a competitor is plan-
ning to bury you. Companies around the world are
going to great lengths to improve themselves. The moment you lapse into smugness or complacency they'll
get you.**

All this means that no matter how well you're doing today,
you have to change — and change fast and continually — if

you're going to *retain* your current market position, let alone thrive and grow. So a constant stream of new ideas is essential.

Watch the big guys

Innovation naturally gets tougher as a company ages. Size, complexity, and bureaucracy all get in its way. So does the fact that people start believing they "know what works in this industry"

But world class companies never rest on their laurels. They constantly rethink all they do. They continually test new products, explore new markets, and change the way they do business.[1] They're difficult to track because while it's often fairly easy to copy a *product* innovation, it's usually hard to detect, never mind copy, a *process* innovation.

Contrary to popular belief, innovation is not the exclusive preserve of young companies. So if you think you can write off competitors who've been around a long time, forget it. *Inc.* magazine reports that "companies, like cows, are regularly 'born again.'" Whether as a result of new management, new techniques, or changes in the marketplace, statistics show that older companies are *more likely* to grow rapidly than even the youngest ones. And surprise, surprise: "The group with the largest concentration of rapid growers consists of companies 75 years and older."[2]

An article in *The Economist* suggests that consistent, persistent efforts are what count in business. "Gone are the super-star entrepreneurs of the enterprise culture," says the magazine. "To the fore has ambled a steadier sort of leader, the type who spends years turning his firm around or pushing it towards greater efficiency. This is the age of the tortoise."[3]

1   Donald K. Clifford, Jr. and Richard E. Cavanaugh, *The Winning Performance*, Bantam Books, 1985
2   David L. Birch, "Late Bloomers," *Inc.*, September 1988
3   "Britain's Hares And Tortoises," *The Economist*, March 25, 1989

Of course, this is not to say that speed isn't important. What it does tell us is that youthful exuberance isn't everything.

Short, sharp bursts of energy won't make you a winner. It's stamina over the long haul — a total dedication to continuous improvement of everything — that leads to victory. And some of the larger companies in every industry are as intent on huge improvements in their performance as are any of their smaller challengers.

Corporate wellness

Customer satisfaction is, in the end, a result of your front line people doing a better job of serving customers. But to get there the entire business needs a rethink. Total corporate wellness must be your aim.

If you as an individual want to be really healthy, exercise alone can't do the trick. Nor can diet. Or medicine. Total wellness demands a whole range of new behaviours: planned exercise, careful eating, mental stimulation, and rest. In the same way, total corporate wellness demands a total strategy.

But where to begin?

Again, let's use health as an analogy. When a doctor examines you he asks questions, feels your pulse, listens to your heart, and perhaps does several other tests as well. And so it is with customer service. A complete and thorough diagnosis is necessary before you begin treatment. Every aspect of your business has to be examined. You have to ask, "Where are we now?" "Where do we want to be?" "How can we get there?"

The basic ingredients

We've already looked at many of the things that keep world class competitors ahead of the pack. Now let's review some of those issues in greater depth, using the "opportunity map." We'll start with the familiar "4 Ps" of the marketing mix —

product, place, price, promotion — still a useful framework, and work outwards.

This is not intended to be a laundry list of "solutions." At best, it's an overview of what the best players are doing, and hopefully a catalyst to spark your own creative thinking. Many excellent books cover these issues in great depth.

The product

If there was a time when you could build a better mousetrap and have customers beat a path to your door, things have changed. Customers don't need to search for better products. They have more than enough options today. This is the Age of Choice. It's hard to get their attention, let alone their business.

Lester Wunderman, chairman of Wunderman Worldwide, a leading direct response marketing agency, says, "The marketer's question of 'Here's what I make. Don't you want it?' will become the consumer's request of 'Here's what I need. Do you have it?'"[4]

> **To have a chance in the marketplace, products must have unique appeal. They must satisfy a need, save money, solve a problem, or enhance the buyer's self-image. They must also be environmentally-friendly. And they must do all that better than the competition.**

The late Konosuke Matsushita, Japan's leading postwar industrialist, put corporate priorities in neat perspective when he said, "Profits should not be a reflection of corporate greed, but a vote of confidence from society that what is offered by the firm is valued."[5] There's only one way to get that vote: *by consistently delivering superior products and services.*

4   In an interview in "Where Will Growth In 1990s Come From?"
    Advertising Age, May 15, 1989
5   "Konusuke Matsushita Is Dead At 94; Japan's Top Postwar Industrialist," *The Herald Tribune*, April 28, 1989

Fast-talking salesmen and slick ads won't satisfy customers. That takes quality, quality, quality. To have any chance at all of survival, products must meet with customers' critical approval. The basic product idea must be a good one. Then, it must be wrapped in value as it progresses from concept to customer.

Most important of all, it must be environmentally friendly. If you can still get away with tardiness in this respect, don't expect your good luck to hold. The "greens" movement is gaining clout. It holds the tickets to entry in most industries. And its attention is spreading rapidly from yesterday's "save the whale" or "save the Amazon" campaigns, to include anything that might help it "save the planet."

Result: everything you do and the way you do everything is under review. Chemical firms like ICI police themselves ruthlessly, because they know there'll be costly repercussions if a toxic product spills or endangers anything it wasn't targeted at. McDonald's has thrown out its foam packaging for hamburgers. Auto makers like BMW and Peugeot are not only testing new materials, but also plan recycling plants for old cars. Coca-Cola sponsors "cans-for-cash" contests to encourage consumers to fight litter. One estimate suggests that the market for environmental equipment and services in Europe alone will hit about $100 billion a year by 1999. "In five or ten years, I think almost all products will call themselves green products," says a leading environmental consultant.[6]

As the opportunity map shows, "the product" is not just "a thing." It embraces a chain of activities: design, production, installation, training, service, and support. It must be backed by some kind of guarantee or warranty to reassure customers,

6 "Clean living: a growing array of firms in Europe are starting to play the green card," *The Wall Street Journal Europe*, 12-13 July, 1991

and perhaps to define your obligations and theirs. And it must be wrapped in imagery.

❑ Does your product (service) offer customers a clear and meaningful benefit?
❑ Is it demonstrably better than competitors' offerings?
❑ Does it offer real value for money?
❑ Do you provide adequate customer support in terms of:
   • Information about your company and your product?
   • Product literature?
   • Customer education and training?
   • Repairs and maintenance? (And spares?)
   • Guarantees? (Money back, or no-questions replacement?)

Design as a competitive weapon

When you wander down a street, browse through a supermarket, check out the latest consumer electronics, or cash a cheque at your bank, one thing is clear: design adds value.

Even the most mundane of products is easy on the eye, easy to handle, easy to use. A recent *Business Week* cover story on design featured several pages of photos of items like these: A Black & Decker stapler, a racing wheelchair by Hall's Wheels, an easy-to-hold baby's bottle from Ansa Bottle Co., Sanyei America's travel iron, and the latest MSA fireman's helmet.

Services, too, are wrapped in design: everything from the basic concept to the delivery process yells, "Buy me!" Banking halls, airline terminals, architects' offices, and hospital reception areas are designed to set their underlying "products" apart. Letterheads and logos, packaging and vehicles all add value. Design makes intangibles tangible.

Says Harvard Business School professor Robert Hayes: "If potential customers are confronted with two products produced by two equally-regarded companies, having essentially the same cost, performance, reliability, and delivery leadtime,

their purchasing decisions will hinge largely on their perceptions of product appearance and ease of use."[7]

Norio Ogha, president of Sony, concurs. "Design may soon
be the only element that distinguishes one product from another," he says.[8]

Ironically, design is attracting a lot of attention even as
companies learn to add value in so many others ways. With
fewer competitors in most categories, with technology leading
to a convergence of standards, and with customers demanding the best from everyone, design can make all the difference
between failure and dramatic success.

Beauty must be more than skin deep

The reason design leads to differentiation is not just an aesthetic one. Good design grabs attention, but it also improves
functionality, and it's a direct cause of lower costs and better
quality.

In most factories, about two-thirds of total manufacturing
costs go on assembly. The Japanese grasped this fact earlier
than most, and they work hard at what they call "mechatro-
nics" or "design-for-assembly" (DFA).

The driving principle is: Simplify! Simplify! Simplify! Cut
out anything that does not have real purpose, that complicates
production, or that gets in the way of customer delight. Rethink processes to have fewer, easier steps; use snap-on, col-
our-coded modules; eliminate screws and bolts.

The main objective of DFA is to cut costs by speeding
assembly and eliminating mistakes and waste. Once IBM
bought dot-matrix printers from Seiko Epson, then the world's

7   Robert H. Hayes, "Design: the emerging competitive battleground,"
    Designing For Product Success, essays and case studies from the TRIAD
    Design Project exhibit, published by the Design Management Institute,
    1989
8   Paul Kunkel, "Beat the competition," in *Competing By Design,* a special
    advertising supplement published by *Business Week* in 1990

low-cost producer; then IBM designed a printer with 65 per cent fewer parts, that could be assembled in just three minutes — a 90 percent time saving. GE cut the number of parts in a refrigerator compressor from 51 to 29 with a new design. The best-selling Swatch quartz watch has just 54 parts, about half the usual number.

Spinoffs of DFA include the need for fewer suppliers, smaller inventories, and greater flexibility. All of which leads, of course, to efficiencies throughout the production and marketing process, to responsiveness to customers' needs, and to easier after-sales service.

But while design alone triggers a stream of benefits, the design *process*, and the way it's integrated with other activities, yields other gains. For example, by adopting a "rugby approach" in which its whole design and engineering team "ran down the field, passing the ball back and forth," Ford slashed the "concept to customer" time of a new car from five years to 40 months.[9]

Out in the marketplace, when products compete for attention, design is the first thing that gets noticed. But good looks are often only skin deep. I recently bought a great looking little pair of Sony speakers for my Walkman, but it's impossible to get the battery cover off. My BMW has a large flat area around the gear shift which should be perfect for holding things like tapes and sunglasses, but there's nothing to stop them sliding off when you accelerate. My Panasonic telephone is jammed with features I've never understood.

Just as it's important to "design-for-assembly," so it's essential to "design-for-use." Products should look good, feel good, be easy to use, and deliver real performance.

9   Paul Kunkel, ibid.

But don't be fooled by the fact that *you* know how to work the products you sell. Your opinion doesn't count. Ricoh recently discovered that 95 per cent of customers never used three features it had carefully built into its fax machines to make them more attractive. According to a survey of VCR owners, only about 3 per cent watch shows they've recorded off the air; most only play rented movies."Manufacturers of consumer products are not only losing the interest of their customers," warned *Business Week* in a cover story on design, "but they're also alienating them."[10]

❑ Does your product have aesthetic appeal?
❑ Is it "user-friendly"?
❑ Does its design allow for:
  • Cost-effective production?
  • Quality production?
  • Easy installation?
  • Easy repair?
  • Easy addition/removal of parts or accessories?
  • Easy upgrading?
❑ Does it have as few components as possible?
❑ Does its design allow it to be made as fast as possible, or can more time be saved?
❑ Can it be sold across cultures and countries? (Is it a "global product?")
❑ Is it made of non-polluting material, in an environmentally-friendly way? (And are you involved in disposing of it after use?)
❑ Does the packaging have "sex appeal?"
❑ Does the packaging:
  • Clearly describe the product features and benefits?
  • Stand out from the competition?
  • Provide easy-to-understand instructions?

10 Bruce Nussbaum, "'I can't work this thing!'" *Business Week*, April 29, 1991

- Provide adequate protection for the product and the buyer?
- Stack well?
- Hold instructions/accessories, guarantee cards, etc?
- Have other uses after the product is unpacked?
❏ Is the packaging environmentally-friendly?

Manufacturing with customers in mind

In December 1980, Honda broke ground for a new American auto plant in Marysville, Ohio. Just 23 months later, the first Accord rolled off the production line.

In November 1983, the then chairman of General Motors, Roger Smith, announced that his company would invest $5 billion in the Saturn project, designed specifically to counter the Japanese threat. Despite the hype, and in spite of the fact that American motor manufacturers were losing market share month after month, GM then took two years to select a site for the new plant. Construction began in mid-1966, and production began in mid-1990. The first Saturn cars hit the market *six years after the project was announced.* Reviews were less than ecstatic. Almost immediately some vehicles had to be recalled.

The difference in the way these critical manufacturing ventures were handled by Honda and GM is a dramatic illustration of what the West is up against in the new competitive arena. Saturn has a good chance of succeeding. It's a state-of-the-art plant, and has adopted many of the best Japanese work practices. But by the time it's fully on stream, and dealers get an adequate supply of cars, the enemy will have gained valuable time.

Manufacturing is where firms begin to create value for customers. If the factory doesn't "get it right first time" the rest of the business gets tied up trying to fix things. Costs accumulated in the plant can never be stripped away. Poor quality triggers a chain of cover-ups. World

class competitors know that being "best of breed" begins at source. They use manufacturing as a springboard for building advantage.

The factory of the future

As more firms seek ways to increase their competitiveness, they'll be forced to explore new technologies and to upgrade their human resources. It's already impossible to compete in many industries — airlines, consumer electronics, retailing, architecture, to name but a few — without a substantial investment in "knowledgeware." Today you might ship production offshore to take advantage of cheap labour in a third world country; but tomorrow a competitor will beat you on costs by using the latest technology in your home market.

Until recently, Matsushita Electric employed 3 000 Japanese housewives on a subcontract basis to wind hair "a little thinner than a human hair" 16 times through a pinhole in a VCR head, then solder it. Now 530 robots do the same job five times faster, and more reliably. And they work 24 hours a day, every day.

Professor Warren Bennis of the University of South California jokes that the factory of the future "will be run by just one man and a dog. The man's job will be to watch the machines; the dog will be there to bite the man if he touches anything!"[11]

In the manufacturing arena, computers control ordering and inventories, manage machines, monitor quality, and handle despatch. They link factories to designers, suppliers, and distributors, so that information captured by one is instantly available to all, and innovations are shared as they occur. Robots boost productivity, cut waste, drive down costs, improve quality, and compensate for skills shortages.

11 Warren Bennis, in a speech before the American Society for Training and Development, Boston, May 1990

Yet despite the obvious benefits of technology, most firms haven't taken full advantage of it. A great deal of the computing power they already have installed is unexploited.

Despite the early promise of automation, there are still only about 256 000 robots in use in the 16 most industrialized nations. Fully two-thirds are in Japan.[12] In 1989 Japan installed $2,5 billion worth of new ones — many designed and made by the firms that use them — compared to just $400 million worth in the U.S.[13] According to Harvard business school professor Ramchandran Jaikumar, American companies make 25 different products on each piece of equipment, while the Japanese turn out 240.[14] His associate, Robert Hayes, maintains that Japanese firms boost productivity not only because they install more robots, but also because they modify them rapidly and continuously once they're up and working.[15]

One study showed that since 1973 white-collar productivity has fallen by some 7 per cent in America while factory productivity has jumped 51 per cent. This despite the fact that 60 million people now work in offices vs. just 20 million in manufacturing.[16] A survey by Deloitte & Touche revealed that under 30 per cent of U.S. manufacturers believed that technology had given them significant gains, down from 60 per cent just two years previously.[17]

One reason things haven't moved faster is that technology doesn't manage itself; it needs highly-trained people. And there's no point in making heavy investments in machines that

12 Ian Rodger, "Factories Where The Future Works," *Financial Times*, Monday January 7, 1991
13 Gary Slutzker, "Why Japan loves robots and we don't," *Forbes*, April 16, 1990
14 Louis S. Richman, "How America can triumph," *Fortune*, December 18, 1989
15 Interview with the author, January 1990
16 Aaron Bernstein, "Quality is becoming job one in the office, too," *Business Week*, April 29, 1991
17 Gary Slutzker, ibid.

simply do the same old things faster or more cheaply than people. Technology's potential is realized only when underlying tasks are changed, when new things are done in revolutionary ways, when different possibilities are explored.

How's your production technology IQ today? Can you compete with your current capabilities, or is it time for a rapid advance?

❑ What have you done in the last 12 months to introduce new technology into your business?

❑ Is your current production technology adequate?

❑ What technology do your customers and suppliers use that you might link into?

❑ What are your competitors doing in this area?

❑ How are your customers using technology today, and what might they expect in the future?

❑ What technology will you need to be competitive tomorrow?

❑ Is your production process "state-of-the-art" — i.e. is "lean production" a reality in your firm?

Smart machines need smart operators

While technology plays a more important role in most production processes today, and its importance will grow as "smart machines" proliferate, people give a plant its edge.

Unfortunately, many of yesterday's production workers are ill-equipped to cope in the new manufacturing environment. Skills and knowledge that once were appropriate are now useless. If employees could once learn tasks by rote, now they must think and reinvent the tasks they do. If once they could rely on a boss to make all their decisions for them, now they must make major decisions for themselves. So in the factory of the future, as everywhere else, new kinds of people are needed. Some of them at least will need advanced engineering skills. Most will need training in statistical process control. All will need to learn how to solve problems, make decisions, and work in teams.

World class factory workers are often more carefully hired than employees elsewhere. In many cases they're now interviewed by the teams they'll work with, and a gruelling process of eight or nine interviews is commonplace. The objective is a comfortable fit, for these teams work closely together, they manage themselves, their members learn each others' jobs, and they're often paid for their group performance.

❑ Do you have the "skillforce" you need to manage tomorrow's production technology?

❑ Do your production people understand the importance of customers?

❑ Do they have regular contact with customers to gain feedback, information, and insights?

❑ Do they see your advertising before it goes out to the rest of the world?

❑ Do they work in flexible, self-managing teams?

❑ Do they have specific quality standards which they've set with management?

❑ Are they "benchmarking" themselves against the best?

❑ Do they aim for the constant improvement of everything they do?

❑ Do they have a chance to use the products they make, and to try competitors' offerings?

Get your suppliers on your side

With the best will in the world, you and your team can't do all this alone. Other stakeholders must be roped in as partners. Customers must be tapped for a continuous flow of information about what they want, how they think you're doing, and how you can improve. . . influencers must be enlisted to help shape customers' perceptions and expectations. . . competitors must be watched because they force you to change and improve . . . and facilitators must be wooed for they make it possible for you to produce, deliver, and support your products.

Most important of all are *suppliers*. When they invest time, energy, and money in adding value to your products, the gains are enormous. Conversely, if they don't deliver the right raw materials or components, of the right quality, at the right time, at the right price, and with total reliability, they can kill your chances of success with customers.

> **Supplier management — also known as "reverse marketing" — is a crucial element of world class performance. Win-win relationships with *customers* hinge on your having mutually rewarding relationships with your suppliers.**

The motor industry has learned this lesson well. Japanese auto makers have convincingly demonstrated the value of close-knit relationships with suppliers. So in recent years virtually all auto manufacturers have changed their buying practices.

Once, they kept the development of new models a close secret. At the very last moment — maybe just three or four months before they went into final production — they'd call for tenders for various parts. Suppliers would fall over each other to meet the buyers' specifications at the lowest possible price. This meant that companies like GM (which spends $30 billion a year with its North American suppliers alone) and Ford (which spends some $17 billion) never got the benefit of the brains in other companies.

Bumper manufacturers would turn out bumpers as required — not the *best* bumpers possible. Makers of windscreen wipers just did as they were asked; they didn't bother to suggest modifications or improvements because that wasn't expected.

The result was predictable: Suppliers got screwed on price. They had to make a quick killing because the relationships lasted for only a short time. The manufacturers — and their customers — got screwed on quality and innovation.

Today, most competitive companies aim to deal with just a few suppliers. Ten years ago, every GM part was bought from at least two or three sources. Now almost all GM's parts are single-sourced. The company aims for what it calls "collective progress" — hooking suppliers into the earliest stages of product development, and treating them almost like internal departments.

Ford started to change the way it managed suppliers in 1980. First it began rating them for quality — and the standards keep rising. More recently it started looking at their R&D strengths and at what they were doing to improve productivity.

Is the pressure good for them?

"If we sell, they sell," says Ford's production head. "It's survival."[18]

A decade ago Ford bought parts from 3 700 different factories. Now they come from 2 100, and the number will probably drop to 1 800 soon. (Ford Europe has just 900!)

For its highly acclaimed Taurus launch, Ford selected about 400 suppliers. Each provided only one component, whereas in the past they'd made several and thus lost their focus. Every supplier got a long-term contract for up to five years.

(Despite this progress, western firms have a long way to go to catch their Japanese competitors. In Europe, Volkswagen has 2 000 suppliers, GM 1 400, and Renault 800. In Japan, Honda has 300, Toyota 230, Mazda 180, and Nissan 160.)[19]

18 "Re-inventing The Wheel," *The Economist*, April 8, 1990
19 John Griffiths, "Next Stop: Europe," *Financial Times*, survey of the Japanese auto industry, Thursday December 20, 1990

Xerox once bought from 5 000 outside vendors. Now it buys from 400, and by 1992 will deal with just 250. One result: 92 per cent of parts were defect-free in 1983, vs. 99,2 per cent today.

Suppliers are potentially valuable partners in winning with your customer. But the relationship needs a rethink. If it's been characterized by distrust and haggling, things must change. New foundations must be laid.

To make this partnership productive, world class firms go to endless lengths to select the best suppliers. Sometimes they actually help suppliers get started. In other cases they provide financing and share risks to demonstrate their good faith.

After Toyota had shortlisted some 400 potential suppliers for its new Derbyshire plant in the U.K., company teams spent ten months checking them on four key criteria: management attitude and strengths; production facilities and investment in technology; quality; and research and development. This gruelling process cut the list to 250, and it was later chopped even further to 150. Toyota then embarked on a series of presentations to its new "partners," to spell out what it expected from them.[20]

Once they've selected their future partners, world class firms invest a great deal of time and money helping them improve. Often they send their own staff into suppliers' organizations to train people, and to help establish systems and standards. Xerox, for example, offers training in statistical process control (SPC), statistical quality control (SQC), just-in-time inventory management (JIT), and total quality control (TQC).

All this is extremely costly. But it means that suppliers really feel they're part of your team, they understand your business from the inside out, and they're equipped to meet

20 John Griffiths, "How Toyota filters its component suppliers," *Financial Times*, April 10, 1991

your requirements. In Xerox's case, production lead times fell from 52 to 18 weeks, new products hit the market twice as fast, and development costs were cut in half.

When suppliers start believing they're on your team, they start thinking about long-term investments in your business. Start work now to build that trust, and watch the benefits on your bottom line.

❑ Do you actively manage your suppliers so they're "on your side?"

❑ Are your suppliers actively involved in helping you improve the way you do business — i.e., do you expect them to come to the party with ideas and suggestions?

❑ Do you share confidential information with them so they know your needs and your expectations, and so they can be effectively innovative?

❑ Are they involved early enough when you start work on new products or projects?

❑ Do you have the right suppliers — and the right number of them?

❑ How secure are they in their relationship with you?

❑ Are they prepared to invest in it for the long term?

❑ Are they familiar with your standards (specifications, quality, delivery times, quantities, etc.), and have you helped them set their own standards?

❑ Do you train their people?

❑ Do you give them regular updates on what's happening in your market, and how you're changing your strategy?

❑ Do you give them fast feedback on how they're doing?

Pricing for market share and profit

In the new competitive arena, prices typically start high for new products, then fall fast. During the introduction phase of the life-cycle, they have to cover hefty development and launch costs. Later, as the firm gains experience and volume, some costs drop and increased turnover makes up for thinner margins.

Price is obviously a major factor in shaping customers' perceptions of value. It's a factor in every buying decision. However, let me underline yet again the fact that being the cheapest supplier in today's competitive markets is seldom a sustainable advantage. For one thing, customers want ever-improving performance *as well as low prices*. Secondly, no matter how much fat you've cut out of your business system, or how efficient it is, aggressive competitors will quickly match your best prices.

Not everyone agrees with this view. In one study, which asked top U.S. executives, "What drives your company?" a colossal 73 per cent said price was the only way to survive.[21] Companies that sell to grocery chains virtually all complain that price is the most important issue for store buyers (but that low prices aren't always passed on to consumers).

Missionaries of death

Studies of many industries show that there are usually huge gaps between what customers expect and what companies *think* they expect. Price is often much less important to customers than is assumed. The table below shows how various factors are typically ranked internally and externally.

21 A survey conducted by Service 1st Corporation of Waltham, Massachusetts, reported in "Do As I Say, Not As I Do," *Training & Development Journal*, December 1988

DIFFERENT VIEWS OF WHAT CUSTOMERS EXPECT

Attribute	Ranked by supplier	Ranked by customer
Price	1	6
Quality	2	1
Supplier's reputation	3	8
Reliable deliveries	4	2
Technical backup	5	3
Frequency of sales calls	6	4
Innovation	7	5
Complaint handling	8	7

Salesmen almost always see price as the No.1 customer concern. When things get tough in the marketplace they all too quickly say, "We can't sell at these prices." Or, "Nobody's going to buy a product like ours unless we give them a really good deal."

Sales managers have a tough time defending their list prices, terms, or discount structures. But often the price argument is just a cop-out. It's a convenient excuse for salespeople who don't understand their customers, their products, or their jobs. If they really got to grips with their customers' perception of value, and if they reinvented their selling methods, they'd be far more effective.

As it is, they cause dangerous ripple effects. When they're rejected "because of high prices" their feedback has a negative impact back at the office. Management is often so out of touch with the realities of the marketplace that sales reports are their only contact with customers. They read them as if they were gospel. Then they spend their lives trying to hype up the sales team instead of adding value to their products and services, and rethinking their promotional programmes.

When price becomes a stumbling block, and appears to be a customer's major concern, it's often because a product's features and benefits haven't been sold hard enough, and the salesman has forgotten to "sell the sizzle, not the steak." The customer doesn't get the information he needs to make a decision. Nor are his emotional needs met. So he compares what he can see — prices. He haggles about money, and the sales person walks into the trap. The selling process becomes a life-or-death struggle about who can screw whom.

Many sales people are their firms' own worst enemies. To make their quotas — and their commissions — they discount their companies to death. Their product knowledge is abysmal, and their aim is to get the whole messy business over as fast and as painlessly as possible.

One motor retailer I worked with was able to double its return on investment in just three months by demanding a minimum margin from its salesmen. They were told, "Get this level of gross profit, or get out!" Most of them quickly found that it was quite easy getting the sticker price. All they had to do was "put more telling into their selling."

A raw materials supplier balanced price and performance in another way. When one of its biggest customers demanded lower prices, the managing director "unbundled" his service package by making a list of all the services that had been added over time, but were now taken for granted. These included an ordering hotline specifically for that customer, technical advice at all hours, deliveries at odd times and in special quantities (which were often small and, on their own, uneconomic), and so on. Then he walked into the customer's office and said to the MD, "I'll be happy to cut my price, but please tell me which of these services you want me to save on." He kept the business — and got his price!

Sometimes price *is* the key issue. Often it's not. Price is always relative. It's always weighed up against other features and benefits.

Price as a promotional weapon

Worldwide, marketers are shifting their emphasis from long-term brand-building to short-term promotions. Most of these involve some kind of price-cut: a direct discount, two products for the price of one, a sample of a different product, entry into a contest with big prizes, or coupons which can be collected and redeemed for other merchandise. Such promotions can be targeted to specific customers, can involve a limited number of distributors, and can be implemented fast. They may be widely publicised through mass media, or focused through tele-sales, direct mail or knock-and-drop campaigns — or even more narrowly through in-store displays or changes to the price on a label. The most obvious advantages are speed, flexibility, and fast feedback. You can use price promotions tactically, and you know almost immediately how they've worked. You can use them to give a new product a fast start or to boost the sales of an older product. And you can test various approaches at the same time.

All of this makes price a powerful weapon — but also a seductive trap. Using it often appears too easy. When cash is tight or a product is losing share, discounting immediately springs to mind as a way to fix things. In the short term, it might be; longer-term, it can have devastating consequences.

Price is just one aspect of a customer's perception of value. But it's an important one, and must be carefully managed because of the impact it has on other buying criteria.

Most customers love bargains, but cutting prices can kill a product's image. A quick promotion can hurt your chances of ever getting the "right" price for your product. One prices start falling, it's hard to push them

**back up without a radical change in the product offer-
ing. And if competitors react with cuts of their own and
a price war erupts, everyone's prices can quickly fall to
uneconomic levels.**

A product's price looks high or low compared to what's
around it. When Sears tried to make a comeback through a
policy of "everyday low prices" in 1989, customers didn't react
as expected. The bargains no longer stood out so shopping was
less fun. Nor were customers convinced that Sears really was
cheaper than the shop down the block.

When you promise the lowest prices, you'd better deliver.
The claim can become a killer. Supermarkets all claim the
lowest prices, but housewives shop around and know who
really delivers the best bargains. And newspapers often run
telling comparison tests. Customers who get mixed messages
seldom side with the advertiser. Word of mouth recommen-
dations, real-life experience, and "independent" views almost
always win.

Inflation pricing

One time that pricing calls for special judgement is under
conditions of inflation. If you don't increase your prices, you
effectively sell at a discount. If your competitors also choose
not to raise their prices, you all lose margin. But of course, the
problem doesn't affect all firms the same way. If you have a
small share of market, your unit costs will probably be higher
than those of bigger players. They might lose more altogether
(more units X lower price), but they'll also be able to weather
the storm more easily than you can. They may not want to get
into a price war with you because it'll cut their profits; but if
they do, you could be even more seriously hurt.

Under some circumstances, price can be a potent competitive weapon, and price cuts can thus be a sensible investment.
But buying market share costs money in the short term, and

can create long-term difficulties. Once you've cut prices, you might not ever be able to get the prices you really want. And your lowest prices might create a new umbrella under which more efficient competitors can fight you for market share.

There can be no doubt that during this decade, price will become more and more important as a competitive weapon. Companies that haven't worried too much about their fixed costs will slash away mercilessly. But at the same time, they'll do more to add to the perceived value of their products. Innovation and constant improvement of everything will make both goals possible.

❑ Is your price reasonable to customers — i.e., are you seen to offer value for money?

❑ Is your price competitive?

❑ Do you charge enough to:
  • Support your product with promotion?
  • Maintain an adequate level of R&D investment?
  • Provide the training your people need?
  • Make your product profitable for your distributors?
  • Give customers information and training?
  • Provide guarantees and warranties?
  • Grow your business?

❑ Does your price add perceived value to your product?

❑ Does your price offer an umbrella under which your competitors can fight you?

❑ Do you aim to continually drive down your price?

❑ As your price falls, can you still afford to maintain your service levels?

❑ What can you do today to cut your fixed costs?

❑ Is your pricing policy flexible enough?

❑ Do you have an attractive discount structure?

❑ Do you offer financing to customers?

Place: the terrain of battle

Where and how you distribute your products or services
makes them worth more or less to customers. As with every
business decision there are any number of "right" answers.
The options deserve careful analysis.

Owning or tightly controlling your distribution channels
gives you maximum say in the customer relationship. It also
ensures a certain volume of business. So franchising is growing at incredible speed, building societies buy significant
stakes in large estate agencies, and many manufacturers tie up
licensing agreements with their distributors.

> **Middlemen generally add costs. Selected and managed
> well, they add value. Often they help *hold down* costs
> by doing some of the things you'd normally do.**

Distribution through independent third parties has its own
advantages. They can provide finance, share risks, store and
fund inventory, offer specialist service, handle deliveries, deal
with complaints, and make repair calls.

The downside is that, if you let them, distributors can
dictate the way you run your business.

When power shifts

Retailing experts believe that within a decade there will be no
more than half a dozen merchants — and possibly as few as
two — making 60 per cent of retail sales in every category in
America. In 1989, Wal-Mart CEO David Glass predicted that
50 per cent of all retailers would vanish by the year 2000. But
given the current rate of change he says, "I might have under-
estimated."[22] The survivors will have immense control over
their suppliers.

22 Bill Saporito, "Is Wal-Mart unstoppable?" *Fortune,* May 6, 1991

The same power shift is especially evident in the grocery trade. Retailers are forming buying co-operatives across Europe, but especially in France and West Germany. By taking over arch-rival Euromarche, France's Carrefour now controls 15 per cent of French hypermarkets. In Britain, the five biggest supermarket chains account for 55 per cent of food sales. Tesco, Argyll, and Sainsbury alone control 40 per cent of grocery sales, and are opening new stores at a frantic pace.

William McKnight, president/CEO of U.S.-based Nabisco Foods recently said, "The top 10 customers of Nabisco Foods represented 25 per cent of total sales in 1980. In 1989, the top 10 will represent more than 44 per cent. The emergence of extra goodies like reclamation centers, co-op advertising fees far in excess of media costs, diverting, slotting allowances and other 'promotional expenses'" have given retailers the edge over marketers."[23]

In South Africa a handful of major firms such as Metro, Makro, and Score dominate the wholesale distribution business. Three chains — Pick 'n Pay, OK Bazaars, and Checkers — account for a healthy chunk of grocery sales. The Edgars Group and Pep Stores have a strong grip on clothing sales.

One way marketers can retain some power is through strong brands. But even here they're up against the chains. "Own brands" account for 57 per cent of grocery sales in the U.K.; Sainsbury alone launches 300 a year. Virtually every product in Marks & Spencer is an "own brand," and the company has built a great reputation for the way it works with manufacturers to develop innovative new products. Carrefour in France, FDB in Denmark, and Ahold in Holland all push their own quality labels.[24] The big South African chains all have house brands. These account for something like 14 per

23 "Grocery Retailers Get Tougher," *Advertising Age*, May 15, 1989
24 "Fat Boys Have More Fun," *The Economist*, April 29, 1989

cent of Pick 'n Pay's grocery sales and 20 per cent at Checkers and OK Bazaars.

The new shopping experience

The key question in planning a distribution strategy is not, "what is best for us?" but "what is best for our customer?" Will your choice of distribution channel make buying from you easier and more pleasant, or harder and less pleasant?

Accessibility and convenience are important issues in almost every buying decision. So are security, comfort, and ambience. The "shopping experience" is shaped by many things: how far people must travel to shop; parking, the appearance and condition of premises, service, the range and mix of merchandise, the way goods are displayed — and even by other shoppers.

Many companies today take convenience very seriously: direct response marketing is growing faster than most other forms. Catalogues, mailers, toll-free phone lines, and coupons all make life easy for stay-at-home shoppers.

Companies such as Land's End, L.L. Bean, and the Book-of-the-Month Club have built enviable reputations for backing their quality merchandise with fast order fulfilment and no-questions-asked guarantees. Dell Computer, which has cut out retailers to avoid becoming embroiled in their price battles, gets top score from customers for its service.

Retailers must sharply revise their habits if they're to compete. So they're staying open longer, they offer improved personal service, and they constantly improve their merchandise mix. Small stores have become more specialised. Large ones introduce "stores within the store" — or boutiques where limited ranges are sold. Many major retailers are also plunging headlong into the catalogue sales business. Shoppers in a hurry can order 24 hours a day, 365 days a year, pay by credit

card, and get their goods within a day courtesy of Federal
Express.

For most retailers, the mass market is history. The industry
is polarizing — into large, cut-price operators at one end and
specialty stores at the other. Tomorrow's best operators will
know precisely who their customers are, and what value they
buy. They'll tap technology to manage display space, monitor
stock levels, and measure the impact of promotions. With the
help of scanners, smart cards, and even sensors on shelves,
they'll get real-time feedback on customers' buying behaviour. This will make them precision marketers, responding
with fantastic speed to their customers' whims. They'll also
gain increasing power over the brands they sell.

New distribution realities change strategic logic

You can treat these changes as a threat or an opportunity. But
you'd better start gearing up, right now, for the new distribution realities. If you don't make creative decisions they'll be
made for you. If you don't burn the midnight oil to foster new
kinds of relationships with your distributors, your competitors will shoulder you aside.

> **The fact is, changes in distribution methods and tech-
> nology are forcing changes in the strategic logic of
> many firms. It seldom happens without warning, but
> it kills companies that either fail to see the signals or
> choose to ignore them.**

The distribution weapon is a powerful one. By looking outside
your business, at emerging trends, you'll surely find a host of
opportunities for using it to your advantage.

❑ Are your premises in the right place?
❑ Are they easily accessible to anyone who visits you?
❑ Does their layout/appearance enhance your business per-
   formance or impede it?

❑ Is your corporate identity clearly visible? Does it convey the image you want? Is it consistent on everything from signs to stationery?

❑ Are your premises well lit, clean, and orderly?

❑ Do your people have the right equipment?

❑ Is it kept in good condition?

❑ Are your distributors in the right place — i.e., as close to the customer as they should be?

❑ Do their premises meet your standards of appearance, safety, convenience, etc.? (Have you spelled out those standards?)

❑ Do you help dealers design/upgrade their premises?

❑ Do you regularly visit their premises to "shop" there?

❑ Do they display your product favourably — in a way that shows it off, and better than competitors' products?

❑ Is your full product range displayed, together with accessories and add-ons?

❑ Is your product displayed near complimentary products?

❑ Are displays continually changed and improved?

Promotion buys share of mind

Since customer satisfaction is so much a matter of perception, promotion plays a major role in the process. In a global marketplace, the fact that customers everywhere recognize the name of a company, a product or a service is worth a lot. Big brands mean big bucks. And while building them still remains more art than science, science is gaining ground.

> Marketers are starting to "micro-manage" their "de-massified" audiences. The objective: one-to-one communication with a red-hot prospect, and fast feedback so the business system can be fine-focused to meet his precise demands.

Deliver the promise

Advertising is one potent tool in the battle for market share. It not only informs people about a product, it also can add value to the product. Names like Marlboro, Coca-Cola, Heinz, IBM, Cartier, and Shell, to name just a few, are worth a fortune. Brand-building will be even more important in the years ahead.

Now here's the danger: to work, advertising must offer something out of the ordinary. It must make a unique and meaningful promise. But if its claims aren't met, it can do a great deal of damage. In fact, the fastest way to guarantee the demise of a poor product or service is to advertise it. Extravagant promises can come back to haunt you.

"We never kid ourselves about the magic of advertising," said legendary advertising man Bill Bernbach. "The magic is in the product. No matter how skilful you are, you can't invent an advantage that doesn't exist."[25]

Rosser Reeves, former chairman of Ted Bates, had this to say in "two of the ultimate laws of reality in advertising":

"1. Advertising stimulates the sales of a good product and accelerates the destruction of a bad product. To make a claim which the product does not possess merely increases the frequency with which the consumer observes its absence.

"2. A campaign that stresses a minuscule difference, which the consumer cannot observe, in actual practice, also accelerates the destruction of the product."[26]

Advertisers continually wrestle with the question of how far to push their claims. They must attract attention, but they also

25 Interviewed by Denis Higgins in *The Art Of Writing Advertising*, Advertising Publications Inc., 1965
26 Rosser Reeves, *Reality In Advertising*, MacGibbon and Kee, 1961

must be truthful. Ads in a recent issue of *U.S. News & World Report* made these promises:

- ❏ "NEC printers. They only stop when you want them to." (NEC Information Systems.)
- ❏ "A tradition of trust." (Merrill Lynch.)
- ❏ "We treat you with respect, concern and understanding. But don't worry, you'll get used to it." (1st Nationwide Network of Member Banks.)
- ❏ "Come. Feel the warmth of Mexico." (Mexico Tourism.)
- ❏ "Toyota quality. Who could ask for anything more!" (Toyota.)
- ❏ "You're somebody special at Ramada." (Ramada Inns.)

Can you believe them? Will they actually deliver? Over-claiming sets a company up for failure. Most people doubt the credibility of advertising, but even so, they expect to get pretty much what they're promised.

Not long ago, a major supermarket boasted about the freshness of its fruit and vegetables in big full-colour ads; but my wife complained that their produce was anything but fresh and stopped shopping there. Similarly, when a specialized newsletter promised me "invaluable insights," and didn't deliver, I asked for my money back.

You can't leave it to the front line

None of those claims can be left to the front line. Delivering on each of them demands a massive and coordinated team effort. Customers are sceptical of advertising at the best of times, and one weak link, anywhere in the value chain, is all the proof they need that they were right.

Ford runs ads proclaiming that "Quality is Job 1." By making this statement it makes quality its property. Any other auto maker who uses the word in a headline runs the risk of a "me-too" position. But what happens if vehicles must be recalled because of a fault? No matter how well it's handled, the advertising is undermined. It takes plenty of dollars to restore integrity. Every ad that the company runs will, for a time at least, be tainted.

International Paper proclaims that "continual product improvement isn't just an idea that gets bandied around our boardroom. It's a here-and-now quality objective that we pursue every day." This is a powerful message to all the company's stakeholders. But customers had better experience the benefits of those efforts; and the firm's employees had better agree that continual quality improvement really is an objective.

Many audiences will be exposed to the International Paper ads. Mass media always have a "halo" effect. They spill messages into unplanned areas.

Ideally, everyone who reads an ad should feel it makes reasonable promises. But this isn't always possible; various stakeholders have different world views, so they read different things into advertising copy.

Managing all of their perceptions is like a juggling act. Getting it 100 per cent right is virtually impossible. But be alert to the problems, and try to target your promotional messages as narrowly as possible. That way, at least, you limit damage from the fallout.

Advertising claims are always risky, and some advertisers really push credibility to the limit.

For example, when Donald Trump took over the New York–Boston shuttle from Eastern Airlines, he announced his new venture in TV commercials and full-page ads in major newspapers such as *The New York Times* and *The Wall Street Journal*.

Copy promised passengers, "This Thursday, you'll find our airplanes scrubbed inside and out, our terminals clean as a whistle and ready for business, our people able to solve problems, our doors closing exactly on time, our whole operation crisp, disciplined, businesslike, and for our customers, truly wonderful."

Trump took a hell of a chance with those promises. His good intentions could easily have been blown out of the water by virtually any employee. (Yet within just four months he claimed 50 per cent market share.)

Six months after he'd taken over, I decided to test the Trump Shuttle. When I tried to get a seat from Boston to New York, the check-in clerk noted that my ticket was for another airline, and the price was different. But without hesitation she said, "Go ahead. The flight's not full so you'll be OK."

I had too much luggage to carry, but she promised I'd get it back within eight minutes of leaving the plane at La Guardia. In fact, my cases were waiting when I got to the baggage claim area maybe three or four minutes after disembarking.

When promises made in advertising aren't kept in real life, customers take everything else the firm says with a pinch of salt. The best advertising in the world can't save a lousy product or cover up bad service. You might persuade customers to try something once, but you can't fool them into buying again. "The consumer is not a moron," said David Ogilvy, in one of advertising's most memorable lines, "she's your wife."

Real success in the marketplace comes through products and services that really do satisfy customers. It comes from innovative concepts, pleasing design, sound engineering, high-quality manufacturing, superb delivery, convenient distribution, affordable pricing, and a host of other factors. Advertising is just the cherry on top of a multi-layered cake.

Manage your message

A brand is a relationship. It is a guarantee of reliability, a symbol of trust, an expression of confidence. Building a brand takes years; destroying one takes seconds. And winning back lost customers is never easy.

With so much competition for your customers' attention, you need a way to stand out in the crowd. Powerful brands do it for you. Everything you do should contribute to their uniqueness and their strength.

Promotional messages play a key role in establishing customers' expectations, so they must be carefully managed. First prize is a narrowly-targeted message that says exactly what you want, under conditions of your choosing. This is becoming more and more difficult to do.

Few sales result from a single, simple push. Even so-called "impulse purchases" have probably been triggered way in advance. Research shows that 61 per cent of supermarket purchases are planned ahead of a visit to the store.[27] Customers see and hear ads, read articles about products and services, and rely heavily on the views of other people. Virtually every sale is the culmination of a complex mix of messages, customer experiences, and the needs and wants they have at a particular moment.

Buying decisions are shaped by many different forms of marketing communication: personal selling, advertising, public relations, and sales promotion (discounts, special displays, incentives, contests, etc.) These activities have seven essential purposes:

1. They gain attention from potential customers, and they keep company, product, or brand names in view.
2. They tell customers what to expect, so they set standards for your firm to meet.
3. They provide information, so they let customers make informed choices (they also help customers *justify* their purchases).

27 "When shoppers decide what to buy," *Advertising Age*, July 16, 1991

4. They "wrap your product or service in value" (this gives your "generic" product an edge over the competition, and can allow you to demand a higher price for it.
5. They spur customers to change, to experiment, to explore new options.
6. They confirm that customers have made sound buying decisions.
7. They build customer loyalty.

Costs out of control

Marketers everywhere wrestle with soaring costs. It takes $150 000 to produce the average TV commercial in America, and millions more to air it. So companies are worried about the effectiveness of their promotional investment. That old saw attributed to Lord Leverhulme, "I'm wasting half my advertising budget, but I don't know which half," is truer now than ever.

Unfortunately, there still is no accurate way to measure mass advertising's impact on sales. Measures of audience awareness, understanding, approval, or even intention to buy, do not automatically translate into sales. The awards that the ad industry gives itself for creativity are seldom an indicator of share gains or added profits for clients.

A lot of advertising is a complete waste. In many cases its only benefit is the control the advertiser has over the *content* of his message. But the moment that ad is published or broadcast it's at the mercy of an increasingly "noisy" environment. The average consumer today is bombarded with messages and confused by a cacophony of promises. Remote-controls and VCRs let viewers tune out and control what they see. Readers of magazines and newspapers flip directly to their favourite pages or to hot items, and ignore the rest.

The result is that astute marketers are spending their budgets elsewhere. According to Gary Tellis, a professor at the

University of Iowa, only about a third of the average marketing budget goes on advertising, down from about half 15 years
ago.[28] John Philip Jones of Syracuse University says that ad-
spend in major media in the U.S. has remained at 1,5 per cent
of GNP since 1984.[29] Promotions account for more than 65 per
cent of most marketing budgets.[30]

Retail chains are seizing control not just of distribution, but
also of manufacturers' promotions. They demand hefty co-op
ad budgets. They charge for displays, and decide when and
how to put them up. And some, such as Boots in the U.K., and
Safeway Stores, Lucky Stores, Save Mart Foods, and Payless
Drug Stores in the U.S., sell advertising time on their own
in-store radio programmes.

These trends will accelerate. They will lead to new marketing techniques and more focused media. Dialogue and flexibility will be the new priorities.

Customer databases are growing; computer lists contain a
rich lode of information, and more companies are capturing
it, combining it and adding value to it, and selling it. Laser
printers make highly personalised mailings possible. Cable
TV offers subscribers the programmes they want without all
the other stuff they "zap." Radio stations specialise in jazz,
rock, talk shows, or news.

New publications appear daily that are directed at specific
audiences: over-50s, teenagers, "greenies," car buffs, trout
fishermen, art directors — the list goes on. One media expert
predicts that "at least 200 new lifestyle and 'niche' magazines
will be introduced each year for the next 10 years."[31]

28 William F. Allman, "Science 1, Advertisers O," *U.S. News & World
    Report*, May 1, 1989
29 Regis McKenna, "Marketing is everything, *Harvard Business Review*,
    January-February 1991
30 Magid M. Abraham and Leonard M. Lodish, "Getting the most out of
    advertising and promotion," *Harvard Business Review*, May-June 1990
31 Allen Banks, executive VP-director of Media at Saatchi & Saatchi, N.Y.,
    "What's ahead for media buyers," *Advertising Age*, November 13, 1989

Local audiences can be reached via regional magazines and split runs of major publications such as *Time, Newsweek, Reader's Digest*, and the *Wall Street Journal*. But astute marketers are calling for even more precise targeting. So journals such as *U.S. News & World Report, Metropolitan Home,* and *Selective Farming* go a step further: using selective binding and ink-jet printing, they have begun customizing certain sections for key audiences — and potentially they can tailor ads for each subscriber.

It currently costs about $400 to make a sales call in the U.S. Marketers must aim to cut the cost of customer contact, and simultaneously make each "touch" more meaningful and profitable. So more money must be spent identifying the best prospects and pre-selling them. Sales training must get more resources. Sales aids must become more impactful, more informative, more involving. Every contact with a customer must be carefully coordinated with all the others.

Add impact, increase complexity

Most companies fight themselves in the battle for customers' attention. Their direct mail shots say one thing, ads another, press releases something else — and their sales people then undo the whole message. What these firms should do is construct their attack in "layers," and come at customers from different directions at once.

The first step is to decide on a core message, and the medium that will carry it best. Then, carefully weigh up the marginal impact of each option that you might add. Keep exploring new ways to drive your message home or to widen the audience it reaches.

Even as you remain mindful of the need for focus, consider how you might reach your customer with an integrated programme: a simultaneous bombardment from many directions; or a press ad today, a radio commercial tomorrow, a mail shot next week. And plan where your sales person fits in; how your sports sponsorship will position you in the public mind; and how your social responsibility investments should reinforce the entire process.

> **Like every other aspect of business today, world class promotion is fast, flexible, opportunistic. It has a long-term purpose and a consistency to it, but continuous feedback and measurement triggers tactical switches. Promotion is an extension of the business system, and whatever it promises is driven by customer needs and wants.**

Zero-base your promotional programme

The promotional effort has a very direct bearing on customer perceptions. It needs to be carefully managed, from zero-base. Every cent that's spent must be an investment in a single-minded message.

❑ Do all your promotional efforts make the same simple, single-minded sales promise?

❑ Do you have the right balance between:
   • Personal selling?
   • Advertising?
   • Public relations?
   • Promotions (i.e., incentives, direct mail offers, displays, sponsorships, etc.)

❑ Do you have specific, measurable objectives for each activity?

❑ Are your various promotional messages focused at clear target audiences?

❑ Do messages "overlap" — i.e., do your various activities support each other?

❑ Do your promotional messages add value to your product?

❑ Do you use the best possible combination of facts and feelings in your messages — i.e., do you appeal to customers' heads and hearts?)

❑ Can you support your claims?

❑ Do your promotional messages create reasonable customer expectations — or demands that you can't meet?

❑ Do they clearly set you apart from your competitors?

❑ Are all of your people exposed to your promotional messages before customers see or hear them?

❑ If you make special offers, are your people equipped to deliver when the time comes?

❑ Do you spend enough money promoting your product?

❑ Do you use the most effective media?

❑ Do you actively encourage word-of-mouth support for your product?

❑ Do you get systematic feedback from stakeholders about your promotional efforts?

CHAPTER FOURTEEN

MANAGING THE PROCESS

Surrounding the "4 Ps" on the opportunity map are another four issues which drive performance. These are leadership, the management style, the organization's structure and systems, and the way front line people act.

Leading from the front

If there's one factor that consistently gets in the way of most companies' attempt to become world class, it's the poor example set by their top executives.

In one large company, the chief executive and his top team all agreed that customer focus was the way to go. All agreed that they had to personally change. Yet after two months of talking, their people were still saying, "Why don't you greet me?" . . . "Why don't you smile?" . . . "Why don't you listen?"

The managing director of another big firm is one of the best speakers on customer service I've ever heard. He says all the right things, says them brilliantly, and has a great deal of charisma. But judging by his behaviour, he either hates or fears customers, or simply doesn't think they're worthy of his time. He never visits them. He never talks to them on the phone. He's always too busy with something else.

There's no quicker way to kill customer service. The leader simply has to model the desired behaviour. Managers at all levels must pick it up and follow his example.

No change will occur until more business leaders become marketing-driven; until they accept that engin-

eering, procurement, accounting, and manufacturing are there in the service of customers; until they personally *act* as though customers were important; and until they learn to treat their people as a real asset.

Jim Burke, CEO of Johnson & Johnson spends 40 per cent of his time communicating the company's credo. SAS president Jan Carlzon had a video monitor installed in his office so he could check that his planes were taking off and landing on time; when they were late, he called the pilot in the cockpit and gave him hell. Sam Walton, 71-year-old founder and chairman of Wal-Mart Stores, America's fastest-growing retailer, suffers from two deadly forms of cancer yet still flies his own twin-engined Cessna around the country to visit his stores. He called on 19 in one day in 1990. A favourite task is to lead his "associates" (he doesn't call them employees) in reciting "the Sam pledge":

> "From this day forward every customer that comes within 10 feet of me, regardless of what I'm doing, in this house, I'm going to look him in the eye, I'm going to smile, I'm going to greet him with a 'Good morning,' or a 'Good afternoon,' or a "What can I do for you?' so help me Sam!"[1]

Corny? Maybe. But it's worked for Walton. Competitors like K mart and Sears wish they could copy his formula.

The point is, all these remarkably successful men are prepared to do things that others consider beneath them. They have a superb grasp of the strategies that make their organizations successful, but they also have the common touch.

Most of today's senior executives are prisoners of the machine age. The world has changed, but they've stood still.

---

1   Vance H. Trimble, ibid. "Sam Walton's hunt for more," *M*, December 1990

They're imprisoned by their own notions of "scientific management." They've made themselves incredibly vulnerable.

A message to leaders

If you're going to point your company at customers, you have to point yourself that way. You have to lead from the front. This means that you have to change your priorities. You have to start spending time in new ways.

John Kotter a professor at the Harvard Business School, and an authority on leadership, says that the inventors of modern management "were trying to produce consistent results on key dimensions expected by customers, stockholders, employees, and other organizational constituencies" so they "created management to help keep a complex organization on time and on budget." Leadership, in contrast, establishes direction . . . aligns people . . . motivates and inspires them . . . and produces change.[2]

This does not mean simply that managers focus on the here and now while leaders look way ahead. There is a tension between the two roles. Managers and leaders share many of the same tasks. But while the former is more concerned about stability, the latter must constantly fight stability and stagnation.

In some circumstances, you'll get the most out of your people by rolling up your sleeves and getting stuck in with the rest of them. You have to talk budgets and challenge tactics and take the lead in customer presentations. Being a "hands-on" operator says that you're not afraid of hard work, and that you're not too important to leave it to others. It also underscores the importance of certain tasks. (And anyway, says professor Abraham Zaleznik, a colleague of Kotter's at the

2   John P. Kotter, *A Force For Change*, The Free Press, 1990

Harvard Business School, "True leaders find romance in the substance of business.")[3]

More often, however, you should do what *you're* employed for: that is, to create an environment in which people can perform, to create the direction they need, and to keep on raising their sights. And above all, to change their sense of possibilities and to make sense of the chaotic environment.

The most effective leaders set almost impossibly high standards for their teams. They demand exceptional performance. They refuse to get bogged down by problems, or to be side-tracked by issues that are interesting but which will take them no nearer their goals. Says UCLA professor Warren Bennis, author of *Leaders* and *On Becoming a Leader*: "Leaders conquer the context — the volatile, turbulent, ambiguous surroundings that sometimes seem to conspire against us and will surely suffocate us if we let them — while managers surrender to it."[4]

This is sometimes frustrating to their people, who feel comfortable with tangible issues, and like to worry nitty-gritty matters like a dog with a bone. When the leader keeps espousing a distant goal that they cannot imagine, they think he's not listening to them, and are likely to drift.

But the leader's purpose is counter this tendency, to sell his vision so compellingly that they adopt it as their own, and to sift through their clamour for the ideas that will help get there.

For the average firm, becoming world class is not even a dream. When you start talking about a goal like this, it's so big that few of your people will even understand it — and they certainly won't see the need for it. So while they might agree to go along for the ride, chances are they'll think you've lost your marbles.

3   Abraham Zaleznik, "What is leadership? Talent and vision!" *World Link*, No.3/1991
4   Warren Bennis, "Managing the dream: leadership in the 21st Century," *Training*, May 1990

Understand this and accept it, but don't be put off by it. The next century will not be won by small thinkers. Wimps won't survive.

Work fast to get some small wins under your belt. Show your people that while the vision might be years away, at least you're making some progress towards it. With enough push and persuasion, with innovation and single-minded action, they'll get the message.

❑ Is customer satisfaction driven from the top in your organization?

❑ Do you visibly go out of your way to show that customers count?

❑ Do you spend enough time clearly spelling out your company's strategy?

❑ Are you accessible to employees and customers?

❑ Do you spend enough time outside your office, talking to them?

❑ Are you a good listener?

❑ Do you encourage and support ideas, and do you act on suggestions?

❑ Do you create a climate of trust throughout the organization?

❑ Do you allow corporate politics to get in the way of performance?

❑ Do you make people feel important?

❑ Do you delegate enough responsibility and authority?

❑ Do you encourage people to take on big challenges, and support them when they make mistakes or fail?

❑ Do you believe in growing people, or do you see them as disposable resources?

❑ Are you an expert in your industry?

❑ Are you alert to changes in the marketplace?

❑ Are you innovative in your responses?

The end of autocracy

If people on the front line are to deliver exceptional service, they've got to managed in a way that makes it possible. They must have not only information and resources, but also the support of the total business system. They must be able to make whatever decisions are needed to positively surprise customers.

One thing everyone needs to perform is a sense of involvement and the ability to make a difference. Managers must move beyond making them *feel* important to making them *important.* The difference is huge, and making it happen is easier said than done.

> **You can make someone feel important with a smile, a pat on the back, a nominal title, or some token reward. To make them really *important,* however, you have to give them meaningful work and the authority to carry it out. You have to let them think, invent novel solutions to problems, take chances, make mistakes, and stretch their limits. Above all, you have to listen to them, and involve them in key decisions.**

Participation still a fad

Since the famous Hawthorne experiment back in 1929–32, human resources experts have pushed the idea that people are more productive when they're involved in decision-making. Concepts such as participative management and empowerment took hold in some companies in the 1980s, and there's abundant evidence that they produce results. Quality circles, one mechanism used to formally encourage participation, are used with apparent success in many countries. More and more companies are shifting their emphasis from individuals to teams. Information is more widely shared.

Yet participative management is still largely a fad. It is non-existent in most firms, and there appears to be little interest in fostering it. (In a survey of 450 senior executives in 335 companies in 11 countries, only the Brazilians rated participative management as a human resources priority. According to *Personnel* magazine, "Japan, the home of quality circles, saw participative management as being outside management's reach — perhaps because Japan has already integrated those ideas so thoroughly."[5])

The "command and control" methods that most senior executives have grown up with are no longer appropriate. Firstly, the people who report to them are products of a generally more liberal age, and they demand a say in whatever affects their lives. Second, "knowledge workers" are valuable precisely because they can think for themselves; to prevent them from doing that, or to hinder them in any way, is to waste their special skill. And third, no manager can keep up with the rapid and complex changes occuring everywhere all the time; even if he could monitor them, it would be impossible to cope with them.

Pave the way for a new management style

If more participation makes sense, why is it not more wide-spread?

Reasons range from top managers' perception that "a firm hand on the tiller" is vital, to the unwillingness of many employees to take responsibility; from yesterday's systems getting in the way, to the apparent poor quality of decisions taken by "the wrong people."

What virtually all the excuses hinge on is summed up in one word: *trust*. Managers don't trust their people to get things right, and employees don't trust themselves either. (Nor do they trust their managers, but that's another issue.) These

5   "A Look At International HR Priorities," *Personnel,* Volume 67, No. 10, October 1990

negative expectations all round cause power — and risk — to be concentrated as high in the organization as possible.

Breaking this "cycle of failure" begins not with pious statements of intent, but with a redesign of the organizational mind. That, in turn, starts with a real change in behaviour.

To say that managers must get their act together, be more imaginative about how things might work, and take some chances with their people, is to state the obvious. It's also too simple.

Their responsibility is to deliver results. They are paid to protect their firms from risk. They cannot just "let go."

The move towards a more participative style of management cannot be taken lightly, and mustn't be rushed. The ground must be carefully prepared.

One factor that has a great impact on performance in Japanese organizations, but that is almost totally ignored in the West, is the way they socialize new recruits. Many of the firms I work with have no induction process at all; a few take newcomers on a quick "tour of the plant," introduce them to people who happen to be nearby, and send them home with a few brochures and perhaps the annual report.

In contrast, consider what happens when someone joins Honda R&D Company, a unit of the Honda Motor Company. About 90 per cent of the company's Japanese recruits are university graduates. They spend two weeks in an orientation programme, three months in the manufacturing division, three months in a dealership, and six months in various R&D centres. Then they move to a technical centre where they work closely with older hands for two years. After that it takes them about eight years to become a fully-fledged engineer, and sometime in the next seven years they might start to manage a few others. But even then, the learning process continues; for several weeks each year they must work in other parts of the company, to learn how things work there.[6]

People who are introduced to an organization this thoroughly need little explicit control. They develop an innate feel for "what counts around here" and "the way we do things around here." They soak up information and they gain new insights; they learn by doing and by watching their *sensei* (master); and they develop an invaluable network of associates in other parts of the firms.

While every company won't follow this laborious practice, the underlying lesson deserves attention. What Honda R&D, and many other Japanese firms teach us is that it takes time for people to become fully-functioning, productive members of a team. Before they can be set free, they must, in a sense, be conditioned to cope with their freedom.

To many managers, participative management implies weakness. They fear it will require them to give up their power. But world class managers know that power is a gift from others, that it must be earned, and that it cements a relationship in a very different way than does coercion.

When a top executive rules "by the gun," those who report to him model his behaviour. People throughout the system do roughly what they're told. They limit contact and communication, and they're cautious about expressing their views or making suggestions.

On the other hand, when circumstances are created which make a new kind of relationship possible, when the leader is able to confidently share responsibility and authority, the ripples of positive change spread fast.

6   Lance Ealey and Leif G. Soderberg, "How Honda cures 'design amnesia,'" *The McKinsey Quarterly*, Spring 1990

Middle managers in the way

The interface between managers and the people who report to them has a direct bearing on the company-customer interface. If the chief executive is the role model, middle managers are the "relays" that carry his example to the outer edges of the organization. And here's where efforts to become world class are most likely to be sabotaged.

People who've worked their way up through an organization have a serious investment in the status quo. Turf is terribly important. Wielding power feels good. Perks aren't easily given up. And of course, egos are always involved.

Middle managers are an endangered species, and they know it. Everywhere they look, their peers are being shoved out of work. So any hint of change presents a serious threat to their status and their security.

When you begin the move towards superior service, it's vital that managers at all levels take ownership of the idea, and really commit themselves to it. But it's not enough to just get their attention and their word. They need to be trained to manage in new ways. This should be started even before front line people are involved.

❑ Do your managers understand your industry well enough to be effective competitors in it?

❑ Do their track records inspire confidence?

❑ Are they aggressive enough as competitors?

❑ Does the management style in your firm empower people to exceed customers' expectations, or does it block performance?

❑ Is participative management:
  • Something people talk about?
  • A reality in some areas only? (Or at some levels?)
  • Widespread practice?
  • Regarded as a lot of nonsense?

❑ Are your managers office-bound, or do they get around to see the people who affect your firm's performance?

❑ Are they task or people oriented?
❑ Do they spend enough time coaching their people?
❑ Are they prepared to bend the rules to help a customer?

Supervisors' skills

Is there a place for supervisors in the firm of the future? No more than for most middle managers. Structures are being flattened, and horizontal cooperation is making hierarchies obsolete. People are being encouraged to work in teams, and they're increasingly empowered to manage themselves. Supervisors are yesterday's link between management and front line people — and often they're the weakest link in the chain. They're poorly selected, inadequately trained, under-supported, and starved of information.

If you can't eliminate their function fast, plan to so as soon as possible (perhaps by reassigning them). Meanwhile, pay more attention to these vital link people. Do everything you can to make sure they're behind your plan to become world class. If you don't, they'll kill your efforts in one way or another.

Supervisors need to learn how to manage knowledge workers. They must be empowered if they're to empower the people reporting to them. They need help to become better communicators, to learn how to listen, and to discover the motivational power in challenging others.

❑ Do your supervisors manage your people in the most positive, constructive way?
❑ Are they prepared to listen to their people — and do they make a habit of it?
❑ Are they committed to your service efforts, or do they get in the way?
❑ Do they believe in your "customer first" philosophy, or do they pay lip service to it and quietly sabotage it?

Architecture that works

The familiar organization chart is a "map" that explains who does what, who talks to whom, and where the power lies. Typically, it's a many-layered pyramid with the thinkers at the top, doers at the bottom. In-between are the middle managers, whose job is to pass instructions down and information up, but who generally trap, filter, and distort messages travelling in both directions. In the traditional organization, front line workers are the lowest form of human life. Getting things done is a nightmare, except by bucking the system and risking their jobs. So people do as they're told, the way they're told to do it. They seldom challenge, question, or answer back. Nor do they test the limits of their potential.

But imagine the organization turned upside-down. The new design offers a dramatically different view of roles, responsibilities, and relationships. Front line people are where they should be — right on top. The CEO supports the whole structure, and people at other levels support the rows above them. Each person has a "customer" whose well-being and performance is all-important. This isn't an original idea: Jan Carlzon did it at SAS, and Nordstrom, the dynamic American retailer, also does it. Nor do you have to actually re-draw your organization chart; imagining it upside down is good enough.

Seeing the organization like this, it's possible to "zero-base" the design of a business system that really delivers. Simply ask, of each person, "What's the very least he needs to serve his customer?"

Inverting the pyramid is one radical way to force fresh thinking about who does what and how. But it's not enough. If the wrong people are in the wrong jobs, and if they don't clearly understand their roles, they simply can't be effective. And they'll drag their colleagues down with them.

What's more, if your organization has too many layers or unduly complex reporting lines, communication will be blocked and bureaucracy will flourish. You can't expect people to respond rapidly and creatively to customers' needs if they have to claw their way through the hierarchy for answers. Nor can you expect them to "achieve extraordinary things" in the face of such adversity.

If you want them to be creative, to think on their feet, and to respond fast and imaginatively to customers' demands, you have to make it possible. That means removing some layers from your organization (three to five should be all that are left), opening doors, and encouraging communication.

It also means you have to cut all that rubber-stamping, and simplify every approval process. Or, best of all, that you give people real responsibility and make them accountable for serious work — and for measurable results.

As Jan Carlzon put it, ". . . by giving more responsibility to the front-line personnel, we are letting them provide the service that they had wanted to provide all along but couldn't because of an inflexible hierarchical structure."[7]

Most organizations not only have far too many layers, but also far too many people in "staff" positions. These "experts" and advisors can't make a damned thing happen. Getting rid of some of them shouldn't be too difficult. Taking a knife to your organization chart will send shudders of fear through the hierarchy, but it has the same effect as pruning a tree: it induces a strong surge of new life into the system.

A network of networks

Okay, so you've slimmed down and got the company standing on its head. But that's still not enough if you expect to keep up with the best. For you're still trapped in a fundamentally unchanged structure. People might have a different understanding of what drives the firm, and of the importance of

7   Jan Carlzon, *Moments of Truth*, Ballinger, 1987

front line people, but they still have their little boxes and their neat reporting lines.

The next step is to abandon your hierarchical organization chart, and think about totally redesigning the way things work in your firm. What should you aim for?

1. Every person should feel informed, involved, and trusted. They should want responsibility, they should be given it, and they should be equipped to handle it.

2. Insofar as is possible, symbols and signals of status should be removed so that people feel good about themselves, feel a sense of equality and fairness, and feel that they're equal contributors to the team's performance.

3. Communication should be made as easy and effective as possible. People should be easily accessible, and talk to each other rather than write memos.

4. People should not feel the need for power plays. Climbing to the top on the backs of others should be impossible.

5. The best people should be matched to each key task. This means that skills and talents can't be confined to departments, divisions, branches, or whatever; instead, they must "go with the flow" of challenges and priorities.

6. People must be trained to do many different tasks, and to perform equally well in a number of functions. They must understand each other's jobs, and it must be easy for them to share the workload, to offer support, or to fill in when a colleague is absent from work.

7. Once they're recruited to handle a project, people shouldn't be trapped in the team forever. When the job's done, they should be free to move off and take on a new assignment.

What all this suggests, of course, is a loose network of skilled people, which comes together as needed, then disbands and re-forms, perhaps with different members. Alvin Toffler called it an "adhocracy." Peter Drucker likens the organization of the future to an orchestra. Charles Handy talks of the "shamrock" organization. Harvard Business School professor D. Quinn Mills refers to "corporate clusters."[8]

As I suggested earlier, it's essential to involve both customers and suppliers in many strategic discussions. However, there's good reason to think even more widely. For given the communicating power of computers, this embryo grouping of teams could tap into an industry network which might include competitors, trade associations, and regulators; and a global network which links all these plus R&D laboratories, customer data banks, freight forwarders, media, and any number of other organizations. The total network thus spans not just departmental, business unit, or corporate boundaries, but also national and even international ones.

The concept of strategic alliances is still in the experimental stage. But the potential for new organizational forms, for networking, for ever more rapid and effective learning, and for subtler communication, is enormous. The first place to build those alliances is right inside your company. But don't stop there. Imagine your firm enmeshed in the densest possible web of information and ideas, and start redesigning it today.

❑ Does your organizational structure facilitate customer service or get in the way of it?

❑ Are the right people in the right roles, with the right responsibility and authority?

❑ Is the organization structure flat enough, or are there too many layers?

❑ Can communication flow easily and effectively through the organization?

❑ Does everyone understand that they have internal customers, who those customers are, and what they need and expect?

8   D. Quinn Mills, *Rebirth of the Corporation*, John Wiley & Sons Inc., 1991

Fix that sluggish system!

Every organization needs controls. They're particularly important in a complex world, when decisions are being made fast and in many places at once, and when mistakes can cost a fortune. On the other hand, too much control slows things down and gets in the way of entrepreneurial action.

Systems, policies, and procedures all affect the way people act. They're either supportive or constraining. Far too often, they're designed to suit some mythical "them," with little or no thought for how they impact on customers. They're defended to the death, like some precious relic of the past.

❏ In a large beverage company, general managers were given budgets for personnel, but couldn't hire anyone without asking a regional director. The policy was irritating, and it stopped managers hiring much-needed help in a hurry because the senior man wasn't always available. But, far worse, it said the the GMs, "You might be responsible for big results, but you'll be second-guessed on the little things."

❏ Not long ago, in a workshop I ran for a telecommunications company, I met a thoroughly demotivated service engineer. One of his major gripes was that he had to drive a truck while his colleagues got cars. The reason? "Ten years ago, the person who did my job had to climb poles to fix the equipment," said the engineer. "So he needed a ladder. And he needed a truck to carry the ladder. But today I carry a briefcase with some printed circuit boards in it. I walk into the customer's premises, remove his faulty circuit board, and replace it with a new one. But still I have the truck!"

It's plainly stupid policies like this that drive people crazy, and get in the way of their performance. When they're enforced, people react in one of two ways: (1) they buck the system, or

(2) they just goof off. After all, if management shows it isn't serious, why should *they* be serious?

But being responsive to customers calls for attention to more mundane issues, too. Any firm that hasn't already started a serious "work out" programme to get rid of paperwork and to streamline the way everything is done, is a victim of its own bureaucracy. If you asked your own people what gets between them and their customers, they'd point out dozens of stupid little tasks that could be killed immediately.

So what are you waiting for?

❑ Do systems exist that make it easy for people to get/understand/use information from the marketplace?

❑ Do all your people get enough information — and the right information?

❑ Do they get information quickly enough, in a digestible form

❑ Could you cut down on paperwork?

❑ Do people get sufficient accurate, honest, and useful feedback on their performance, and on how the company as a whole is doing?

The technology revolution

The information age is about four decades old. During that brief time technology has extended the boundaries of what we can do, and transformed the way we do things. Yet still we have a lot to learn about how to tap the awesome potential of thinking machines in the service of our customers.

Computers allow marketers to collect vast amounts of information about consumers and their shopping habits. Over 90 per cent of American products now bar-coded. More than 50 per cent of U.S. supermarket purchases, and about one-third of British ones, occur in stores where scanners read those codes. Store debit cards give instant feedback on who's buying

what. "People meters" monitor how much television customers watch, and which programmes they tune in to.

British retailers like Laura Ashley, Littlewoods, and Asda,
the supermarket chain, use customer data to build win-win
relationships with both customers and suppliers. Buy a dress
from Laura Ashley today, and pay for it with a store card, and
within six months you can expect a mailshot promoting another one. Asda's scanning information is sold to manufacturers of fast-moving consumer goods, who use it to evaluate
new products, pricing, and displays.

Eagle Star Direct, the direct marketing arm of the Eagle Star
insurance group, has built a database of some 900 000 existing
and potential clients. The firm captures client profiles from
their application forms. Postcodes give useful clues as to the
socio-economic status of policyholders. By analyzing client
profiles, Eagle Star can learn what kinds of promotion they
respond to (for example, press ads or mail drops), and how
they respond (by phone or by coupon). The company uses the
information to attract new clients, renew policies with existing
clients, and track the performance of new products.[9]

Industrial marketers are also using technology to get right
under the skin of their customers. Their sales people use
laptops to call up key data, to monitor stock levels, to place
orders, and to manage their time, their territories, and their
expenses.

**Computers speed up processes, and give virtually
everyone easy access to facts and records. (They even
check their own health, and call for help when there's
a problem.) Electronic mail speeds up communication.
Organizations have become "transparent." With the
aid of technology, you can see right through them. This**

9 Dave Madden, "Shoppers' minds are on the cards," *Financial Times*, July
4, 1991

has significant implications for every aspect of management.

As John Naisbitt pointed out in *Megatrends,* this high-tech world calls for more "high-touch." Machines can do a lot of things better, faster, and cheaper than people, but customers want personal attention. They want to be loved and cared for.

And of course, just as computers benefit marketers, so they also benefit customers. For one thing, they let customers hook directly into supplier networks to check prices, delivery dates, and so on. They also expand customers' options, by enabling them to rapidly compare the offerings of various suppliers. And when they've made a choice, they can order and pay at the touch of a button.

Technology holds the promise of greater productivity in almost every industry. But superior technology doesn't necessarily lead to superior service or cut jobs. "Computers often fall short of their apparent productivity-enhancing potential," says the *Wall Street Journal.* "Some industries even find that new technologies increase their need for labor rather than diminish it."[10]

Getting the best from technology doesn't hinge only on getting the *best* technology. It's far more complicated than that. Harvard Business School professor Shoshana Zuboff does a fine job of analyzing the problem in her seminal book *In The Age Of The Smart Machine.* Conducting research in a bank, for instance, she heard managers talk about "meaning as a central challenge in the informated organization." What they recognized, of course, was the futility of employing people who just looked at screens without understanding what they were seeing.

10 "Working Smart : With Labor Scarce, Service Firms Strive To Raise Productivity," *The Wall Street Journal,* June 1, 1989

She also heard them call for people who were "more oriented toward abstract thinking"; people who could switch from thinking of products as material things to thinking of them as "conceptual innovations"; people who were "conceptualizers . . . not afraid to think in abstractions and learn through analysis"; people skilled in "data-based inferential reasoning" and with a solid theoretical understanding of the business to help them "navigate" in the information-rich environment.[11]

Advances in technology offer many opportunities for better service. But don't ever expect machines to rescue you from a lousy way of doing things. If people can't make a system or a process work, investing in computers or robots will make things worse, not better.

Differentiation through data

One of the key uses of technology is to differentiate your product or service in the minds of customers. Knowledge is embedded in more and more products, and plays a growing role in service marketing. Information about buyers lets you customize what you do for them.

"From my point of view," says John Watson, director of information management at British Airways, "the aircraft is a commodity. Airlines fly to the same places, use the same fuel. The only differentials are the customer service, management skills and staff we employ — and the computer systems we use."[12]

Nedlloyd, a Dutch freight firm, sees itself as a "distribution architect," using computers to assign cargoes to low-cost, independent operators.[13]

11 Shoshana Zuboff, *In The Age Of The Smart Machine*, Basic Books, Inc., 1988
12 John Lawless, "King Of The Jet Set," *Business*, February 1989
13 "Teasing Goliath," *The Economist*, December 9, 1989

R.R. Donnelley & Sons, America's biggest printer, sees itself in competition not just with other printers, but with anyone who can help clients communicate. With the help of satellites, it can print documents simultaneously in the U.S., Europe, and Japan. Digital technology lets it print on paper, magnetic disc, or compact disc.[14]

McKesson Corporation, America's largest wholesale pharmaceutical distributor, uses computers to redefine the function of the middleman. A strategy review in the 1970s revealed that the company had to do something different to survive and grow in the 1980s. The company's turnover wasn't growing, and its customers — independent pharmacies — were being killed by the chains. Management first set out to make its own operations super-efficient, then began devising ways to make its DP capabilities useful to suppliers and customers. In effect, McKesson became part of their marketing teams.[15] Today, after a $125 million investment, computers impact on every step in the value chain. They not only link suppliers and retailers, but transform their relationship. McKesson helps suppliers analyze markets, manage stock, and plan new products. And it helps retailers order effectively, plan their displays, and control prices.

Computers are changing the possibilities of business. But again, speed is of the essence: once you get left behind in the technology game, it's hard to catch up.

Fare wars

Investment in technology by service businesses is rising to match that in manufacturing. In many industries, it's vital to being able to compete, and thus presents a daunting barrier to entry. Hotels, retailers, architects, and accountants spend

14 Ronald Henkoff, "How to plan for 1995," *Fortune*, December 31, 1991
15 "Foremost-McKesson : The Computer Moves Distribution To Center Stage," *Business Week*, December 7, 1981

heavily to become more competitive. But the biggest spenders of all are the airlines.

In 1976 American Airlines spent $350 million (then the cost of seven DC-10 jets) on its Sabre booking system. Within five years, 8 000 travel agents were sitting in front of leased terminals, and could instantly call up flight information about American and other airlines, make reservations, and issue tickets. As a bonus, Sabre also automated the travel agents' accounting systems. Other airlines didn't move as fast, and were severely hurt. (In 1982 the marketing vice president of Braniff complained that American had used Sabre to put his company out of business by cancelling reservations and switching passengers to American's flights.[16] People Express disappeared in 1986 because it failed to keep up with the new technology.)

Today, there are 85 000 Sabre terminals in 47 countries. The system is driven by seven giant IBM mainframes, and provides information on 665 airlines, 20 000 hotels, and 52 car rental companies.

Sabre benefits American Airlines in many ways. In the first ten years, it greatly increased the company's share of travel agency business. It also helped earn almost $340 million in revenues — mostly from other airlines, who paid $1,75 for every leg of a flight booked through Sabre.

During a fare price war, American changes almost 1,5 million fares in Sabre each day. The system automatically monitors travel by 11 million American Advantage frequent flyers, calculates flight plans for 2 300 flights a day, and controls a stock of close to 1 billion spare parts for the company's aircraft.[17]

16 "How To Keep Customers Happy Captives," *Fortune,* September 2, 1985
17 Kenneth Labich, "American Takes On The World," *Fortune,* September 24, 1990

The key challenge to any airline is to fill as many seats as possible on every flight. The seat that stays empty today can't be sold twice tomorrow — its revenue is lost forever. The problem is that passengers who pay the highest (and most profitable) fares can cancel at the last moment. So airlines compare historical loads with actual daily bookings, and try to reach a reasonable forecast of how many people will board each flight. For insurance, they over-book — but this is risky, since passengers who get "bumped" expect hefty compensation.

In 1989–90, British Airways carried 25,2 million passengers on 274 000 flights to 164 destinations in 75 countries. It offers 26 fare levels, in currencies from each of those countries. A flight leaves from somewhere in the world every two minutes. To manage the complex process of satisfying all those customers, and still stay the world's most profitable airline, BA spends £150 million a year — the cost of two Boeing 747s — on information technology. The airline has 15 mainframe computers and 200 mid-size computers attached to 200 000 terminals. Almost 5 per cent of its people work in this area. Today, BA's most valuable invisible asset is its huge lode of customer information.[18]

Push-button finance

Today money is an electronic impulse. It travels around the world as fast as you can blink. Computers have become essential in every area of finance, from credit cards to banking to stock exchanges.

In the early 1980s banks began offering computer links with corporate clients. More recently, they've started introducing the same opportunity to individuals, so banking by phone is now commonplace. Here again, getting in first — and

18 Lynton McLain, "Computers Climb Into The Hot Seat," *Financial Times*, Tuesday January 8, 1991

fast — is vital to success. Once customers are tied into a system, it's not easy to uncouple them.

To stay ahead in the cut-throat capital markets, Banker's Trust spends "hundreds of millions of dollars a year" on technology. In 1986, the London office needed 60 people to handle 400 to 500 foreign-exchange tickets a day. Now one-third of the people deal with three times the volume.[19]

Citibank spends $1,5 *billion* a year on information technology — which adds up to $19 000 a year for each person employed.[20]

In South Africa, the Standard Bank has built a commanding lead in technology by investing heavily for many years. The recent amalgamation of the United, Allied, Volkskas, and Sage was prompted in large part by the need to exploit technology. The problem for all these firms will be (*a*) to continue inventing new products, and (*b*) to manage them and to sell them effectively. They will have to segment their markets far more finely than they do today, while making life easier for both their customers and themselves.

It all comes together on the front line

Here's where your customers experience those all-important "moments of truth." And here's where special effort is required to manage your customers' perceptions.

Not long ago, says *Fortune*, an executive phoned a Nordstrom store in Seattle "to order a basket of fruit for the family of a friend who'd died on the West Coast. The store didn't offer food baskets, but a salesclerk found a specialty shop that did and arranged to have it send the basket."[21]

19 "Screen Wars," *The Economist*, July 21, 1990
20 Alan Caine, "IT investment a one-way street," *Financial Times*, September 25, 1990
21 Stanley J. Winkleman, "Why Big-Name Stores Are Losing Out," *Fortune*, January 16, 1989

How do you put a price on behaviour like that? Simple answer: you can't! How do you train people to act like that? Some cynics would say you can't, but it's worth a try.

❏ Jan Carlzon showed the way by training all his 20 000 people in customer service. Later, they spent a day learning to read SAS's financial statements so they'd understand their influence on the airline's profit.

❏ New drivers at Federal Express get four weeks' full-time tuition before they deliver their first package. Then they must pass a formal test every six months, to check that they understand and can practise the 12 key factors that the company stresses in its customer relationships.

❏ Before McDonald's opened in Moscow, the top four Soviet managers spent four months at Hamburger University in Chicago, followed by more than 1 000 hours of on-the-job training. Their 25 assistant managers each got three months of training in Toronto. Students who work part-time in the Moscow store all spend hours watching videos of smiling staff in western restaurants, and learning to say, "Have a nice day."[22]

❏ Disney World puts all its "hosts" through an intensive, three-week induction programme, in which they learn how to give "guests" a great time. Classroom sessions are supplemented with on-the-job learning. Throughout the process, Disney managers treat the newcomers with extreme courtesy and care — to show how good it feels.

❏ British Airways sent all 37 000 of its employees through a two-day "Putting People First" programme. The workshops not only gave them key skills for dealing with customers, but also bolstered their self-image.

As with SAS, that was just the start. Other workshops followed. BA people volunteered to join "customer first

22 Quentin Peel and Mark Nicholson, "Mac Attack in Pushkin Square," *Financial Times*, January 31, 1991

teams" which met to talk ideas. One group suggested that starters, main courses, and coffee should be offered on separate trays, to increase the number of contacts with each customer. Now, on a flight between London and New York, business-class passengers get 16 personalized "touches" from a stewardess.[23]

Another group suggested that children travelling alone be called "young flyers" instead of "unaccompanied minors." The next step was a Young Flyers Programme, with pre-flight briefings, special souvenir tickets, special meals, and even a visit to the flight deck.[24]

If training your own people is necessary, it's often equally rewarding to train your *distributors'* employees. Hartmarx, the manufacturer of Hickey Freeman and Hart Schaffner & Marx apparel, is doing just that. Its own college, "Hart Schaffner & Marx U," teaches department store sales people how to sell an expensive suit. "There's too much clerking and not enough selling," says Hartmarx CEO Harvey Weinberg. "We're going to fix that."[25]

Another apparel firm, $650-million-a-year Warnaco, shows equal commitment. Says CEO Linda Wachner: "We're treating the retailers as our partners in selling. . . . In the new environment we have to listen to what retailers want, and we have to make it happen."[26] Among other strategies, she talks of assigning merchandisers to a group of stores, to make daily checks of stock volumes and displays.

Training people to smile or deal politely with angry customers isn't nearly enough. There's far more to su-

23 "British Air : Bigger And Better," *International Herald Tribune*, May 8, 1989
24 Karl Albrecht, *At America's Service*, Dow Jones-Irwin, 1988
25 Bill Saporito, "Retailing's Winners & Losers," *Fortune*, December 18, 1990
26 Susan Caminiti, "Treating the retailers as partners," *Fortune*, December 18, 1989

**perior service than good manners or a pleasing person-
ality. This kind of training is important, but the way
people act is a direct reflection of how you hire, manage, promote, and retire (or fire) them.**

In other words, you should review not just every interaction
between them and their customers, but also every interaction
between them and the firm.

A lot of effort went into training BA people. But they were
also highly motivated to put what they'd learned into action.
When the company was privatized, 94 per cent of employees
bought shares. Almost all staff get a chunk of profits.

These are the things you have to think about. Becoming
world class isn't just another "tweak" of an otherwise finely-
tuned system. It's a complex and serious job, with serious
ramifications.

Training for tomorrow's advantage

I don't recall dealing with a single company where managers
don't say, "People are our most important asset." Nor do I
know many where employees say this statement is true. The
fact is, we squander our people power.

One key reason for the relative decline of the West is the
failure of basic education. *Business Week* says that America has
been "scrimping on human capital." A September 1988 cover
story concluded: "The $150 billion yearly trade deficit and a
foreign debt of half a trillion dollars reflect the inability of a
large percentage of the American work force to compete effectively in an integrated world economy."[27]

An American Management Association poll of 1 633 firms
revealed that one job applicant in four failed basic reading and

27 "Needed : Human Capital," *Business Week,* September 19, 1988

mathematics tests. The failure rate soared to a startling 36% when people were tested just for reading skills.[28]

A report on a joint study by the U.S. Department of Labor and the American Society for Training and Development says that education and training are vital not only to individuals, but also to the productivity and competitive advantage of organizations and nations. All signs are that "the economic importance of schooling and learning on the job is increasing. The economic history of the modern world shows acquired human skills inexorably replacing natural and machine resources as the basic building blocks of production and service delivery."[29]

The situation in Britain is not much better. A wide-ranging debate is under way on how to raise standards in schools, technical colleges, and universities. The National Training Awards get increasing publicity and interest. Companies are spending more and more to upgrade their people, and often to make up for inadequate schooling. Currently only 7 per cent of Britain's 2,5 million managers are university graduates. A mere 2 per cent hold a business degree or management qualification. A stunning seven out of ten managers never get any training at all for their roles.[30]

According to *The Economist*, the average westerner scores 100 in standard intelligence tests, while Japanese pupils score 117, and a Japanese high school diploma may be equal to an American undergraduate degree. The reason has nothing to do with genetics, and everything to do with effort.

28 "Poll of firms says 25% of U.S. job applicants fail basic skills tests," *The Wall Street Journal Europe*, May 23, 1991
29 Anthony P Carnevale and Leila J. Gainer, *The Learning Enterprise*, The American Society For Training & Development and the U.S. Department of Labor Employment & Training Administration 1989
30 "Skills level must improve," *Management Today*, February 1987

In Japan compulsory education ends in junior high school, but 94 per cent of children attend high school. They put in an average of two hours a day on homework compared to just 30 minutes by Americans. And some 72 per cent of Japanese kids in junior high take extra lessons two or three times a week for two or three hours at a time.[31]

American children spend 180 days a year in school; German and French Children spend 220; and Japanese 240! So U.S. companies spend about $30 *billion* a year making up for basic skills deficiencies alone.

Early attempts to fix the competitiveness problem centred on technology. Hundreds of billions of dollars went into capital equipment; computers and robots appeared all over the place. But the results were disappointing. (GM has even *removed* robots from some high-tech plants!) Corporate restructuring and a cheaper dollar have helped slow the economic decline, but companies are learning that only trained and motivated people can reverse it.[32]

So now, more money is going into training and development — and not a moment too soon. *Training* magazine estimates that 124 840 American organizations with 100 or more employees delivered around 1,2 *billion* hours of formal training to 37,5 million people in 1988. The magazine's 1988 "Industry Report" reveals that 63,6 per cent of all U.S. companies with 100 or more employees offer customer service training. Expenditure in virtually every other category was up over 1987.[33]

This isn't happening only in the U.S. Employees everywhere are getting more training today then ever before. They're also being exposed to a *wider range* of courses, workshops, and seminars. Employers worldwide are waking up to

31 "Japan's Schools: Why Can't Little Taro Think?" *The Economist*, April 21, 1990
32 "Needed : Human Capital," *Business Week*, September 19, 1988
33 Jack Gordon, "Who Is Being Trained?" *Training*, October 1988

the fact that people are a scarce commodity and must be looked after.

Training in the 1990s will be very different from that which is delivered today. Here are some emerging trends:

1. Training will increasingly be used as a tool for implementing strategy.

As we've seen, the development of core skills is a key factor in strategy. So managers will increasingly talk about training needs while they formulate their strategies, and they'll include training personnel in these discussions. This, in turn, will demand a new level of input from trainers, who'll have to take responsibility for results in a way they've never done before.

In the past, training was the poor sister of business activities. But now it's being recognized as a key to organizational change. When people learn new skills they widen their horizons. With the right encouragement and support from management, they experiment with new behaviours. That experience, in turn, is yet another learning process.

Some firms still conduct training on an ad hoc basis. They do it only when there's a pressing need — which usually means that they're in some kind of crisis. They treat training as an emergency measure, and of course it never gives the results they expect.

To be effective, training must be continuous. This doesn't mean that people must forever be hauled off work to attend courses. Most useful learning takes place on the job, not in the classroom. But to facilitate it, managers must take the time and make the effort to coach people, and employees must be open to learning.

Real-time training is a key factor in corporate renewal. World class managers use it as a tool to grow their people, and to create an environment in which they can manage the future.

2. Training will become more relevant and practical.

"Soft" leadership and human relations skills are critical to improve business performance. Yet management training still gives undue emphasis to "hard" issues such as quantitative analysis, finance, and strategy.

Our complex environment demands that people at all levels be equipped with a wide range of skills. For some, this means lessons in literacy and arithmetic. For others, it means specific job skills. And almost everyone needs to learn about product and service quality, productivity, problem solving, teamwork, creativity, and cost control.

3. Needs will be more carefully defined — and probably by line managers.

Too much training treats people like cattle: they all get the same stuff when they enter the training room. But companies now work harder to determine individuals' specific developmental needs, to prepare them for training, to measure what it does for them, and to help them decide what they need next.

Competency-based training and learning contracts are becoming more widely used. Programmes are learner-driven. People are given responsibility for their own development, counselling to help them plan for the future, and help over the humps.

In the past, human resources specialists were responsible for training. In future, line managers — and the trainees themselves — will do it.

4. Training will be more tailored.

People don't all learn the same way, so there's no "one best way" to train them. New methods — interactive video, computer aided instruction, etc.— will give people more control over the way they learn.

In addition, more companies will use methods and materials designed especially to meet their own objectives. "Packages" sell, but training won't escape "demassification."

5. Training will be driven by line management.

In the past, trainers had to sell their wares to often reluctant line managers. Today an increasing number of managers really believe in training as a tool to improve performance. Tomorrow more of them will initiate, deliver, and often control training.

Transferring new skills and knowledge from the classroom to the workplace has always been a problem area. Newly-trained people have often bumped heads with managers resistant to their new ideas, or resentful of their new skills. But when managers "own" the development process, training will become an integral part of work.

6. A wider range of issues will be addressed.

Until now, people at various levels were given different types of training. Front line people got technical training, supervisors learned people skills, and middle managers got a mix of concepts and methods.

From now on, more people will get a mix of knowledge and skills, delivered in a wider variety of ways. They'll learn general management, finance, and strategy. Also, how to build relationships, how to solve problems, make decisions, and cope with conflict and stress. Some of their learning will take place in the classroom; most will occur on the job or in seminars and workshops where their input is a key factor.

In addition, more companies will offer courses or financial support to employees who want to learn about *non-business subjects*. There's a growing belief that development of the "whole person" equips people better to deal with complex tasks and surprising change. It also helps make up for the fact that everyone can't occupy the top office: job enrichment is a powerful form of compensation.

❑ Have all your people been trained to do their jobs properly?

❑ Have they been *cross-trained*, so they understand the context in which they work, and so they can do other jobs which impact on their performance?

❑ Do you spend enough on training?

❑ Do line managers have a say in its planning and delivery?

❑ Do the recipients of training have a say in the training they get?

❑ Do you regularly and effectively measure its impact?

> **You can't over-train people. You can't spend too much on their development. This is one area where you'll never run the risk of being over-capitalized. So train them and train them and train them. Then, start again!**

Job descriptions and performance evaluations

Most job descriptions aren't worth the paper they're written on. Most performance reviews aren't worth the effort. If you use either, maybe now's the time for a rethink.

In theory, job descriptions make a lot of sense because they define an employee's purpose. People who're used to having them may feel uneasy when, for example, they switch jobs and don't immediately get that piece of paper. Managers feel a sense of unease without this "contract." And, of course, personnel departments feel robbed if they can't file it.

In practice, job descriptions tend to focus on *activities* rather than on *results*. They're often idealistic instead of realistic. They describe what should happen in a make-believe world; seldom if ever do they underline the importance of creating value for internal and external customers. And worst of all, they're often written for yesterday's needs — a new person in a job has no say in the tasks they define or the challenges they offer.

Job descriptions are dangerously confining in world where flexibility, adaptability, and constant learning are imperatives. They might have had some purpose in a machine age, when specialization and routine were the norm. Today, however, they may be a mental straightjacket. They're also a weapon that can be misused by, for example, trade unions, who still argue about "the wage for the job," and fiercely resist people sharing tasks or crossing the bounds of their boxes on the organization chart.

Performance reviews are even worse. In too many firms they're worthless rituals that everyone hates. The problem is not reviews as such, but rather the way they are done. The process is driven by the personnel department and the calendar, rather than by a rational management need. And like much strategic planning, it's tied to the budget — in this case, annual wage and salary increases.

Performance reviews create paperwork, and force managers and their staff to lie to each other. If they're supposed to help decide who gets paid what, they fail hopelessly.

But consider the real purpose of job descriptions and performance reviews. Both are tools to encourage human growth through learning and continuous self-improvement. The first provides an early benchmark, a starting point, a rough description of an individual's "territory." The second gives feedback, advice, encouragement — and, where necessary, criticism; over time, it should redefine the worker's "territory."

Seen in this light, it's clear that firms must rethink what they expect from both of these well-worn aids. Managers must learn to use them in new, constructive ways, and employees must learn about their benefits.

As a first step, managers must recast themselves in the role of coach and facilitator. They must understand that perhaps the larger part of their work is *leadership* — that is, to create an enabling environment in which people can and will extend their potential. So in addition to providing a solid base of information and training to start with, they must also keep raising people's sights and pushing them to learn. The key is ongoing communication in its purest form: *dialogue*, not *monologue*.

❏ What purpose do your job descriptions and performance reviews really serve?

❏ What do you expect from them?

❏ How are they perceived by your people?

❏ What else could you do that would make better use of the time these activities take, and the paperwork they generate?

❏ How could you redesign these management tools to get the most from them?

❏ How would managers have to change to use them properly?

❏ How would you sell them to your employees?

❏ What would employees need to know to (*a*) accept them, and (*b*) help make them work?

The employee information system

Communication has come up many times in this book as a central theme. Here are just a few of the questions that have already been raised in one way or another:

❏ Do your people get enough information — and the right information?

❏ Are they really in touch with what's happening in your firm, and in the world outside?

❏ Do they get information quickly enough, in a digestible form?

❏ Do they get sufficient accurate, honest, and useful feedback on their performance and on how the company as a whole is doing?

Put a team together to analyze these questions. Set a goal of eliminating a specific percentage of all paperwork. Get out of your office and talk to people — and *listen* to them. Replace formality with informality. Show by your example that people don't need to put everything in writing just to protect themselves, and that short memos and punchy letters and reports score most points with everyone.

The reward system

When you start talking about new efforts at customer care, people assume you're asking them to do "something else," something extra, something for which they're not already paid.

They need to understand that what you want them to do is simply operate in the most effective way possible. You have to show them that customer care is good business sense, not another gimmick you want them to add to their job descriptions.

That said, the reward system plays a powerful part in shaping behaviour. It's a tool which must be used in a deliberate way. (We'll look at it in much more depth in Chapter 15.)

❏ Does your reward system pay people to do the right things the right way — or just for turning up each day?
❏ Does it take into account the fact that individual initiative and teamwork are both important, and therefore should both be rewarded?
❏ Is it seen as fair?
❏ Are the rewards big enough and meaningful enough to really motivate people?

The physical arrangements in your firm

These include the location of premises; office, reception, and showroom decor; workshop and factory layouts; where people are situated; cleanliness; tools and equipment, etc.

Almost any company worth its salt has a decent corporate identity. But remember the iceberg factor? There's more to customer service than sexy signs or embossed letterheads.

Customers' perceptions are affected whenever they visit a company's premises. What they see is often as important as how they're treated. First impressions do last.

Every organization doesn't have to look like something out of *Architectural Digest*, or be as clean as a hospital operating theatre. (David Glass, president of Wal-Mart, describes the decor of his firm's head office as "early bus station."[34]) But tidiness is vital. People must be taught that "there's a place for everything, and everything has its place."

Not long ago, when I arrived at 6.00 a.m. to check in for a TWA flight from New York to Boston, I waited in line for 25 minutes while a clerk hunted for a rubber stamp. The person who'd closed up the night before had been careless about putting it away. Before it was found, there were about 60 irritated customers waiting to board the plane.

When you put your mind to it, there are many ways to make customers feel welcome when they visit you. A service station near me offers fresh filter coffee when you check your car in. My local video hire shop goes one better, with delicious chocolate cake. (And they don't pre-slice it — you cut as much as you like!)

Doctors could take a hint from such welcoming touches. Their waiting rooms are generally a disaster. You don't want to be there in the first place, and they make sure you hate sitting there. The chairs are usually old and broken, don't

34 Vance H. Trimble, ibid.

match, and clash with the wallpaper; the magazines ·are ancient and thumbed; and the receptionist is a dragon lady.

Unlike many medical facilities, the Worthing District Health Authority is run as a business, so it treats cataract patients as guests. They're put up in the Berkely Hotel for five nights with full use of all amenities — including the bar. They're responsible for taking their own medicines, and are allowed to have relatives to stay. Result: they get better much faster, so more cases can be handled.[35]

Good housekeeping makes for efficiency. When people know where their tools are, when equipment is clean and close at hand, when there's adequate filing space and comfortable chairs, and when the lighting level is right, then they can get on with what counts. Just as hygiene factors — pay, benefits, etc. — underpin individual performance, so do all these other issues. So ask:

❏ Are your premises in the right place?
❏ What do they look like?
❏ Does your corporate identity convey the image you want?
❏ Is your image consistent on everything from signs to sta-
tionery?
❏ Do your people have the right equipment?
❏ Is it kept in good condition?

It all comes back to empowerment

It's evident that empowering people to deal in a responsive, creative way with customers is a massive job. There are no short-cuts. The entire business system has to be redesigned to make it happen.

❏ Do you recruit carefully enough for front line jobs? (It's
easier to recruit "nice" people and train them in the necess-

---

35 "Guests Under The Knife," *The Economist*, February 18, 1989

ary skills, than to improve the attitudes of skilled people. So start with good raw material!)

❑ Are people interviewed by their future managers and other colleagues? (Or does Personnel do the job?)

❑ Do they get enough information about your company, the job you're hiring for, and exactly what you expect of them?

❑ Do they go through a careful, structured induction process?

❑ Do they know where to turn for help — especially when they're new?

❑ Do your front line people continue to get enough information about your business to represent it effectively?

❑ Do they show initiative in "going the extra mile" for customers?

❑ Are they positive about their jobs?

❑ Are they allowed and encouraged to take rapid decisions, and to act without getting tied up in red tape?

Hopefully, you and your team will have been using this book as a workbook, and you've already started on the road to improvement by working through the checklists and using some of the ideas you've read about. If so, you've already begun to change. And the fact that you're doing it, and perhaps seeing some of the positive effects, is proof that there's room for improvement in your organization — and that your team can make it happen.

In the final chapters, however, we'll look at a structured change process, and at the all-important issue of how you reward people for their contribution to it.

CHAPTER FIFTEEN
MAKING CHANGE A WAY OF LIFE

The road to world class performance is a rough one. For most firms, getting there is a brand new challenge with a definite starting point. Too often, it also has an end date — e.g., "we'll achieve this goal by June 31, 1992." It becomes a project, sometimes with its own budget. An individual or a small team is charged with making it happen.

And this is precisely the wrong way to go about it. Becoming world class is not something you take on today, and finish tomorrow. It's a way of life from here on. If it's not begun in that spirit, it'll almost certainly peter out and fail.

Along the way, you'll have to change many things. People throughout your organization will have to learn to think for themselves and take responsibility for themselves. And they'll have to re-learn virtually everything they know about business.

Change is not just a good idea for the 1990s, nor is the need for change debatable. To survive and thrive, every organism undergoes change. And every organization must change itself, before the pressure for change becomes unbearable, and the process becomes a reaction rather than a strategy.

Winning with the customer is a foreign idea in most companies. To make it happen means that many people — perhaps *everyone* — must do new things in new ways. What's more, they must get used to the idea of *kaizen* — continuous improvement. This goes right against our nature. We almost instinctively grope for stability. We like things to "settle down" after any upheaval. Human beings are astonishingly adaptable and inventive, yet most seem intent on keeping things the way they are. In addition, we have been conditioned in countless ways to resist change. The longer we've been in a job, the longer we've done things in a particular way, the more comfortable we get. We like the status quo, because we know how it works.

So, says Kenichi Ohmae, managing Director of McKinsey and Co.'s Tokyo office, the focus in most companies is on doing "more better." Radical change is avoided at all costs — and almost always until a crisis forces it.

During the 1980s, things got so tough for many firms, and the environment became so threatening, that they embarked on ambitious change projects. Often these efforts were led by new or extremely charismatic leaders. These executives created a lot of excitement, lit fires under a lot of people, and generally raised their organizations' energy level. A flurry of activity followed: new projects, new products, and a good deal of tinkering with the business system. (All driven by strategy retreats, corporate videos, mission statements, and the generous use of terms such as "towards the future," "towards 2000," or "leading the way to tomorrow.")

Unfortunately, all those good intentions didn't pan out. In fact, the vast majority have resulted in no more than a marginal change in most firms. Managing change is an appealing idea, but it's far harder than it looks.

A model for change agents

Change is a messy and often unstructured business. *Managed* change hinges on four steps. They may or may not occur in the following sequence, and one or more of them might even happen at the same time, but all four are vital. Managers often overlook the need to take people through these steps, and then wonder why things grind to a halt.

Step 1: Create dissatisfaction with the status quo.

Step 2: Debate possible futures.

Step 3: Implement to learn.

Step 4: Evaluate and recreate.

Step 1: Create dissatisfaction with the status quo

The first step needs special emphasis. It's the "de-freezing" step that Kurt Lewin talked about. If you skip it and rush straight into discussion about the future, you'll leave people behind. Until they internalize the need for change, until they deeply feel that the way things are just isn't good enough, they won't let go of the past.

Emotion plays a big role in change. Individuals need to feel comfortable disengaging themselves from what they're used to. The pain of the present must be outweighed by the possible gain of a different future.

As long as people are satisfied with the way things are, they won't change or they'll get in the way of change. They might hamper the process *actively*, by deliberately blocking it or slowing it down. Or they might foul up the process in a *passive* way, by seeming to agree with it, but doing nothing that will move it along. So the starting point is to shake up their world, and make them feel a deep need to do something different.

Sometimes this is done for you: a crisis grabs people's attention and spurs them to action. At other times, you have to create your own earthquake. You can do this in a number of ways:

❏ Through *discussion* of the issues — what's changed, what's likely to change, how will we be affected?

❏ By providing *information* that shows why more of the same won't do (using guest speakers, statistics, articles, books, etc.).

❏ By exposing people to *examples* of how other firms have changed (through plant visits, videos, etc.).

People throughout an organization are unlikely to be equally ready for change. Some assessment should be made of their various degrees of readiness, and strategies must then be created for dealing with different needs.

The "easiest" targets should then be aimed at first, to get them on your side as "missionaries" for change. Once a critical mass of favourable opinion builds up, the "tough nuts" often give up their opposition and crack quite easily.

Step 2: Debate possible futures

While some negative data can be used to get people agreeing that change is needed, they must rapidly be involved in creative, *positive* thinking about the way things "might be." The sooner they can start thinking about a vision of the future, the sooner they'll start to move.

Key players must feel that something better can be achieved, that they have some control over the new direction, and that making it happen is in their best interests.

"People always believe their own data," says American training expert Bob Pike. They must be able to take ownership of "new" facts as quickly and easily as possible. So exercises like brainstorming, in which they not only share ideas but also generate their own, are very helpful.

The goal of the first two steps is to start mentally moving away from "where we are now," towards consensus about "where we want to be." But important as they are, and much as planning can smooth the way to later action, it's essential to spend as little time as possible *talking* and as much as possible *doing* new things.

Step 3: Implement to learn

Even before the new direction is absolutely clear, people should start experimenting. When they act, they learn. Their experience suggests new possibilities and triggers yet more creative thinking. It also allows them to prove to themselves that their old views and behaviours were not necessarily best.

> **Until people start testing possibilities, the future is pure theory. When they do start trying things, they often surprise themselves. Good ideas pop out of nowhere, and small successes become stepping stones to bigger ones.**

To get the most out of new activities and experiments, however, the new insights and knowledge that come from them must somehow be captured and internalized. Feedback is useless if it simply washes over people or if it's not recognized and used. So this step is closely linked with the next one.

Step 4: Evaluate and recreate

No change strategy is born perfect. Feedback and review are vital in keeping the process dynamic and relevant. As people learn what works and what doesn't, the change process must be refined and redesigned. Managers must ask, "What did we set out to do? How are we doing? What happened? Are the results what we expected, and if not, why? What further opportunities can we now see? What else can we do? Who else can we involve?"

Brutal honesty is especially important at this stage. Projects take on a life of their own. Resources and egos are committed to them. People lose sight of other options for themselves, and cover up when things go wrong, because they think their careers hinge on taking things to a successful conclusion.

Hopefully, in reviewing progress, you and your team will once again "create dissatisfaction with the status quo." And so the process continues.

The improvement process

The improvement process itself has five stages:

Step 1: Gain top management commitment.
Step 2: Create a clear strategy.
Step 3: Involve others.
Step 4: Fine-tune.
Step 5: Review and revise.

Step 1: Gain top management commitment

Ideally, the CEO should initiate any significant corporate change. Ironically, however, the first move towards better customer service often comes from somewhere else in the organization:

❏ The export director of a large, multi-divisional industrial company wants a "package" that he can introduce into one division, and which can then be picked up by others if they see the need. From his front-line exposure to international customers and competitors, he's acutely aware of what the firm is up against.

❏ A training manager in an electronics firm identifies customer care as a serious weakness. He feels that sales staff can do with a new "angle" on selling. He has read a number of articles on customer care, and several mailshots on the subject have crossed his desk.

❏ The sales manager of a fast-moving consumer goods firm wants to improve relations between his department and the marketing department. He sees customer care as the "glue" that might do it.

All of these are legitimate needs. The fact that each is so different, and that customer service is seen as the "solution" in each case, shows just how fuzzy the notion of customer service is. It also shows just how superficially managers see the issue. But most condemning of all, it points to top managers' near total lack of appreciation for the customer end of their businesses, and for the holistic nature of the change that's needed to create and keep customers in this fast-changing world.

So a word of caution: *If you're the boss, and you want to improve customer service, understand that this isn't something you can fool around with. It's not something the top does to the bottom. Piecemeal stabs at it might be worse than none at all.*

Equally, if you're not the boss, start lobbying for his support before you press the "go" button yourself.

Tom Peters suggests that people can create "pockets of excellence" wherever they are in an organization, and perhaps get the attention of others. A recent Harvard study of change in six large companies showed that the successful efforts "started at the periphery of the corporation in a few plants and divisions far from corporate headquarters. And they were lead by the general managers of those units, not by the CEO or corporate staff people."[1]

Maybe so. But the same study points out that the reason many change efforts fail is that the CEO is too remote from what's actually going on in the trenches; change programmes are too generalized; and when one fails, another is quickly tried.

Superior customer service requires more than just a few "pockets of excellence." It really is everybody's business. And it has to be the leader's No.1 preoccupation. When it's not, everyone knows it was just another fad, and that getting involved really isn't worth a row of beans.

1   Michael Beer, Russel A. Eisenstat, and Bert Spector, "Why Change Programs Don't Produce Change," *Harvard Business Review,* November-December 1990

The first step in changing a company is to create a sense of dissatisfaction with the status quo. The top man must be the prime mover in this process. After that, his job is to keep people focused on the company's vision of the future — and on day-to-day superior service.

Step 2: Create a clear strategy

As I've pointed out so many times already, better customer service doesn't come through bitty efforts. It cannot be treated as a stop-start project or one that's implemented only in certain parts of the firm. Tinkering doesn't lead to genuine improvement.

Tactical moves might give you a short-term advantage in the marketplace. You can cut prices, increase advertising, run a consumer promotion, or offer special sales incentives — but those all have a limited impact.

To bring about real, structural change in the way your company works, you need a solid strategy.

It must include specific, clear objectives, it must identify the key players, and it must spell out precisely how the process will be acted out. It must take into account possible obstacles, and it must include contingency plans.

Above all, however, the strategy must be based on a critical mass of resources — money, management time, energy — which are always in short supply, and easily diverted elsewhere. For if one thing is certain, it's that world class customer service doesn't just happen by decree. It takes money, time, and hard work.

Costs must be budgeted for. Management time must be specifically assigned to this process. And the total effort must be big enough to make an impact.

Efforts to improve customer service often fail because they're fragmented or under-supported. Managers who know just how much has to go into their business strategies are often quick to short-change the customer service strategy. This is a big mistake. If you're going to do it, do it properly and do it well.

At the outset, the customer service strategy is likely to be seen as separate from the overall business strategy. However, the clear intention must be to make superior customer service the focus of all activities, and the central concern of the firm. So as soon as possible *it must become the main thrust of the total strategy*.

The way it's sold up front will either make this possible or relegate customer service forever to "poor sister" status. If you don't convince people that all future business planning will be done with a view to its impact on customer service, they'll always treat it as just another task they can start or stop at will.

Step 3: Involve others

Customer service becomes reality only when the customer feels it. So once a strategy has been agreed to, people throughout the company should be rapidly involved in making it happen.

Talking about great service might give people in the executive suite a nice warm feeling. Slogans and rah-rah meetings might help sell the idea. But nothing beats the personal touch. The best way to spread the gospel is through managers who see themselves as missionaries.

They must get out of their offices and talk to their people. Even more important, they must *listen* — to both staff and their customers.

This is always easier said than done. MBWA is a great idea and makes a lot of sense. But it's hard to do, so in many companies MBWA means managing by walking *away!*

Most of the managers I talk to are under terrific stress. A growing range of issues and problems calls for their attention.

They're under pressure to produce short-term results. They're inundated with paperwork. And an endless stream of people waits for their advice, opinions, recognition, and go-ahead.

Given these realities, managers shut their doors and try to close out the world. It's the worst possible route.

One reason for managerial stress is that many managers are "doers" rather than leaders. They're bogged down with operational details. They forget that their priority has to be to manage others — to create a climate in which ordinary people can do extraordinary things. So they don't delegate, they don't coach others, they don't share the load.

In some situations — e.g., in repetitive tasks — creative thinking isn't too important. So it makes good sense to give people instructions and precise standards, and to monitor them carefully.

But superior customer service sooner or later requires that the people who deliver it show extraordinary initiative, and take unusual responsibility. Front line or service staff must be able to think fast. They must be prepared to bend the rules when necessary, to see the customer's point of view, and to go the extra mile for customers.

To do this, they must be thoroughly trained — but then they must be *empowered* to perform. They must be given both responsibility and authority, plus whatever backup they need to do what you expect of them.

Who to involve

A difficult decision is which people to involve, and when. As soon as you have more than about 100 people you need some kind of plan for unrolling the improvement effort. Only in the very smallest of firms can everyone be involved at once.

Who to involve depends on many factors: not just the size of your firm, but also its structure, the location of various units, and so on.

In a small firm, one might decide to have a single, concentrated launch. You might be able to get everyone together for an initial seminar or workshop to get things moving.

In a larger company, you might want to spread the word in phases: first the top team, then middle management, then various departments. Or you might introduce the process into one division at a time, or into individual work teams.

Yet another option is to take diagonal slices through the organization, so that people from different levels and with different horizontal relationships wind up in the same group. This results in the greatest possible cross-pollination of ideas. It also enhances people's understanding of each other's roles, and it highlights the need for close cooperation up, down, and sideways throughout the organization.

Related to the decision of how to group your various audiences, is the question of what to say to each of them. You need to ask:

❑ What must they know?
❑ What *else* must they know?
❑ What information must they get on an ongoing basis?
❑ How should they be told?

Many change efforts flounder because stakeholders don't get enough information. On the other hand, the process often leaps forward when people do know what's happening, what's required of them, and how they're doing.

How fast should all this happen?
There are two things we know about change management:

1. It always takes longer than expected.
2. Quick fixes are essential catalysts in the process.

Because most change efforts are triggered by some sort of crisis, there's usually a need for speed. The top team gets fired up about a new direction, and wants to make it happen overnight. (Alan Kennedy, author of the best-selling book, *Corpor-*

ate Cultures, tells how one of his speeches enthused the CEO of a major company. As Kennedy finished speaking, the man turned to his personnel director, and said, "Let's have a new culture. And let's do it by Monday!")

Making world class performance a reality in most companies is like turning the QEII. It's a long, slow business. (After eight years of intense effort, General Electric CEO Jack Welch believed that his views were shared by his 2 000 top managers; but that left 99,33 per cent of his massive organization "still to conquer."[2])

But with enough energy behind the process, early results can be achieved. So while it must be approached with extreme patience, a sense of urgency is also needed.

When people are told that things are about to change, they greet the news with very mixed feelings. Some are excited. Some are frightened. Most are cautious and sceptical. They take a "wait-and-see" view, because they know from past experience that in the long run nothing will change. They send the leader mixed signals, appearing to be right behind him but in reality working hard to preserve the status quo.

If people are told too early that things are about to change, they might be unprepared to cope with the news, unwilling to help the change along, or *unable* to do so.

Good intentions alone cannot make superior customer service a reality. They must be backed by action — and people must be equipped to do the right things in the right way.

So while you might elect to tell your people early on that you're about to launch a new effort to improve customer service, you might also have to give some of them specific training.

You'll almost certainly have to review your company's objectives, and the standards set for each job.

---

2   Stratford P. Sherman, "Inside The Mind Of Jack Welch," *Fortune,* March 27, 1989

And you'll need to look again at the kind of information people get, the form they get it in, and how they use it.

Step 4: Fine-tune

There's no such thing as a perfect change process. They always unfold in surprising ways. They always trigger unexpected consequences. They always go wrong, at least in part.

No matter how well you've thought through and designed your effort, it must be tweaked as you go along. New opportunities will crop up, and they must be accommodated. New problems will present themselves, and they must be dealt with.

From the moment top managers start talking about customer service as a way of life, other people will have ideas about it. The faster they can be shown that management is serious, and the faster they *experience* participation, the faster it'll become ingrained.

No matter how well thought-out your strategy, it must be tested in the real world. And it must be continually improved — like everything else.

Fine-tuning is an endless process. As the strategy unfolds, new needs will become apparent, new moves will be needed. And as adjustments are made, they'll trigger yet more ideas.

Fine-tuning must be a *deliberate* process. It must be planned and managed like the other phases of the change process. It cannot be merely spontaneous — something "we'll do if we need to" or "if we have time."

Fine-tuning will throw up both positive and negative views. Some people will suggest ways of improving the strategy, or making it work more effectively, while others are sure to find fault with it. But remember that the purpose of fine-tuning is to *hone* the strategy — not change it entirely. Its central thrust, its main theme, must be retained.

One vital source of ideas for improvement is obviously customers themselves. The question always is: how early should they be made aware that you're trying to change? You'll also want to think about how to involve them, and how much to tell them.

Customers are the final judge of how well your strategy works. They can be of immense help in designing it. There's no reason at all for not using them as a sounding board as you go along.

If they know you're trying to change to their advantage, they'll help. Winning *with* the customer means total teamwork and an intimate partnership. Just as trust and open communication must be fostered inside your firm, so it must be encouraged with your customers.

Some companies make the error of publicly announcing their new interest in customers as soon as they start thinking about the benefits. This can be self-destructive. The new "product" should exist before it's launched with bells and whistles to the wider world. Beware of making extravagant promises or bold claims before you can deliver.

Step 5: Review and revise

While fine-tuning is a day-by-day task, it makes sense to occasionally pause and critically review how you're doing. To ask: What's working? What's not? Are we on course? Should we stick to our original plan, or deviate from it?

I'm dead against making any planning exercise too structured. Business just is not a structured process; it's as messy as hell. But time out from everyday issues, time for reflection and for creative thinking, is vital.

The thing to remember is that you should probably be trying less for a massive big-bang change than for the 1 000 tiny improvements that happen throughout your firm. So formal strategy reviews should focus on creating more new ideas, rather than shoving your plan back on track.

After the change process has been moving for a reasonable time — one month is soon enough, three months is too long — the strategy should be carefully reviewed, and progress checked. The team responsible for designing it, together with everyone who has a key role in implementing it, must look at the objectives, look at what's actually happened, and think hard about the future.

The main players should meet for at least half a day, and preferably a full day, at an off-site venue. They should be briefed to report thoroughly on what they have done to make the strategy work. Also, to offer their views of its current state of health: how their people have reacted to it, what they're doing to support it, any resistance to it, and special problems or opportunities in their part of the business.

They should also be asked to explain in some detail how they're going to push it along in the future. Some, at least, will try to get away with being vague; they'll offer the sketchiest possible outlines so they can't be tied down. They'll avoid hard facts, dates, deadlines.

But they must be pinned down. Their commitment to specifics is important. They must learn early that they'll be held accountable for the success of the change effort. They must learn to be hard on themselves. This meeting sets the trend for future get-togethers, and the ground rules must be clearly established.

This is a delicate stage in the life of a change strategy. Any temptation to change course must be resisted.

The strategy must be put on trial for its life. It must be critically talked through and tested. But it must not be destroyed.

The purpose of this meeting is to *improve implementation* — not to redesign the whole process. So the discussion must be headed by a strong leader, and probably kept on course by a facilitator. (An outsider will almost always be best.)

The tone should be positive and constructive. While open criticism must be allowed, the participants should be reminded that there's no turning back — that if they throw out the strategy at this crucial juncture, their own personal credibility will be called into question. Any trust they might have earned will be immediately destroyed.

I've never seen any change effort begun with all a company's employees right behind it, or believing that management is really serious. There are always sceptics. They're just waiting to say, "I told you so."

If you oblige by calling a halt or deviating significantly from the strategy, they'll grab the opportunity. And any future change effort will be greeted with immediate cynicism and a total lack of commitment.

Changing a company is always difficult. Far more than symbols or slogans are at stake. Familiar and comfortable behaviour must be given up. Plenty of people will watch for lapses. Management has to play a very visible, extremely positive role.

Pulling it all together

Winning with the customer starts with a sensitivity to customer needs, and hinges on many people in different areas doing things superbly. Front line sales people must naturally be involved, but so must people in purchasing, administration, manufacturing, and the rest. The quality and productivity of every function must be raised.

Better customer service thus means total change. It's always a much bigger process than most people expect. Answering the phone on or before the third ring is not

evidence of superior customer service. It's just one tiny measure of one person's performance.

If you want your company to be a world class competitor in the years ahead, be prepared to invest what's needed for total wellness. Start work now to strengthen every link in your value chain.

CHAPTER SIXTEEN

"WHAT'S IN IT FOR ME?"

Changing a company's performance means that a lot of people have to change the way they do things. For some, this means new objectives; for others it means new tasks; for many it means new methods; and occasionally it even means harder work. All of which adds up to a change in job descriptions — and thus a change in what people believe they get paid for.

When this happens, people assume that if you happily paid them for yesterday's behaviour, a bigger reward is due for something new. And one reason change efforts get stuck or fail is that management doesn't give enough thought to the remuneration aspect.

So watch what happens. The CEO stands up in front of his people and announces a new drive for quality or cost savings. A few people giggle nervously or say, "Great idea . . . but what do *we* get out of it?"

The CEO is caught off balance. He says, "Don't worry, we're looking into it," or "We'll have a new incentive plan for the supervisors by next May." Or he retorts, "Your job, that's what's in it for you!"

The result is that (a) people are turned off before the process even begins; (b) they do nothing until the incentive plan actually starts; and (c) they walk away feeling that they've scored points at management's expense.

In most companies, there's no incentive for most people to stretch a little further or try a little harder. People get paid for turning up rather than for quality performance.

If there is a bonus scheme, it benefits a few senior executives. Sales staff might take home some or all of their compensation in the form of commission. No one else can easily influence their pay cheque.

This practice might have been O.K. in an era of labour over-supply, but it's not good enough when there's a skills shortage. So an increasing number of progressive companies are introducing performance-linked financial incentives.

In Japan, 75 per cent of workers earn more than half of their take-home pay in the form of performance bonuses. Workers at British Steel earn up to 18 per cent of their pay that way. The 6 000 factory workers at Steelcase Inc., a Michigan office furniture manufacturer, earn low basic wages — about $17 000 a year — but get another 35 per cent for piecework and 69 per cent more in profit-sharing bonuses.

In the U.S., some 1,5 million employees now belong to more than 1 500 employee stock option schemes (ESOPs), and the number is growing rapidly. And almost everywhere you look, firms are introducing rewards for suggestions, cafeteria benefit packages, flexitime, and other innovations.

Compensation is an issue too important to overlook in the quest for superior customer service. Paying people according to the grade they've reached might make the accountants' job easy, but it does nothing to make a firm competitive.

The power of "please" and "thank you" and "well done!"

Money is a powerful motivator. It can move mountains. But put it in context. Frederick Hertzberg called it a "hygiene factor." Abraham Maslow labelled it a "survival need." It's one of the basics that everyone works for, but it's not everything.

As psychologist Edgar Schein points out, employees have both a *financial* and a *psychological* contract with the firms they work for. They work for money, but they also want satisfaction. The higher up the ladder they go, the more important psychological rewards become. Quite often, when people complain that they're not paid enough, what they really want is not more money, but more *recognition.*

We spend far too much time looking for mistakes, and criticizing bad work, and far too little stroking people and praising them (and making them important!) Yet these "warm fuzzies" can be an important factor in transforming the climate in a workplace, and can give an organization a sound foundation on which to build other competitive strengths.

Making incentives motivational

Incentive programmes that work meet ten important criteria. Try to launch a programme with anything less, and it'll be bound to fail. Here are the golden rules:
1. Reward people for the right things.
2. Start small.
3. Set specific, measurable goals.
4. Make rewards immediate.
5. Make them appropriate.
6. Reward everyone who made a contribution.
7. Communicate the programme clearly and loudly.
8. Celebrate with gusto.
9. If the reward isn't earned, don't give it.
10. Think long-term.

1. Reward people for the right things.
People always do what they're rewarded for. So make sure you know what "the right things" are, and make sure everyone understands.

Take sales incentives, for example. They're usually based on units sold, market share gains, or some similar measurement. They reward sales people for immediate results, not for long-term customer satisfaction.

Thus in the motor car industry, sales staff shoot for sales at all costs. Most of them are short-term hustlers. They're loners rather than team players, and more often than not they're in conflict with colleagues in the workshops or in credit control. They rush customers out of the dealership as fast as possible because they don't want to get into too much detail about a vehicle's shortcomings, or have the customer see a scratch or hear a squeak. Given half a chance, they're not above snatching a colleague's customers.

But it's not only sales staff who're affected by ill-conceived incentives. Nor are material rewards the only factors that influence behaviour.

When a manager acts in an aggressive, autocratic fashion, subordinates think that copying him is the right thing to do. If the CEO is secretive with information, and likes to label things "confidential," his people will do the same. If a boss turns a blind eye to dishonesty, they'll take the cue. When someone is promoted shortly after an unexceptional effort, people interpret that as meaning that O.K. is good enough.

2. Start small.

A fatal error many firms make is to launch their incentive programmes with the biggest possible bang. They make the announcement at a lavish celebration, and they offer huge prizes right off.

Managers in those companies should ask themselves, "What are we going to do for our *next* act?" For that's precisely the question their people will ask.

Creating initial excitement is an important goal. But don't go overboard. Keep something in reserve. Don't start off too lavishly, and then find you're forced to cut back.

Also, consider what you're actually trying to achieve. One manager recently tried to make his company more customer-conscious by starting with a highly-publicized suggestion scheme. He specified a cut-off date for judging, and planned a massive celebration.

The problem is, once you begin like this it's hard to keep going. When there's a closing date for entries, people assume that's the end of the entire effort. They rush to submit a few entries, then fold their arms. They totally miss the point management is trying to make: that new behaviour is wanted *forever*, and suggestions should keep coming.

An exciting start may be just what your particular effort needs. But a modest beginning is much likelier to lead to long-term success.

Any change effort always hinges on a few key players. It's vital to get them totally on side as quickly as possible. Once they're with you, it's much easier to roll out the process.

So focus your early efforts. Pick your targets, and involve them in developing the strategy. Give them a feeling of ownership, and they'll help you rather than get in the way.

3. Set specific, measurable goals.

Every job should be measurable, or it shouldn't be done. So right up front, get people to specify precisely what they do to create value for their customers. Establish clear performance criteria, and tailor incentives to those.

Insurance companies are hot on incentives for their sales people. Those in administration are left out. One justification is that their contribution is difficult to measure. But this is no reason at all; it's sloppiness. If managers can't agree on measurable goals with their staff, how on earth can those people know when they're doing well or badly?

Just as the company needs a service strategy, so do individuals need one. And just as the company's strategy must be based on measurable goals, so must the individual's. Everyone needs to know exactly what's required of them, to what standard, by when, and perhaps at what cost.

4. To make rewards meaningful, make them immediate.

When your dog performs a trick, it's no good waiting three days before you give him a pat or a bone. In the same way, it's absolutely useless recognizing a person's performance too long after the event.

Meaningful rewards are immediate. The best managers go out of their way to give people immediate, positive feedback.

A major incentive programme might offer prizes each week, each month, or even each year. The trouble is, when the horizon is too far out, people don't try hard early enough. They wait until the end is in sight.

When you design an incentive programme, think about both the short term and the long term. Consider making some awards at short intervals. At the same time, think about a longer-term build-up.

5. Make rewards appropriate.

In deciding what kind of reward to give, consider these issues:

❑ Does its perceived value match the effort that earned it?
❑ Will it really appeal to the person who gets it?

While a pat on the back, a "thank you," or even a simple smile may be a powerful motivator, a small cash award or a cheap prize might make you appear stingy. So if you want to keep the lid on your incentive budget, either give fewer, bigger awards or give symbolic items.

Certificates, cuff links, tie pins, brooches, scarves, or necklaces all make excellent awards. People accept them and wear them with pride. Their value lies in their exclusivity rather than their price. They signal special achievement and they last virtually forever. (A word of caution: if you use such items, don't make them available except for the specified exceptional performance. Don't give them to buddies, to the board of directors, or to anyone who "nearly" earned one!)

The second issue — the appropriateness of the award — is equally important. If you choose not to give money (which everyone likes) or symbolic awards, ask your people how they feel about whatever else you might have in mind.

One person might love the idea of a trip to Disney World, while another might prefer a motor car. One might be turned on by luggage, while another might go for jewellery. And while a long weekend at a luxury resort might be one person's dream, another might make huge efforts to earn a new dress, a microwave oven, or a stereo set.

When you select awards you don't get a second chance. So get it right first time. Don't try to surprise people. Rather ask their advice, get their input, and give them what they really want.

6. Reward everyone who made a contribution.

As I've said so many times, superior customer service comes from a team effort. Sales force incentives are important, but the sales force can't succeed on its own. So count others in; show them they're also important; share the rewards.

And share them as widely as possible. *Everyone* should be on an incentive plan of some sort. Pay for turning up should be replaced by pay for performance. There are countless ways to structure people's packages; investigate the options, and use an imaginative one.

7. Announce the programme and communicate results loudly and clearly.

When you consider an incentive programme, tell your people you're doing so. Then tell them when you actually introduce it. And tell them when anyone gains from it. Providing the awards are worthwhile, you can't over-publicize what you're doing.

8. Celebrate with gusto.

A great part of the value in any award is the recognition and praise that goes with it. People love being cheered. You can't make too much noise about someone's success, but you can easily make too little.

Once again, this aspect of any incentive programme demands careful thought and meticulous planning. A slapdash ceremony might be better than none at all, but it might cost as much as a really good one.

One of your managers might fancy himself as a public speaker, but it might be far better to hire a professional. And though the ladies in your office might get a kick out of preparing snacks, it might pay to get a professional caterer and do the job properly.

9. If the award isn't earned, don't give it.

Not long ago, the head of a large industrial firm told me how his suggestion programme had deteriorated over the years. "Today," he said, "we give the monthly prize as a matter of course. Most of the suggestions are so poor they're useless, but we feel we have to keep it up."

Doing this totally debases the incentive programme. People aren't fools. When cash or other incentives are given for mediocre efforts, everyone finds out very quickly. The awards become meaningless. No one feels good earning them, and they don't spur anyone to try harder. Nor are the winners admired; in fact, their colleagues laugh at them.

10. Think long-term.

Making superior customer service a way of life can't be done in a year, except in the very smallest of firms. Nor should you set a deadline for making "it" happen. Rather, aim for specific improvements by specific times, and keep ratcheting your sights upwards.

Your incentive package must match this extended effort. Even if you elect to make short-term awards — monthly, quarterly, half-yearly, or whatever — always see each of them as part of a whole. Don't make them in isolation. Remember, the goal is to change the everyday behaviour of your people.

NOW, IT'S OVER TO YOU

As a consultant, I've sat through countless meetings and listened to any number of managers wrestle with the question: *how to take customer service beyond quick fix status and make it a way of life?* I've spent endless hours reflecting on the problem, and reviewing other people's "solutions." In the process I've become convinced that:

1. The task is a lot bigger than anyone suspects.
2. The chances of failure are better than the chances of success.
3. A big "customer care" budget guarantees nothing.
4. Customer service does not provide a magical route to a sustainable competitive advantage.
5. If the overall business strategy is not driven by customers, it will never be effective.
6. If the chief executive doesn't lead the charge, nobody will believe it's serious.

To create a world class customer satisfaction strategy, and to drive the ethic deep through the organization, you need to take a new look at some old tools. You need to *begin* with an approach that will improve your chances of success. Starting in the wrong place, and in the wrong way, simply causes confusion and resistance.

When you get down to it, your place in the business arena is determined by the value you offer. The way you package that value — the service you wrap around it — will turn customers on, or send them away.

In their search for solutions to the competitiveness problem, companies have suddenly latched onto the idea of superior customer service. More will do so in the next decade. If you don't start doing something about your service today, you'll be out off the game.

The good news is, most of your competitors will treat customer service as just another quick fix. They'll make superficial efforts to improve it, and will pay lip service to the changes it demands.

Don't fall into the same trap. The rewards for those firms that really do change will be tremendous. When customer service becomes the focus of attention, everything else falls into place. People start doing the right things, the right way, right on time, and right every time.

Winning with the customer is a long-term task. It calls for consistent, focused attention to key issues over a period of years rather than months. One-night stands give only brief satisfaction; long-term relationships are hard work, but worth it in the end.

What the winners do

Companies that do well in the eyes of their customers do many things well. They work incredibly hard at shaping their customers' expectations and moulding their perceptions. Everyone seems to have a sense of purpose.

Ten essential beliefs drive the process of becoming a world class competitor:

1. The customer is the ultimate judge of business performance. Success or failure hinges on the management of customer perceptions.
2. Superior service is everybody's business.
3. The effort must be led from the top.
4. Long-term continuous improvement and short-term quick- fixes are both crucial goals.
5. There is always a better way to do everything.

6. Problems must be prevented, not fixed. (i.e. Customer satisfaction must be built in step-by-step — not inspected in at the end of the line.)
7. Every employee must aim to do the right things the right way, right first time, on time, every time.
8. All employees must be cross-trained and encouraged to make learning a lifetime process.
9. All stakeholders must become partners.
10. Information must be widely and openly shared.

There's an 11th principle to keep in the back of your mind. It's the old "K.I.S.S." idea.

Whatever you do to get better, don't get too clever. Don't look for over-sophisticated concepts. And don't waste time searching for the answer that's precisely right.

Companies run into trouble, and their improvement efforts come unstuck, when they look for the perfect answer, and when they fall in love with current fads.

There are many ways to improve your business performance. The ones that will work best for you are the ones that you and your team invent yourselves. World class performance does not occur when extraordinary people do one thing 1 000 per cent better. It happens when ordinary people do thousands of little things 1 per cent better — and then another 1 per cent better tomorrow.

Go for it!

I hope in these pages that I've conveyed to you a sense of excitement, of challenge, and of adventure. This is altogether a most wonderful age. The next decade will be even more testing. So get into shape for it now. Set your sights on becoming world class! Make winning with *your* customer a way of life!

DRAFT AGENDA: TOP MANAGEMENT WORKSHOP

DAY 1

08h30–08h50	Introduction — why we're here and what we hope to achieve	CEO
08h50–10h30	Where we are now — presentations by individual managers	Individuals
10h30–10h50	TEA BREAK	
10h50–12h00	The new business arena : issues we must manage	Facilitator
12h00–13h00	Discussion: the need for change in our company	Group
13h00–14h00	LUNCH BREAK	
14h00–15h00	Our vision, mission, and values	Group
15h00–15h30	Film on participative management	
15h30–15h45	TEA BREAK	
15h45–16h15	How well we're doing in the "7 Cs" now	Syndicates
16h15–17h00	Syndicate presentations	Syndicate leaders

DAY 2

08h30–08h50	Review: how we're doing	Group
08h50–09h30	Film on change management	
09h30–09h45	Discussion: how these ideas apply to our company	Group
09h45–10h30	How we can improve our performance against the "7 Cs"	Syndicates
10h30–10h50	TEA BREAK	
10h50–12h00	Syndicate presentations	Syndicate leaders
12h00–13h00	Discussion: defining priorities	Group
13h00–14h00	LUNCH BREAK	
14h00–15h00	Objective setting	Group
15h00–15h30	Action plan	Group
15h30–15h45	TEA BREAK	
15h45–16h30	Next steps: strategy for cascading the process down through the organization	Group
16h30–16h45	Summary/close	CEO

CUSTOMER PROFILE (DISTRIBUTOR)

This questionnaire is designed to help you build win–win relationships with distributors of your products. It will help you and your team explore what you know about your distributors, and what you need to find out. When you work through it, you'll probably discover that in your minds and your data banks you already have a surprising amount of this information. The questionnaire gives you a framework for systematically uncovering this invisible asset.

1. Company name and address

_____

_____

_____

_____

_____

_____

2. Key contacts

Name	Title	Business phone	Home phone

3. Nature of business
   (How would customer describe "what business we're in"?)

   _____

   _____

   _____

4. How good is our relationship? (1 = poor, 10 = excellent)

   1   2   3   4   5   6   7   8   9   10

   Describe it (What's especially good or bad about it, who
   are the key players on both sides, who has problems with
   whom, are things getting better or worse? etc.)

   _____

   _____

   _____

   _____

   _____

   _____

   _____

   _____

   _____

   _____

   _____

   _____

5. What is the history of our relationship?

   _____

   _____

   _____

   _____

   _____

   _____

   _____

6. Customer's financial structure/history/stability

   _____
   _____
   _____
   _____
   _____
   _____
   _____

7. Business objectives (1 year and 5 years)

   _____
   _____
   _____
   _____
   _____
   _____
   _____

8. Business strategy

   _____
   _____
   _____
   _____
   _____
   _____

9. Past performance (sales, market share, profits, etc., for 1 year and 3 years)

   _____
   _____
   _____
   _____
   _____

10. Key competitors

_____

_____

_____

_____

_____

_____

_____

_____

_____

10. Strengths

_____

_____

_____

_____

_____

_____

_____

11. Weaknesses

_____

_____

_____

_____

_____

_____

_____

_____

_____

12. Opportunities (as customer sees them)

_____

_____

_____

_____

_____

_____

_____

_____

13. Opportunities for customer (as we see them)

_____

_____

_____

_____

_____

_____

_____

_____

14. Target market/s
   • Demographics

_____

_____

_____

_____

_____

_____

   • Psychographics

_____

_____

_____

_____

_____

_____

15. Target market potential

_____
_____
_____
_____
_____
_____

16. Promotional promise

_____
_____
_____
_____
_____

17. Promotional strategy

_____
_____
_____
_____
_____
_____
_____

18. Promotional media used

_____
_____
_____
_____
_____
_____
_____
_____
_____

19. Promotional budget

_____

_____

_____

_____

20. Where are promotional decisions made?

_____

_____

_____

_____

_____

_____

21. Who makes promotional decisions?

_____

_____

_____

_____

22. How can we influence promotional decisions?

_____

_____

_____

_____

_____

_____

23. Organization structure (draw rough chart)

24. Number/location/size of outlets

_____
_____
_____
_____
_____
_____
_____

25. What is the merchandise mix?

_____
_____
_____
_____
_____
_____

26. Where is buying done?

_____
_____
_____
_____
_____
_____
_____

27. Who does the buying?

_____
_____
_____
_____

28. When is buying done?

_____
_____
_____
_____
_____

29. For what period is buying done?

_____

_____

_____

_____

_____

29. How firm are orders? (i.e., Can we rely on them?)

Yes ☐   No ☐

30. Where/how must deliveries be made?

_____

_____

_____

_____

_____

_____

31. What financial arrangements does the customer demand?

_____

_____

_____

_____

_____

_____

32. What other special demands is this customer likely to make?

_____

_____

_____

_____

_____

_____

3. What corporate policies might impact on our relationship?

_____
_____
_____
_____
_____
_____
_____
_____
_____

34. What does this customer expect from us altogether?

_____
_____
_____
_____
_____
_____
_____
_____
_____
_____
_____
_____
_____
_____
_____
_____
_____
_____
_____
_____

35. What can we do immediately to improve this relationship?
    Action   By (person)   Date

_____

_____

_____

_____

_____

_____

_____

_____

36. What can we do in the long-term to improve it?
    Action   By (person)   Date

_____

_____

_____

_____

_____

_____

_____

_____

_____

37. Comments/suggestions

_____

_____

_____

_____

_____

_____

_____

_____

CUSTOMER PROFILE (KEY CONTACT)

This questionnaire can be used together with the preceding one to add more personal details of a key individual within a distributor firm, or of your end customer. Again, you probably know a lot of this stuff, but thinking about it systematically will show up the holes in your knowledge, and spark ideas for dealing with this person.

1. Name
_____

2. Nickname
_____

3. Preferred title
   Mr ☐   Mrs ☐   Dr ☐

4. Address
_____
_____
_____
_____

5. Home phone
_____

6. Company name and address
_____
_____
_____
_____
_____
_____
_____
_____

7. Business phone

_____

8. Date of birth

_____

9. Home language

_____

10. Other languages spoken

_____

11. Names of spouse and children

_____

_____

_____

_____

_____

_____

_____

12. Date of wedding anniversary

_____

13. Does he/she read a lot?

_____

14. Favourite reading material

_____

_____

_____

_____

_____

15. Favourite TV programmes

_____

_____

_____

_____

_____

16. Is there anything this person is particularly sensistive/em-
barrassed about?

_____

_____

17. State of health/past history

_____

_____

_____

18. Hobbies/sports played or watched

_____

_____

_____

_____

_____

_____

19. Clubs/professional, or business associations

_____

_____

_____

20. Education

_____

_____

_____

_____

_____

21. Military service/dates

_____

_____

_____

_____

22. Career history

_____
_____
_____
_____
_____
_____

23. Favourite holiday destination

_____
_____

24. Work habits

_____
_____

25. Favourite food

_____
_____

26. Favourite resaurant/s

_____
_____

27. Does he/she enjoy business entertaining?

_____
_____

28. Proudest achievement

_____
_____

29. Why does this customer like dealing with us?

_____
_____
_____
_____
_____

30. Is this person an experimenter?

_____

31. How important is image (brand names) to this person?

_____

_____

32. Would you describe this person as:

    1   2   3   4   5

INTROVERT   EXTROVERT

33. Is this person generally an optimist or a pessimist?

_____

34. What is the history of our relationship?

_____

_____

_____

_____

_____

_____

_____

35. Customer's financial situation/history/stability

_____

_____

_____

_____

_____

_____

_____

36. Customer's personal objectives (1 year and 5 years)

_____

_____

_____

_____

_____

37. What is this person doing to reach his/her objectives

_____

_____

_____

_____

_____

_____

_____

_____

_____

38. What does customer buy from us?

Product   Volume   Discount   Terms

_____

_____

_____

_____

_____

_____

_____

_____

39. Why does customer buy from us?

_____

_____

_____

_____

_____

_____

_____

_____

_____

_____

41. Who else does customer buy from
    (who competes with us)?

    _____

    _____

    _____

    _____

    _____

    _____

    _____

    _____

    _____

42. Where does customer buy?

    _____

    _____

    _____

    _____

    _____

    _____

    _____

    _____

43. When does customer buy?

    _____

    _____

    _____

44. How often does customer buy?

    _____

    _____

    _____

45 What financial arrangements does the customer demand?

_____
_____
_____
_____
_____
_____

46. What other special demands is this customer likely to make?

_____
_____
_____
_____
_____
_____

47. What does this customer expect from us altogether?

_____
_____
_____
_____

48. What can we do immediately to improve this relationship?
Action   By (person)   Date

_____
_____
_____
_____
_____
_____
_____

_____

_____

_____

_____

_____

_____

_____

_____

49. What can we do in the long-term to improve it?
    Action   By (person)   Date

_____

_____

_____

_____

_____

_____

_____

_____

_____

_____

_____

50. Comments/suggestions

_____

_____

_____

_____

_____

_____

_____

_____

HOW TO HANDLE ANGRY CUSTOMERS

1. Keep your cool.

Don't be become defensive or respond with anger. Let your customer blow off steam. Remember, when people are upset, what they want most of all is to be heard. If they get personal, they're probably angry at your company, not at you. So be polite. Show that you respect them.

2. Listen empathically.

Put yourself in your customer's shoes. Don't rush into a routine response. Probe for the real problem. Listen for what's *not being said*, as well as to what is being said. Use open-ended questions to get to the nub of the matter.

3. Let the customer sound off.

Angry customers want to be heard. Don't be in a hurry to cut them off or to offer a solution. Let them finish what they have to say.

4. Apologize . . . then move towards areas of agreement.

Look for "win-win" opportunities.

5. Focus on facts, not on personalities.

Don't cover up, deny responsibility, or pass the buck. Don't try to prove the customer wrong. Don't get personal, and if the customer gets personal with you, don't get drawn into the trap. Instead, talk facts.

6. Act fast to solve the problem.

Most people don't complain; when someone does, take them seriously. Agree with them what you'll do to fix things. If necessary, call the real problem-solver, your boss, or someone else who can help you.

7. Don't expect to win 'em all.

You can't. Some customers are just plain unpleasant or unreasonable. But more often than not, even they can be turned around if you show you're on their side.

PERSONAL PERFORMANCE MEASUREMENT
(What can you do to improve customer service?)

When we talk about customers, we usually refer to the outsiders who buy our goods or services. But each of us has
internal "customers" as well: fellow employees, a boss, or subordinates.

How well are you doing in your job? How can you improve? What can you do to become a more valuable member
of your work team? The key to success is to focus on the "value"
you create for your colleagues. In other words, to think of them
as "customers" who depend on you. These internal customers
include people at your own level, as well as your boss or
people who report to you.

This questionnaire will help you (a) identify your internal
customers; (b) agree with them what results you should aim
for; (c) develop a personal improvement strategy, and (d)
measure your progress.

How to use this questionnaire

Work through the questions on your own, and answer them
as well as you can. Then talk to your "customers", and check
how they feel. You might need to get various people's views,
to get an accurate picture.) Then write an action plan for
improvement, and if necessary, discuss it with your boss.

1. Who are *your* internal customers?

    _____
    _____
    _____
    _____
    _____

2. What do they expect of you? (*Ask them*, if you aren't sure!)

    _____

    _____

    _____

    _____

3. What will they expect of you in the future — i.e., how might
    their needs change *your* job?

    _____

    _____

    _____

    _____

4. How well do you satisfy your customers? Rate yourself on
    a scale from 1 - 10 (1 being poor, 10 being excellent.)

    1 2 3 4 5 6 7 8 9 10

    Now ask your customers to rate you.

    1 2 3 4 5 6 7 8 9 10

5. What affects your performance? (i.e. what happens inside
    your company that lets you do your job well, and what
    stops you from doing as well as you might? Consider
    issues such as training, systems, policies and procedures,
    equipment, workload, management style, conflicts, etc.)

    _____

    _____

    _____

    _____

    _____

6. What do you need to learn about your customers' needs ...
    and what should you tell them about your job?

    _____

    _____

    _____

    _____

7. Do you get the information, resources, and support you need to do as good a job as you're capable of?
Yes ☐   No ☐

What's missing?

_____

_____

_____

_____

8. Do you need any specific training?
Yes ☐   No ☐

What kind?

_____

_____

_____

_____

9. Do you get enough feedback on your performance?
Yes ☐   No ☐

What would you like to know? What would help you do a better job?

_____

_____

_____

10. What else will help you improve your performance
   • From *your* point of view?

_____

_____

_____

_____

- From your customers' point of view? (Remember to ask them!)

  _____

  _____

  _____

  _____

11. What can you do right away to improve your service?

    1. _____
    2. _____
    3 _____
    4. _____
    5. _____
    6. _____

12. What can you do in the next 12 months?

    1. _____
    2. _____
    3. _____
    4. _____
    5. _____
    6. _____
    7. _____
    8. _____
    9. _____
    10. _____

13. What will you do on your next day back at work?

    1. _____
    2. _____
    3. _____

LEADER'S CHECKLIST
10 Steps to Superior Performance

1. Listen to customers. Let them help you define "superior service."

2. Establish a clear service strategy, and make sure all your people buy into it.

3. Set specific, high standards ... measure and review performance regularly.

4. Recruit carefully and over-train your people.

5. Empower them to perform — i.e., give them the information, resources, and support they need, and give them room to get on with it.

6. Publicize what you're doing and how you're doing . . . inside and outside of your firm.

7. Recognize and reward superior service.

8. Make rapid, creative response a way of life.

9. Don't ever stop trying to improve everything. Remember, "there's always a better way!"

10. Go back and check how your customers think you're doing.

HOW TO SELL YOURSELF AND YOUR COMPANY
The 10 Commandments of Customer Service

1. *Know your customer.* Listen! Listen! Listen! Remember, you're in business courtesy of your customers. Pay attention to what they say. Use them as a source of new ideas. Talk facts . . . but listen for feelings.

2. *Know your company and its products/services.* Bone up on the details: history, success stories, facilities, features, and benefits.

3. *Know your competition.* Keep an eye on them . . . but never become paranoid about them.

4. *Cut your response time.* Make fast action a way of life. When a customer calls, or when you have an idea to share, do something about it. Show that you're interested, and that you're willing to go the extra mile to help.

5. *Watch your appearance.* Remember, you never have a second chance to make a good first impression. Good grooming, well-cut, clean clothes, and a shine on your shoes all add up to a professional appearance. Also make sure that offices, sales aids, and promotional materials all support the image you're trying to convey.

6. *Be prepared.* Never go into a meeting with a customer without knowing how you want to come out. Set clear objectives. Take the right support materials. If possible, have an agenda. And above all, know your stuff!

7. *Make people feel good about being your customer.* When you see them, acknowledge them. Let them know you know they're there. Be polite. Smile. Be sincere. It's almost always a surprise to be treated this way, and your customers will love it.

8. *Aim at building long-term relationships.* Customers are the
    most precious invisible asset any company has. They're
    expensive to get, and even more expensive to lose. So never
    aim for a one-off sale; always think of the long-term, and
    see the effort you make on your customer's behalf as an
    investment in your future.

9. *Make continuous learning and improvement a way of life.* No
    matter how much you know about your industry, your
    company, your customers, or your competitors, you can
    learn more . . . and you can improve your performance
    over and over again. So every day, seek to do just a little
    better in every way.

10. *Become a master of change.* Anticipate the future. Watch
    trends, and spend time in creative dreaming. Stay one step
    ahead of your customers, and offer them a steady stream
    of new insights, new opportunities, new solutions to their
    problems. Never accept the status quo. Dare to be different.

USING CUSTOMER INFORMATION CONSTRUCTIVELY

1. Remember the KISS principle — "Keep It Simple, Stupid!"
2. Get it fast . . . discuss it fast . . . act on it fast!
3. Get it often! Aim for *continual improvement!*
4. Collect both facts and feelings. Remember, service is a *customer perception!*
5. Measure your competitors, too. Performance is always relative!
6. Don't use information to embarrass, criticize, or punish employees. If you do, they'll make sure you can't get it!
7. Share information widely. You never know where ideas for improvement will come from!

MAKE YOUR VALUES LIVE

What can you do to make the "7 Cs" live in your company? Talking about them is important, but *acting* them out, day after day, is even more vital.

Round 1

How important are each of the "7 Cs" to your performance? Rank each (1 - least important, 10 - most important) and use a solid line to join the numbers.

Round 2

How are you doing? Join the numbers with a dotted line (or another colour).

1. CUSTOMERS 1 2 3 4 5 6 7 8 9 10

2. COMPETITION 1 2 3 4 5 6 7 8 9 10

3. CHALLENGES 1 2 3 4 5 6 7 8 9 10

4. COOPERATION 1 2 3 4 5 6 7 8 9 10

5. CREATIVITY 1 2 3 4 5 6 7 8 9 10

6. COSTS 1 2 3 4 5 6 7 8 9 10

7. COMMUNICATION 1 2 3 4 5 6 7 8 9 10

10 KEYS TO WORLD CLASS PERFORMANCE

These 10 characteristics appear in most World class companies. Use this checklist to get a quick fix on how your company rates — and to identify areas for attention.

Round 1

How important are the following issues to your performance? Rank each (1 — least important, 10 — most important) and use a solid line to join the numbers.

Round 2

How are you doing? Join the numbers with a dotted line (or another colour).

1. VISION 1 2 3 4 5 6 7 8 9 10

2. BOLDNESS 1 2 3 4 5 6 7 8 9 10

3. ANTICIPATION 1 2 3 4 5 6 7 8 9 10

4. RESPONSIVENESS 1 2 3 4 5 6 7 8 9 10

5. FOCUS 1 2 3 4 5 6 7 8 9 10

6. COMMITMENT 1 2 3 4 5 6 7 8 9 10

7. FLEXIBILITY 1 2 3 4 5 6 7 8 9 10

8. CREATIVITY 1 2 3 4 5 6 7 8 9 10

9. KNOWLEDGE 1 2 3 4 5 6 7 8 9 10

10. COMMUNICATION 1 2 3 4 5 6 7 8 9 10

MANAGEMENT TITLES FROM JUTA

GETTING IT RIGHT — The Manager's Guide to Business Communication

ADEY & ANDREW

This work is more an introduction to business practice than a book about theoretical communication. Management, marketing, advertising, and industrial relations are approached from the perspective of business communication. Each chapter has a summary of concepts and terms, as well as case studies that test the understanding of these concepts. The syllabi of the diplomas of various professional institutes, including that of the communication Course of the Diploma in Business Administration as examined by the SA Institute of Management, are covered.

MARKETING MANAGEMENT

MARX & VAN DER WALT

Written to suit South African conditions, the style of this text is easy, while figures and tables are used liberally to explain complicated concepts. While characterised by a practical approach, the content is scientifically founded. The twenty chapters are divided into four parts. The first is a general introduction providing a broad perspective; the second deals with the marketing environment; the third with marketing decisions and the fourth part, including topics such as the product life cycle, marketing warfare, strategical marketing, product portfolio etc, deals with the integrated marketing strategy. This work is also available in Afrikaans.

COMMUNICATING FOR CHANGE — A Guide to Managing the Future of South African Organisations

A D MANNING

Communicating for Change is based upon this simple idea: 'Business has a serious responsibility to remain viable, create wealth, and generate jobs and opportunities for personal growth; to sensitise people to the need for change; and to help them learn new behaviours and thus bring about change.' This book not only shows the reader how to increase profits, but it also addresses the all-important changes in our South African society and shows how a climate for change can be created in every workplace.

NEGOTIATING CONFLICT — Insights and Skills for Negotiators and Peacemakers

M ANSTEY

This book takes a realistic look at the dynamics of conflict and the prospects of negotiation. It seeks to provide an understanding of existing conflict and it supplies negotiators and peacemakers with the requisite tools to promote effective settlement between parties in dispute. It supplies essential content and process information for practitioners in the fields of labour, community and political conflict.

The publication of NEGOTIATING CONFLICT could not come at a more fortuitous time. Its immediate relevance and the contribution it makes towards enabling South Africans to realise a peaceful and negotiated future make it essential reading.

TRENDS TRANSFORMING SOUTH AFRICA

A D MANNING

This title provides an unique collection of views covering a wide range of issues, from some of the leading experts in key fields. It ranges across politics, economics, the youth, labour, education and technology, illiteracy, international status, AIDS, and the environment. Leading South Africans provide key scenarios for the future —a future in which these issues will have to be addressed if there is to be any real peace or prosperity. This book is essential reading for all South African businessmen and women — indeed for anyone with a stake in the future of this country.

INDUSTRIAL MARKETING

C VAN VEIJEREN

Background on industrial marketing is combined with a description of the strategic marketing planning process in this book which enables the reader to put it all together into an integrated strategic marketing plan. While implementation and the need for a strategic planning system that will ensure continuous rejuvenation are dealt with in depth, the interfaces between industrial marketing and competitive strategic marketing are explicitly considered. This is both a handbook and reference source for the practitioner and the student or academic.

Publication September 1991

MARKETING TO BLACK TOWNSHIPS

R MORRIS

Robin Morris offers penetrating insights into the rapidly growing Black market. He also provides a detailed programme which focuses on distribution and sales maximisation. The book is sales driven and the concepts that are discussed and analysed are all designed for one purpose — the long term growth of sales and the securing of a profitable position for any given product. The author eliminates the complexities inherent in this huge domestic market and shows the reader just how accessible, how affordable, and how luctrative it actually is.

Publication end 1991

THE MARKETING DECISION-MAKER

L F PITT & D BROMFIELD

The organisation, management, and control of information is a prerequisite for business success. These processes are fundamental to marketing. Effective marketers and customer-oriented organisations require not only information, but information that is timely, organised, useful, and in a form that can be understood and manipulated so that decisions can be made. Information technology has revolutionised the handling of information. This book focuses on the harnessing of technological developments to enable marketers to gather, and use, information to retain competitive superiority.

STARTING MANAGEMENT SCIENCE

D R SNADDON

This book is an introduction to management science and, while it does not compete with large introductory texts, its treatment of the subject is far from superficial. It calls for active participation — problems and tutorial questions graded from simple to those of an examination standard are utilised as 'cues' to think. It is a necessary and valuable addition to the literature available to lecturers and students.

Publication end 1991

THESE BOOKS ARE AVAILABLE FROM JUTA BOOK-SHOPS OR LEADING BOOKSELLERS COUNTRYWIDE